P9-DHT-901

Biblical Revelation—
The Foundation of
Christian Theology

Biblical Revelation—The Foundation of Christian Theology

by

CLARK H. PINNOCK

Wipf and Stock Publishers
150 West Broadway • Eugene OR 97401
1998

Biblical Revelation
The Foundation of Christian Theology

By Pinnock, Clark H.

ISBN: 1-57910-126-7

Printed by *Wipf and Stock Publishers* *1998*
150 West Broadway • Eugene OR 97401

Previously Published by Moody Press, 1971.

ACKNOWLEDGMENT

The author gratefully acknowledges the assistance of Grant R. Osborne, who compiled the indexes.

Dedicated to
that remnant of faithful men
who long for
a new reformation,
Spring, 1970.

CONTENTS

INTRODUCTION

Modern theology of almost every shade is in crisis. While there is no lack of religious verbosity, a sure word resonant with divine authority is scarcely to be heard. There is "a famine . . . of hearing the words of the Lord" (Amos 8:11). Contemporary theology has become relativistic and hesitating. The gravity of the crisis for the churches should not be underestimated. The foundations have been shaken. Men are told that all that exists is a human word, colored by the conditions of language, culture and environment. It is a word which is wholly immanent, uttered by man from within the socially conditioned human situation. The transcendent norms of the biblical revelation have been relativized so that they no longer possess the power to provide an absolute standpoint in the midst of the flux. Such a theology which lacks a conceptual ground in divine revelation continually finds the categories for expressing its thought elusive, and is compelled to resort to ambiguity in order to gain an appeal. It is reduced either to manipulating bare symbols with hazy referents, or to the production of an endless stream of innovation and speculation which bear the unmistakable marks of their modern genesis. Modern theology is virtually discredited.

A major cause of the ferment in contemporary theology is the breakdown in liberal and neoorthodox proposals due to severe internal weaknesses. Classical liberalism, while seeking to be relevant, became deeply involved in nineteenth century romantic thought. When the spirit of the times changed early in this century, liberalism found herself suddenly outmoded and old-fashioned. Her decline sparked the rise of a theology more sympathetic to the growing realism and irrationalism of the twentieth century. But this neoorthodox theology did not repudiate liberalism's assumption of a universe closed to divine intervention and disclosure. As a result the new theology sought to wed two incompatible entities: the secular world view of liberalism, and the supernatural outlook of the Bible. In order still to speak of the "acts of God," neoorthodoxy was compelled to relegate them to an existential never-never land. Inevitably the truth began to dawn upon perceptive students that a saving event which did not occur in ordinary space-time history like other events was itself a pseudo-event. Similarly, because neoorthodoxy did not repudiate liberal criticism of Scripture, her claim to the possession of God's "Word" began to wear a little thin. After all, what is "God's Word" if it cannot be identified with any extant text? How does it identify itself? What content does it convey? The time has never been more propitious for the development of a viable evangelical proposal in systematic theology. Into the vacuum left by the demise of these recently influential positions, Evangelicals are called to step with a consistent, biblical construction of Christian truth which will provide our searching generation with a map to lead them out of the tangle of modern theological confusion.[1]

The principal cause of the modern theological sickness is a crisis in valid authority, and at the heart of the matter is the question as to *what constitutes revelation data.* The nature of the theological enterprise has become obscured. Its moorings in a truth base have become loose. Men are unsure whether there has been a genuine self-disclosure of God. The link between divine revelation and the Hebrew-Christian Scriptures, which formerly was almost universally accepted, is

1. For an evangelical overview, see Harold O. J. Brown, *The Protest of a Troubled Protestant.* One of the most helpful books to appear which analyzes the causes behind the breakup of the current nonevangelical theologies is Langdon Gilkey's *Naming the Whirlwind: The Renewal of God-Language.*

now hotly disputed, and has become a vigorously debated issue. The problem of revelation and inspiration is momentous, and central to every theological question.[2] The authority of Scripture is the watershed of theological conviction, and its importance to a sound methodology is incalculable. Clearly a decision regarding revelation and truth is of pressing urgency in relation to the church's mission in the world, for all theology is at stake—indeed, the very proclamation of the gospel. The central problem for theology is *its own epistemological base.* From what fountainhead does theology acquire the information from which she forms her doctrinal models and tests her hypotheses? What is the *principium theologiae* which measures and authenticates the subject matter for theology and preaching? No endeavor in theology can *begin* until some kind of answer is given. The sheer weight of this crucial question has kept, and will continue to keep, the debate over biblical authority at the center of the theological arena in our era. All issues pale before this one. It is the continental divide in Christian theology. Everything hangs on our solution to it. Differences between Christians over matters of biblical interpretation are minor compared with the current dispute over the nature of revelation and inspiration. The whole of Christianity gets drawn into this discussion. If our high regard for Scripture fails, all the ancient controversies and heresies will reappear and receive new life. When the lawful standard is gone, all is permitted.

Behind the massive assault on the orthodox doctrine of Scripture by countless theologians today stands more than a genial attempt to instruct us concerning the true nature of the Bible. There is a concerted effort to substitute for the message of evangelical Christianity "another gospel," one stripped of normative doctrinal truth, and evacuated of ascertainable content. It is a choice between two versions of Christianity. Instead of Scripture being the source and norm

2. William Temple, "Revelation," in *Revelation,* ed. John Baillie and Hugh Martin, p. 83; and H. D. McDonald, *Theories of Revelation,* p. 7.

of faith, subjective faith has become the source and norm of theology. The issues run very deep. The surface differences on this issue will not be glossed over, for they extend down to the very foundations of faith. Indeed, the spiritual vacuum that exists throughout every branch of the Christian church can also be largely blamed on the loss of biblical authority. When the Word of God is lost, the effects are felt at first by the theologians, but then quickly by the whole church. Revelation used to be found in Scripture; now it is not found at all. The common people argue, "If the theologians do not believe, why should we?" And the surveys clearly show the erosion of traditional belief among church members.[3] Since Kant, the objectivity and rationality of divine revelation have been philosophically questioned and, because of the rise of negative biblical criticism during the same period, a new method of establishing theology has had to be found. These factors have created an enormous crisis for theology and faith. Preaching and teaching have been undermined. Doubts and perplexities have discouraged the faithful, and Christians are tossed to and fro by every wind of doctrine that blows. The solution is a return to the historic Christian position on divine revelation as an objective and intelligible disclosure inscripturated in the Bible. The issue of biblical inspiration and authority lies at the heart of Christian theology; whether a man stands on the divine authorship and integrity of the Scriptures ultimately determines the nature and content of the gospel he preaches to the world. Therefore, we must increase the clarity and precision of our convictions regarding it. Exponents of a radical and speculative theology speak with increasing arrogance and impunity from beneath the umbrellas of the historic denominations. This pretended autonomy of theological thought, this egoistic, first-person theology, must be challenged with a vigorous evangelical al-

3. See C. Y. Glock and R. Stark, *American Piety: The Nature of Religious Commitment*, vol. 1. Martin E. Marty points to the proliferation of cultic and parareligious belief and an acceleration of pluralism as typical of American religion today in "The American Situation in 1969," in *The Religious Situation 1969*, ed. Donald R. Cutler, pp. 25-43.

ternative. The chaos in contemporary theology can be traced to its roots in the rejection of biblical infallibility. Having spun free from the controls of biblical revelation, theology has been reduced to wandering in the wastelands of subjectivity. Now is the time to lead her gently back to firmer ground.

The relevance of the doctrine of Scripture extends far beyond the circumference of theology and touches issues central to the mission of the church. Few are unaware of the intellectual and cultural malaise of our time. There is widespread despair about the possibility of arriving at truth and of finding any solid meaning to life itself. The longing cry is audible on every side; if only there were some anchorage beyond the world of flux in which our lives might be rooted! Malcolm, the biographer of Ludwig Wittgenstein, recalled, "Often as we walked together he would stop and exclaim, 'Oh, my God!', looking at me almost piteously, as if imploring a divine intervention in human events."[4] In the *Tractatus Logico-Philosophicus* he had written, "The sense of the world must lie outside the world"; "If there is any value that does have value, it must lie outside the whole sphere of what happens and is the case"; "The solution of the riddle of life in space and time lies *outside* space and time."[5] Humanism is caught in an inescapable relativism. If we are ever to discover the clue to the meaning of reality, history, and life itself, it must come to us from beyond the flux of the human situation. *And it has!* God's personal Word has entered the empirical realm where He may be met and known, and has left a precious gift for His people, a written transcript of the greatest of all facts, the truly liberating fact, the good news of a salvation from sin (1 Ti 1:15). Ours is a revolutionary message which turned the world upside down once (Ac 17:6) and can do it again.[6]

4. Norman Malcolm, *Ludwig Wittgenstein, A Memoir,* p. 32.
5. Ludwig Wittgenstein, *Tractatus Logico-Philosophicus,* 6:41, 4312.
6. John Warwick Montgomery has written along these lines with great brilliance. See "The Relevance of Scripture Today," in *The Living Word of Revelation,* ed. Merrill C. Tenney, pp. 201-18.

Scripture is not only relevant to the need in theology of a proper epistemological base, and to the need in philosophy of an empirical anchor to resolve the truth question, it is a particularly compelling solution to man's *existential* dilemmas. The metaphysical wasteland in which man is presently languishing was created by the tragic loss of God's reality and His sure Word. "Cut off from his metaphysical, religious, and transcendental roots, man is lost," writes Ionesco. "Two times anything equals zero," says Beckett. There is a vacancy in man's world view and self-conception which only Christ can fill. Our sensitive artists and writers have repeatedly shown that this vale of tears is insufficient to satisfy the intellect or appetites of man (cf. Pr 8:35-36).[7] Man's dignity and identity rest upon a religious commitment. Only Christ can answer the question, Is there life after birth? In the text of Scripture the liberating word is to be found. Scripture is relevant to a disenchanted era, for it holds the only hope of its deliverance. The so-called absence of God reflects, not *His* unavailability to us, but *our* inability to speak of Him authentically and with authority. When the note of valid authority is restored to our proclamation, the philosophers, writers and common folk will hear us gladly. Secular man's long day's journey into night can be changed by Jesus Christ into a long night's journey into day, his metaphysical wasteland turned into a land flowing with milk and honey.[8]

In a sense this book makes no claim to novelty. The belief it expounds and defends has stood now for two millennia, and not without eminent grounds. It is simply a matter of adducing the reasons underlying this historic conviction in

7. For works in cultural apologetics, see Stuart Barton Babbage, *The Mark of Cain;* Hilda Graef, *Modern Gloom and Christian Hope;* John Killinger, *The Failure of Theology in Modern Literature;* Francis A. Schaeffer, *Escape from Reason* and *The God Who Is There;* Charles I. Glicksberg, *Modern Literature and the Death of God.*

8. Gilkey sketches the outline of the twentieth century's cultural "Geist" with consummate skill in *Naming the Whirlwind* chap. 2. See Clark H. Pinnock, "Cultural Apologetics: An Evangelical Standpoint," *Bibliotheca Sacra* 127 (Jan.-Mar. 1970):58-63, and "The Secular Wasteland," *His* (May 1970); and "A Long Night's Journey into Day," *His* (June 1970).

terms of the contemporary climate of thought. However, when a theology is incapable of fresh thought, and of forging new intellectual tools for explicating its content, it is sterile and frail, content to repeat the old formulas, the "trophies" of the past. We cannot be complacent with the slogans of orthodoxy, if that is all they are. A study is needed which will demonstrate the adequacy of the historic doctrine of inspiration in the light of current discussion. The well of evangelical thought has not dried up. Greater precision can be injected into the traditional position. It is not so much new information which is needed, as a more careful arrangement of what we already know in the face of current challenges. Warfield and Gaussen cannot be relied on exclusively for answers to some of the new questions. The time is ripe for a fresh examination from an orthodox Protestant perspective which will sharpen and improve the case for plenary inspiration.[9] We take seriously a warning by Carl F. H. Henry:

> If evangelical Protestants do not overcome their preoccupation with negative criticism of contemporary theological deviations at the expense of the construction of preferable alternatives to these, they will not be much of a doctrinal force in the decade ahead.[10]

Sir Isaac Newton formulated a law of motion which held that a body remains at rest unless acted upon by an external force. The same could be said of evangelical theology. Only when she is goaded into it does she bestir herself to refine and improve her doctrinal formulations. But the task is by no means disagreeable, since, compared with the newer proposals on inspiration, the Evangelical is in an enviable position both to defend and to expound his own. The project is twice welcome in view of the fact that the question of in-

9. There are pitfalls to avoid: the neoliberal inability to see beyond the marks of human genius to divine authorship; the neoorthodox reluctance to do justice to the cognitive side of our encounter with God; the fundamentalist tendency to overbelief in the matter of inspiration. See the author's book, *A Defense of Biblical Infallibility.*

10. Carl F. H. Henry, ed., *Jesus of Nazareth: Saviour and Lord,* p. 9.

spiration is at the heart of the entire theological endeavor and such a study affords the opportunity to diagnose the ills that weaken theology today and prescribe an effective remedy.

Our study brings together three related topics: *revelation, inspiration* and *theology.* The central thesis is that our understanding of revelation radically affects our view of Scripture (its medium and witness) and, in turn, our conception of the character and role of theology. *Christian theology is the articulation of the truth content implicit in divine revelation mediated in Scripture.* The question of inspiration is all-important. But before it can be properly defined, the shape and pattern of revelation must be traced. The view held concerning the material content of revelation proves decisive in the matter of the formal category of inspiration. The chaos in modern theology and the rejection of plenary inspiration both result from the unbiblical and novel manner in which revelation is conceived by neo-Protestantism. Therefore, we shall delve down to the roots of biblical inspiration. Revelation is the fundamental datum which supports inspiration and theology. Before theology begins, it ought to establish the basis of its speaking. Unfortunately many works in theology proceed from a starting point not yet defined, or make crucial methodological decisions under the table which go on to determine the shape of all that follows. Evangelical theology operates on the basis of a doctrine of Scripture *inductively* constructed out of the materials of redemptive revelation. The high doctrine of inspiration is not an a priori dogma, assumed arbitrarily to suit a particular view of God and truth. It is the conclusion of an examination of what revelation *is,* a divine self-disclosure which generates a documentary residue, inspired by the Spirit.

Inevitably the truth question gets drawn into the discussion. There must be a close interplay between theology and apologetics. It is not enough to approach revelation descriptively, to ask what sort of revelation it is which the Bible describes, unless the truth claim can be grounded in reality.

For there are numerous claims to revelation, most of which must be false. If theology is not an exercise in personal prejudice, the question why it should be taken seriously cannot be avoided. Christian theology rests upon an attested, historical revelation. We shall attempt, therefore, to indicate not only what view of inspiration should be held if Christianity were true, but also on what basis its truthfulness securely rests. A theologian must be something of an apologist lest his labors should seem irrelevant, even as an apologist must be something of a theologian lest his passion for truth appear merely sophistic. This book is both polemical and didactic: it attempts both to vindicate and to expound the revelational data concerning biblical inspiration.

The orthodox view of Scripture is not without difficulties to face. This book hopes to show that these difficulties are seldom quite those which our opponents suppose, and are in fact less intractable and obstinate than those which plague the various current alternatives. We are pessimistic about convincing those who are deeply committed emotionally and intellectually to the existentially oriented theologies. But perhaps this book will suffice to persuade numerous students of the Christian faith not to discard the historic conviction of the church concerning Scripture, and help them see that in this instance the old wine is better than the new.

Unfortunately, in a book which aims to explore the very foundations of Christian theology and to consider the doctrine of biblical inspiration on a broad canvas and in the light of the extensive modern discussion, many topics will seem to have been lightly passed over. Many questions, such as the historical question of the rise of the New Testament canon and its acceptance, a complete exegetical analysis of the biblical texts bearing upon inspiration, or an extended attempt to vindicate Scripture against the many charges of error that have been leveled against her, have not been accorded the patient consideration they deserve in this work. But they have all been faced in the course of the discussion, and sufficient comment with reference to further resource material, has been made, so that the matters of importance we have elected to discuss deserve a fair hearing.

The first three chapters are the most important. The first treats the Christian claim that history yields an attested and meaningful revelation. The second defines the kind of Scripture generated by revelation. The third explores the implications for theology which this holds. The remaining chapters bear upon the central thesis from different angles. By means of this plan it is confidently hoped that the historic high doctrine of inspiration can be set forth in a manner that reveals its strengths and comprehensive character. The effort is supremely worthwhile because the Bible is the greatest guarantee that the church will not in the course of time substitute another gospel for the apostolic message. A good deal is at stake.

Quite literally this study is a *radical* one (Latin *radix*, "root"). Indeed, the word *radical* and the word *fundamental* are two metaphors for the same thing. They indicate getting into the essential core of something. In one sense the argument is "fundamental": it is a testing of the soundness of the evangelical *foundations*. In another sense it is "radical": it involves some fresh digging around the *roots* of the biblical faith. In a day in which all is in question, it is a vital effort which can demonstrate to Christian believers the healthy integrity of their spiritual ground.

1

THE PATTERN OF DIVINE REVELATION

> Everything else in the New Testament depends upon the idea of revelation. The writers believe that God reveals himself, that he has made his final revelation in Christ, that they have been enabled by the Spirit to receive and impart that revelation. They nowhere define their idea of revelation, and perhaps did not consciously reflect on it; nevertheless, it forms the basis of all their thinking.[1]

CHRISTIANITY CLAIMS to be a revealed religion. The Creator Himself has removed the obstacles to understanding and revealed Himself to men (Heb 1:1-5). In the works of creation (Ps 19:1) and in the acts of redemption (Ac 2:11) the sovereign Lord has disclosed something of His character and purposes (Deu 29:29) so that men might enter into covenant with Himself (Jn 17:3). Revelation is a gracious divine activity, a free and voluntary gift which has as its end the salvation of sinners (1 Ti 1:15). Because of revelation we have been privileged to see "the light of the knowledge of the glory of God in the face of Jesus Christ" (2 Co 4:6).

F. Gerald Downing has asked the question, *Has Christianity a Revelation?* in an important recent book. His purpose is not so much to challenge the validity of the Christian truth claim as to question whether the Bible makes any claim to revelation at all. He notes that theologians differ consider-

1. E. F. Scott, *The New Testament Idea of Revelation,* p. v.

ably as to what they consider revelation to be, and often fail to demonstrate that Scripture claims to contain a revelation.

Downing is certainly right in saying that neoorthodox writers do speak of revelation in a curious way owing to their existential commitments. But it is not possible to deduce from this a denial that Scripture itself confronts us with a revelation claim. For the Lord has made Himself known (Ps 9:16). The glory of God has shone forth in the face of Jesus Christ (2 Co 4:6). The point that needs to be made however, is that "the ultimate divine confirmation of Jesus will take place only in the occurrence of his return."[2] The revelation in Jesus had a proleptic element. God's kingdom was now and, paradoxically, not yet. Only at the end time will the revelation of God in Christ shine with all its irresistible glory. For this apocalypse we wait (1 Co 1:7; 1 Pe 1:5, 7). And yet, revelation, while partial, is revelation still. Now we "know in part" (1 Co 13:12). Plenary theological knowledge is future and eschatological. The full verification and vindication are still to come. What we have in the New Testament is a partial but valid revelation on its way to becoming a complete and perfect revelation in that celestial city. Downing is correct to point out the futurity of revelation (though he interprets it wrongly). However, he then goes on to pit "salvation" over against "revelation." Granted, salvation is an important biblical concept; but it should not be contrasted with revelation. For revelation is precisely the locus of the saving message and its presupposition. Indeed, revelation is soteric in its intent (2 Ti 3:15). "He appeared to take away sins" (1 Jn 3:5, ASV). Revelation is certainly not given to satisfy curiosity, but for the sake of salvation and life. "The history of revelation and the history of salvation are the same history."[3]

The context in which biblical inspiration should be viewed is that of divine revelation, and Scripture should not be con-

2. W. Pannenberg, *Jesus—God and Man*, p. 108.
3. P. Tillich, *Systematic Theology*, 1:144.

sidered apart from it. The Bible is a witness to t
activity in history, and a record of divine speaking. Indeed, in itself, Scripture is a product of that revealing work. Scripture is the written embodiment, the grammatical residue, as it were, of redemptive revelation. Inspiration is not to be taken as an independent datum and isolated from revelation. The Bible should *not* be regarded as a sort of philosophical axiom, or a priori necessary construct whose inerrancy is required. Such models of biblical inspiration are alien to the historical character of Christian faith and distort it. Historical revelation and biblical inspiration are organically related and, if wrenched apart, suffer morphological change. Scripture is the divinely given culmination of the process of special revelation, the capstone of God's revealing activity. Warfield comments that Scripture is

> not merely the record of the redemptive acts by which God is saving the world, but itself one of these redemptive acts, having its own part to play in the great work of establishing and building up the kingdom of God.[4]

Although he may not quite do justice to the divine character of the witness, Karl Barth deserves our praise for his insistence against much opposition that the Bible is the only authoritative witness to revelation.[5] The reason Scripture is relevant to us and binding on us is because it belongs to the organism of divine revelation itself.

Because revelation and inspiration are correlative ideas, our view of divine revelation is decisive for our understanding of inspiration. John Hick, from the neoorthodox side, alerts us to the magnitude of the question:

> The non-propositional view of revelation also tends to be accompanied by a different conception of the function of

4. B. B. Warfield, *The Inspiration and Authority of the Bible,* p. 161. Two excellent books which relate inspiration and revelation properly are B. Ramm, *Special Revelation and the Word of God;* and J. I. Packer, *God Speaks to Man.*
5. Karl Barth, *Church Dogmatics,* vol. 1, pt. 2, pp. 457-72.

> theology from that operating in the propositional system of ideas. . . . The notion of revealed theology is rejected on the ground that revelation means God disclosing *himself* (rather than a set of theological propositions) to man.[6]

In effect, Hick reduces the affirmative teaching of the biblical writers to human guesswork on the basis of certain religious insights or experiences they had. *Revelation* is taken to denote a nonconceptual, ecstatic experience of mystery to which the Bible and theology pose an attempted human interpretation. The cognitive side of divine revelation is left up to the genius of man, and its truth content is caught in the flux of human opinion and remains forever relative.

The Neo-Protestant View of Revelation

Hick's comment points to a considerable shift of theological opinion in regard to revelation. In the English-speaking world, John Baillie's *The Idea of Revelation in Recent Thought* documents this important transition, the shift from a propositional act-word theory to a nonpropositional, existential one. Baillie candidly remarks, "there is a general awareness among us that it [the question of revelation] is being answered in a way that sounds very differently from the traditional formulations."[7] It is just as well Baillie noted this fact before his orthodox critics did. More neoorthodox writers should recognize the extent of their deviations from historic Christianity at this point. Traditionally, revelation and the Bible were for all practical purposes identified. Scripture was taken to be the locus of the divine speaking. Now revelation and the Bible have been wrenched apart with devastating results for theology and faith.[8] Baillie, however, cannot be credited (or blamed) for this considerable revision of evangelical theology. The roots of it penetrate deep into the history of recent Western thought. Many factors played a role: there was

6. John Hick, *Philosophy of Religion*, p. 76.
7. Baillie, *The Idea of Revelation in Recent Thought*, p. 3.
8. For the history of this unfortunate development, see McDonald, chap. 5.

Kant's denial that theological realities can be grasped by the mind and that such doctrines enjoy universal validity; there was Schleiermacher's insistence that God revealed Himself, not truths about Himself; and there was Kierkegaard's stress on the radical disjunction of finite and infinite, a virtual metaphysical dualism which made objective divine revelation impossible. These influences and many more helped to prepare the stage for the neo-Protestant view of revelation. Each in its way undermined confidence in the intelligibility and objectivity of divine revelation in Scripture. It was only a matter of time before theologians would awaken to the fact that on this basis no one could know what the Word of God was, or wherein it consisted. *Revelation bereft of content is the bane of contemporary theology.*

With the rejection of any direct correlation between revelation and inspiration, modern theology has been forced to relocate the locus of God's Word away from an exclusive connection to the text of Scripture onto some other ground. That locus has been shifted in *two* directions primarily: from the propositional to the personal, and from literature to history. In both cases the shift involves a faulty construction placed upon a valid biblical motif which Protestant orthodoxy never denied (the personal and the historical). The result is a twofold assault on the truth character of divine revelation. The neo-Protestant view of revelation generally oscillates between these two poles, often incorporating both for good measure as Baillie does. The shift from the propositional to the personal is the favorite of the systematic theologians, and the shift from literature to history is preferred by the biblical scholars.[9]

REVELATION AS SUBJECT TO SUBJECT ENCOUNTER

Revelation is not a question of information communicated

9. Robert Preus has described the true character of the neo-Protestant view of revelation with great precision in an article, "The Doctrine of Revelation in Contemporary Theology," in *Crisis in Lutheran Theology,* 2:18-29.

from God to man, Baillie notes, but a matter of God's revealing Himself personally. Temple writes,

> There is no such thing as revealed truth. There are truths of revelation, that is to say, propositions which express the results of correct thinking concerning revelation; but they are not themselves directly revealed.[10]

Theological propositions, even those of the New Testament, are only "explications of the understanding inherent in faith," according to Bultmann. Barth makes it abundantly clear that God may be known only as *subject* and not at all as object. Brunner considers the identifying of revelation with revealed doctrines a fundamental error. In the entire neoorthodox movement there is a strong depreciation of the noetic content of revelation, without an apparent awareness of the nihilistic implications of this for theology. There is a *crisis of content* here. Although credit is given ostensibly to the sovereignty of divine revelation, the result is virtual mysticism, for there are no objective criteria whereby the content of the divine imperative or the character of the divine claimant may be determined. Whereas the Bible tells of God whispering to His servants the prophets, and informing men of His person and plans, in this theory there is a meeting without a knowing and, consequently, no way whereby errant human notions about revelation may be tested and corrected. In the biblical framework, on the other hand, personal revelation takes place in the context of *truth revelation*. Revelation *about* God is crucial to the knowledge *of* God. Content of the divine imperative is inseparable from the demand itself.

In addition to the crisis of content, there is a *crisis of meaningfulness*. Revelation claims are not self-validating. Many voices are urging us to bow to their claims to authority. Discrimination between them is a necessity. A mere claim to

10. Temple, *Nature, Man and God*, p. 317. Temple consistently opposes any form of propositional revelation. "What is offered to man's apprehension in a specific revelation is not truth concerning God but the living God himself" (p. 322). See McDonald, pp. 162 ff.

revelation may reflect nothing more than a psychological experience or, indeed, demonic influence. Experience alone is quite insufficient as a basis for theology and apologetics, for the experience may be divine, demonic, or merely human in origin. Furthermore, it fails to convey substantive truth not already believed by the experiencing subject, and is incapable of validating its claims to truth over those of countless alternate religious experiences.[11] In short, the subject-to-subject theory lacks both content and credibility.

REVELATION AS DIVINE ACTIVITY

Revelation consists, according to this interpretation, of a series of disclosure situations in history, in which God's hand is seen to be at work by faith.[12] The Bible contains a recital of events interpreted redemptively by believing hearts, and functioning sacramentally of divine revelation. The more conservative members of the *Heilsgeschichte* school insist God's saving acts are truly factual and miraculous, the interpretation of which is left up to human genius and insight (a kind of divine charade). More often, however, the issue of the miraculous is skirted altogether. Where it is not denied outright (e.g., Bultmann), miracle is relegated to the mysterious realm of supra-history (*Geschichte*) where it is historically unverifiable. In either case, the explicit biblical emphasis (Ac 1:3; Ro 1:4; 1 Co 15:14) on the factual objectivity of the redemptive acts of God is denied.[13] In essence, the viewpoint seems to be that normal historical occurrences were creatively transformed by faith into "the acts of God"; in which case it is something of an exaggeration to say "God acted in history" when all that is meant is that some men

11. See C. B. Martin, "A Religious Way of Knowing," in *New Essays in Philosophical Theology*, pp. 76-95; Montgomery, *The Shape of the Past*, pp. 257-311; Pinnock, *Set Forth Your Case*, pp. 69-76.
12. See G. E. Wright and R. H. Fuller, *The Book of the Acts of God*.
13. See K. S. Kantzer, "The Christ-Revelation as Act and Interpretation," in *Jesus of Nazareth: Saviour and Lord*, pp. 241-64. See J. Barr, "Revelation Through History in the OT and in Modern Theology," *Princeton Seminary Bulletin* 56(May 1963): 4-14.

imagined He did. Revelation refers rather to a psychological event than to miraculous divine action. Even "Christ" becomes the name of an event occurring, not in history, but over and over again in existential experience (e.g., H. Braun). At best Scripture seems reduced to "what St. Luke couldn't help fancying someone's having said he thought he remembered St. Peter's having told him," as A. Farrer puts it. It simply will not do for those who emphasize the presence of human error in the writers' mind not to recognize it in the believers' psyches as well.

The two views, revelation as encounter and revelation as activity, are more similar than dissimilar. They both leave the nature of Scripture vague and vulnerable, and both play down the noetic side of revelation to the point of virtual mysticism. The two theories are too narrow to do justice to the pattern of divine revelation in Scripture. They make it impossible to define the content or defend the validity of divine revelation. The liberal idea of the Bible as a record of religious experiences lives on in the neoorthodox concept of revelation as an ecstatic, personal encounter. It is subjectivity again trying to pose as Christianity. The neo-Protestant view of revelation is foreign to the historic Christian understanding of it. Revelation includes a web of divine truths from Him who has spoken by the prophets (*qui locutus est per prophetas* [Nicea]).

The neo-Protestant view of revelation sees God as coming within the orbit of human experience in a divine-human, personal encounter. Theology and the Bible represent the human response to revelation, the attempt at understanding the significance of revelatory events. Faith is a voluntary recognition of revelation, a creative response which elects to *see* events in a certain way, a religious *Blik* (Hare). Thus a religious interpretation is superimposed upon the ambiguous data of history by the act of faith. For Hick, as for Tillich, happenings became revealing events through response.[14]

14. Hick, pp. 70-77; Tillich, 1:35.

Theology and the Bible are but fallible human attempts to understand the data of faith. As Macquarrie puts it, "The person who receives revelation sees the same things *in a different way.*"[15] Thus, in effect, poetic and religious expression coincide.[16] Each is emotive and metaphorical, and not literal or factual. Under this interpretation, Scripture is the "literary outburst" of one particular poetic-religious vision, which vision is the vitality and justification of the myths employed in the literature. Even religious experience is naturalized. *Revelation* becomes the vision that makes one more alive. Whereas the earlier Heidegger (Bultmann's idol) had viewed language as the expression of one's subjectivity, the later Heidegger understands language as called into existence by Being itself, its "revelation." The language event of Fuchs or word event of Ebeling is a meaningful happening which contains the existential "genie" of authentic self-understanding. It is hoped that a linguistic millennium will follow the intrapersonal *agape* relationships set up by a series of such events!

The deepest issues are raised when the nature of divine revelation is discussed. A chasm exists between this mode of thinking about revelation, faith and theology, and the orthodox standpoints. The Roman Catholic theology is just as deeply affected. Braaten observes:

> Roman Catholic theology today is catching up with Protestant theology; it is no longer sure of what it means by revelation. Ever since the decline of Protestant orthodoxy,

15. John Macquarrie, *Principles of Christian Theology*, p. 80. G. D. Kaufman writes: "Revelation refers, then, to that locus in experience through which men discover themselves in relation to the *ultimately real*" *(Systematic Theology: A Historicist Perspective)*, p. 19. See also Hick, "Revelation," in *Encyclopedia of Philosophy*, ed. Paul Edwards, 7:189-91. Needless to say, this view corresponds exactly to the materialistic objection to our religion, that it is but an arbitrary series of interpretive hypotheses laid upon the experienced world.

16. Ernst Cassirer points out that man employs "poetic imagination" in formulating his experience of reality. Tillich has picked this up in support of his view that the Bible uses myth as symbol for expressing existential reality. Thus he contradicts the biblical insistence on factual history and employs the category of *myth* for what the New Testament repudiates as pagan (cf. 1 Ti 4:7; 2 Pe 1:16).

> theology has been in search of a category by which to define revelation. The search continues today.[17]

This is true, and Roman Catholics have our sympathies. For whatever the errors of the Trent-type Catholicism, they are nothing in comparison with the doctrinal atrocities we may expect from a Catholicism of an existential-humanistic persuasion. The issue at stake is *the orthodox method of building theology*. How on this basis can theology even start? Divinely revealed truth does not exist. Inevitably faith is mystical and theology emotive. There is no way to recognize truth or error. Preaching is dead. Although we can sympathize with those who (because of what they consider to be the assured results of biblical criticism) desire to be rid of the theory of an infallible Bible, we must hasten to point out the high cost of such convenience: namely, the lack of any definite word from God, and only rough approximations of it, with nothing solid on which to stand. It is fatal to surrender the objective biblical authority of God speaking. The authority of pope or council or scholar or religious expert is never quite the same. When the standard of the written Word is discarded, sentimentality becomes the canon. Ramm is right:

> A wordless revelation in mysticism and a merely human word in religious experience cannot yield a *logia tou theou*. Theology is possible only as a word comes to us from beyond ourselves. . . .[18]

Biblical preaching is more than subjective testimony about a meaningful psychological event. It is to be the proclamation of divine doctrine and revealed truth.

17. Carl E. Braaten, *History and Hermeneutics*, p. 11.

18. Ramm, p. 159. The gospel requires that we distinguish it sharply from myth. It is more than a groping after the numinous. Myth is an important aspect in human religion. It represents a longing after the incomparable reality at the core of things. But divine revelation is the hard fact corresponding to the inconsolate longing, and should not be equated with it. It is the divine elixir which satisfies the eternal *Sehnsucht*. To equate the gospel and mythology is to deny that the reality which mythology seeks has come.

The Biblical Conception of Revelation

The category *revelation,* which covers the semantic breadth of numerous biblical terms, refers to the divine self-disclosure, the purpose of which is, by intervention in history and communication in language, the calling of men into fellowship with God.[19] These terms signify the removal of obstacles to the perception of divine truth. No single term adequately represents our theological term *revelation,* which describes the whole process by which God has made Himself known to man. While Scripture undoubtedly alludes to a general revelation of God in the created order, its predominant emphasis is upon special revelation. Remedial redemptive revelation enjoys centrality in the Bible. It is soteric, restorative and therapeutic. The invisible, hidden and transcendent God, whom no man has seen nor can see, has planted His Word in the human situation that sinners might be brought nigh unto God. Redemptive revelation is logically and chronologically prior to Scripture, whose task it is to make us wise unto salvation which is in Christ Jesus.[20]

We do not encounter special revelation in the form of propositional theology, but in a historical mode. For revelation unfolds itself in progressive installments, in a series of disclosure situations in history. All revelation is "incarnational," immersed in human history and language. It is an organic growth from seedling to fully mature plant, from earliest

19. Ramm lists the verbs and nouns denoting special revelation, pp. 161-65. Warfield discusses biblical terminology too, pp. 97-101. See especially Albrecht Oepke, "apokalupsis," in *Theological Dictionary of the New Testament* (hereafter, *TDNT*), 3:563-92; Hannelis Schulte, *Der Begriff der Offenbarung im Neuen Testament.*

20. Westminster Confession 1:1: "Although the light of nature, and the works of creation and providence, do so far manifest the goodness, wisdom, and power of God, so as to leave men inexcusable; yet are they not sufficient to give that knowledge of God, and of his will, which is necessary unto salvation; therefore it pleased the Lord, at sundry times, and in divers manners, to reveal Himself, and to declare that His will unto the Church; and afterwards for the better preserving and propagating of the truth, and for the more sure establishment and comfort of the church against the corruption of the flesh, and the malice of Satan and of the world, to commit the same wholly unto writing: which maketh the Holy Scripture to be most necessary; those former ways of God's revealing His will unto His people being now ceased."

beginnings in the book of Genesis to the glory of the new covenant of our Lord. Revelation is mediated in numerous modalities, and steadily advances in fullness until the crowning and final edition is published in Jesus Christ.[21]

The moving cause of revelation is the grace of God. His attitude of unmerited favor toward sinners moved Him to disclose saving purposes for man and beckon him into covenant (Gen 12:3; Ex 19:5-6; Deu 7:7-8; Titus 3:5). Revelation is Christocentric to the core (Jn 5:39) and redemptive in intention (Gal 4:4-7). The purpose of revelation is to enable us to know God personally (Phil 3:10).[22]

The means by which the infinite God was able to reveal Himself to finite, sinful men involved the humble stooping down of the divine majesty. An entity of our universe of discourse was chosen to represent an element of God's. Revelation makes sacramental use of our universe in order that genuine communication might take place. Revelation thus enters into the human orbit *authentically,* clothing itself in the linguistic and cultural garb of that time. Joseph dreamed Palestinian dreams, and Nebuchadnezzar, Babylonian dreams! Revelation is adapted to the world of the persons to which it comes. It is concrete, historical and particular. Revelation is aptly fitted to our condition so that it might function as revelation to us. The ontological chasm was bridged by the divine willingness to stoop to the use of anthropic media, most clearly seen in the greatest of all revelation modalities, the incarnation. Mankind is enmeshed in the finite and the contingent, and cannot look on the face of God. It is imperative that revelation be cosmically mediated that we might receive it. In the face of Jesus Christ, the divinely accredited Emissary, we can see the reflected glory of God (Heb 1:3).[23]

21. Gerhardus Vos, *Biblical Theology,* had a particularly vivid grasp of this truth.

22. A superb article on revelation by J. I. Packer is in *The New Bible Dictionary,* ed. J. D. Douglas, pp. 1090-93.

23. Ramm, chap. 2, "The Modality of the Divine Condescension." The concept of *analogy* has been employed by theologians who wish to avoid the

Two Chief Facets

REVELATION BY DEED

At the core of the biblical conception is revelation as divine activity in history. God reveals Himself by acts of mighty power (Ex 20:1). Israel is called to remember what happened in the past so that she "may know the righteous acts of Jehovah" (Mic 6:5, ASV). Psalm 78 is a recital of the glorious deeds of the Lord (v. 4). The gospel is a story of God's mighty works (Ac 2:11). "The Word became flesh, and dwelt among us" (Jn 1:14, ASV). Revelation is concrete and historical in mode. It frequently involves God's transcending the alphabet of human power in order to make His name known upon earth. Throughout the Bible, God's mighty acts are celebrated. "You must revere the LORD, who brought you from the land of Egypt with mighty power and with an outstretched arm; you must worship Him" (2 Ki 17:36, Berkeley). The *existential* import of these works is dependent on their *historical factuality*.[24] Whereas for much modern biblical theology, as Gilkey has pointed out, faith is accorded a *creative* role, so that the Bible does not really contain a record of the acts of God so much as an anthology of creative religious opinions by assorted Hebrews! Whereas *God* is the subject of the verbs describing His activity in the Bible, Hebrew *faith* has become the subject of the verbs in modern discussions.[25] There is no doubt that the biblical writers considered the mighty acts they were relating to be

agnostic pitfall without falling into the anthropomorphic pitfall. In Christianity, God selects the images with which men may speak of Him. See E. Bevan, *Symbolism and Belief;* E. L. Mascall, *Existence and Analogy.* The effect of conceiving God as wholly Other in the neoorthodox theology, has been to cast doubt on any and all conceptions of God which man may have. Whatever language describes, that God is not.

24. Biblical writers, unlike modern theologians, do not place the existential cart before the historical horse. See the author's *Set Forth Your Case,* pp. 61-68.

25. Gilkey, "Cosmology, Ontology, and the Travail of Biblical Language," *The Journal of Religion* 40(1961): 197.

historically factual.[26] Existential historiography was not part of their mental framework. "If Christ has not been raised, then your faith is futile; you are still in your sins" (1 Co 15:17, Berkeley). The *kerygma* is dependent upon historical facts, upon the supernatural acts of God. If we may speak of *God*, we may speak of *miracle*. It is odd that those who feel themselves unable, because of a naturalistic bias, to believe in miracles, continue to refer to God, who is by all standards the largest supernatural entity in the biblical record. If God exists, miracles are not a problem. And, we may add, if God does not exist, everything everywhere is a problem. Precisely by His acts of power, the biblical God has demonstrated His existence (Deu 3:24). Jehovah, not the idols, is Master over the stuff of the universe. The "power" of God is capable of vanquishing every foe and bringing salvation to sinners (Ex 15:6; Ro 1:16). The miracles of Jesus were "signs" of His deity and Messianic office (Mt 11:2-6; Jn 20:30-31). His glorious acts cause a ripple in history. They confront the mind with evidence of the truth of God and the gospel. History is the medium of the divine self-disclosure. The supreme example of revelation in history was the incarnation. "But when the time was completed, God sent forth His Son" (Gal 4:4, Berkeley). God's eternal Son, the final and perfect Word, stepped forth into the empirical realm where He might be met and known (1 Jn 1:1-3). He came as Saviour (the *soteric* purpose) and as Revealer (the *epistemological* purpose). "No one has ever seen God; the only Son, Deity Himself, who lies upon His Father's breast, has made him known" (Jn 1:18, Williams). The Bible does not contain a finer picture of what cosmic-mediated revelation is. In Christ's character and teaching there is an authentic mirroring of the divine nature. To Him the Scriptures witness (Lk 24:27; 2 Ti 3:15). For *He* is the heart of the revelation they display and the substance of their good news. The Scriptures are the record

26. See J. Barton Payne, "Faith and History in the Old Testament," *Journal of the Evangelical Theological Society* 11(1968): 111-120.

of this event. They are "the perpetuation within the Church of the apostolic experience of the incarnation."[27] God, having performed His mighty acts, did not leave the understanding of them nor the testimony to them to chance, but graciously assisted in the illumination of minds and the inspiration of pens, so that the infallible Scripture might result. The Bible represents the concluding redemptive act, which by its testimony to Jesus Christ renders divine revelation continually effective in men's lives.

REVELATION BY WORD

Act and word are perfectly blended in the biblical pattern of revelation. Event and interpretation are bound together in indivisible unity. Kantzer remarks:

> The revelation of mighty deeds of God without revelation of the meaning of those deeds is like a television show without sound track; it throws man helplessly back upon his own human guesses as to the meaning of what God is doing.[28]

The Bible gives an important place to the divine *speaking*. The author of Hebrews refers to the entire Old Testament revelation in terms of God's speech (1:1). "The Lord God hath spoken, who can but prophesy?" (Amos 3:8). God's *Word* is central in the biblical concept of divine revelation.[29] Pagan idols are dumb, but the Lord is a living, speaking God. Revelation is mediated through language. Man and God have become speech partners. Language is the basis of culture, and written language is durable, objective and transmissible. Scripture grew out of the divine speaking as it was cast into writing for the welfare of God's people. God-inspired Scripture is an extension of the modality of the divine speaking. Writing has revelational significance in the Bible.[30] Moses wrote down the law for a witness (Deu 31:24-26).

27. Ramm, p. 115.
28. Kantzer, p. 252.
29. See *TDNT*, 4:91-136.
30. See ibid., 1:744-46.

Scripture was written for our learning (Ro 15:4). John was ordered to write (Rev 1:11). The New Testament phrase "it is written" is the equivalent of saying "Thus saith the Lord."

"What Scripture says, God says." The divine Word is cast into permanent form in Scripture, which is the durable vehicle of special revelation and provides the conceptual framework in which we meet and comprehend God. *Truth is fundamental to trust.* Our encounter with God takes place within the context of mutual knowledge. Faith is walking in the light of the divine promises.

The word-deed complex in divine revelation must not be shattered. God did not act without speaking, nor speak without acting. His mighty deeds of redemption are clothed with a word of interpretation. "Christ died [act] for our sins [meaning]" (1 Co 15:3). God told Moses what He would do before *and* after the events (Ex 4:28-31). Ladd comments,

> The deeds could not be understood unless accompanied by the divine word; and the word would seem powerless unless accompanied by the mighty works. Both the acts and the words are divine events, coming from God. In fact, it would be better to speak of the revealing deed-word event, for the two belong together and form an inseparable unity.[31]

The Bible is both a record of the historical acts of redemption and the transcript of the prophetic Word of God. Scripture is *vere et proprie* (truly and exclusively) God's Word, His utterances (*logia*) and the product of His breath (*theopneustos*). It is arbitrary to limit revelation to an "encounter" with God or to His mighty acts in history, as though the divine speaking lacked full revelation status. Revealed *truth* belongs to special revelation and is of divine origin.

31. George E. Ladd, *The New Testament and Criticism*, p. 27. Otto W. Heick expresses the oft-repeated neoorthodox notion that the subject matter of Scripture is somehow incapable of being expressed in propositions. "Biblical Inerrancy and the Hebrew Mode of Speech," *Lutheran Quarterly* 20 (1968): 7-19. This is superb metaphysical dualism, but bad theology.

The Place of Scripture in Revelation

The Bible is the witness to and the graphical residue of the divine act-word event, the locus in which God's revealing activity now takes place. It represents both the culmination of revelation and its primary *product.* The Holy Spirit created *graphe* (writing) that revelation might be conveyed in a written form (Heb 3:7; 2 Pe 1:21). By the Scriptures God speaks to His church (Mt 22:43; Ac 28:25; Heb 10:15). The Bible is the embodiment of extant revelation, the deposit of divine truth for the doctrinal, moral and spiritual welfare of God's people. *Inspiration* refers to the miracle of *conservation* whereby the Spirit has preserved and conserved divine revelation (cf. Is 30:8). Revelation *generates* Scripture! Inspiration settles its actual form that the text might serve as an "adequate, authentic, and sufficient vehicle of special revelation."[32] Revelation and inspiration are inseparable, though they are not identical. The creation of *graphe* is the final stage in quite an extended process of divine revelation. Revelation is the act of God revealing Himself; inspiration is a recording of the revelation in writing, so that Scripture is the authentic expression of it.

Scripture is a gift of God for the good of His church and gospel, a gift well suited to the need of sinful man. "How necessary it was," Calvin writes, "to make such a depository of doctrine as would secure it from either perishing by the neglect, vanishing away amid the errors, or being corrupted by the presumptuous audacity of men."[33] Theologians have often speculated as to the relative or absolute necessity of Scripture. Barth comments,

> Of course it might also have pleased God to give his Church the canon in the form of an unwritten prophetic and apostolic tradition, propagating itself from spirit to spirit and from mouth to mouth.[34]

32. Ramm, p. 179.
33. John Calvin, *Institutes,* 1:6:3.
34. Barth, vol. 1, pt. 1, p. 117. See also Warfield, pp. 210-11; and J. Orr, *Revelation and Inspiration,* p. 155.

If this had been so, he quickly observes, the church could scarcely have distinguished God's Word from her own. Scripture is for the *bene esse* (well-being) of the church. It is important to distinguish, however, the absolute importance of the redemptive revelation in Christ on which salvation rests, and the relative importance of the Scripture which is its vehicle and record. There could be a gospel without inspired Scripture. The Bible is not a necessary rational postulate required for the gospel to survive; it is a witness to revelation and generated by it, and a text which enjoys its validity on the basis of the prior validity of the gospel it attests.

The question is somewhat theoretical, for revelation comes to us clothed manifestly in the garb of Scripture. It was in *fact* given by God and authenticated by Christ (Jn 10:35). To deny the divine authority of Scripture in the light of the actual pattern of revelation would be an act of impiety and unbelief. No doubt many factors were involved in the *wisdom* of creating Scripture: the danger of God's message being corrupted by unscrupulous men, the need for its international distribution, the frailty of human memory, the complexity of divine truth to be transmitted, the church's need of its reforming impact. So it pleased God to instruct and edify His people by the provision of inspired *graphe*. The near anarchy of modern theology is proof of its pastoral necessity.[35]

The *purpose* of Scripture is identical with the purpose of revelation itself: to witness to Jesus as the Christ (2 Ti 3:15). It is not an almanac of sundry information, nor a book of historical curiosities. It is at heart Christocentric. He is the hub of its message, and the fulfillment of its hope (Ac 17:2-3; 28:23).[36] Because Scripture is Christological, it is soteriological. It belongs to the divine plan for redeeming sinners. Its role is to witness *truly* to the divine activity and the divine

35. See Packer, "The Necessity of the Revealed Word," in *The Bible: The Living Word of Revelation*, ed. Tenney, pp. 31-49; Preus, *The Inspiration of Scripture*, pp. 23-25.
36. *TDNT*, 1:758-59.

speaking. Christ is the hermeneutical *Guide* to the meaning of Scripture, not its critical scalpel. The fact that the Bible focuses on Christ gives no basis for critical mutilation of its text. Scripture is a seamless robe of truth-telling language. We have no right to delete passages we regard as unessential or incidental. Christ's attitude to Scripture was one of total trust. The Bible testifies to Christ precisely by being truthful in every part.

The reason Christians love and reverence Holy Scripture is because it is the locus of their confrontation with the living Word. It is the vehicle of the saving truth of the gospel. We love the Bible because we worship the Saviour. It is the transcript of the glad tidings of reconciliation and peace with God. The Bible is truly written revelation, the inscripturated Word of God. The divine revelation in Christ is the ultimate datum which Scripture documents. At the same time it is itself the culminating facet of holy history.

The Credibility of Revelation

How may a person reach the assurance that revelation is authentic and true, and the Scripture trustworthy and authoritative? Many religious claims are in the world competing for the allegiance of men. The mere claim to authority is not self-validating. Claims to divine revelation need to be checked and screened for their truth value. Since faith stands in relation to an object, it is imperative that the object be worthy. For many false prophets have gone out into the world, and Satan himself is clever at disguises. The testing of revelation claims is essential (1 Jn 4:1-6).

For some time there has been a vigorous tug of war between the "fideists" who believe that Scripture and the revelation it contains are *autopistic* (self-authenticating), and the "revelation-empiricists" who stress the intrinsic credibility of revelation and Scripture, that is, its *axiopistic* character (worthy of belief). The disagreement appears in a striking fashion in the reprinting of Warfield's various articles on inspiration, to which Cornelius Van Til supplies a lengthy introduction in which he repudiates a historical apologetic of the Butler type.[37] To establish the truth of revelation apart from first presupposing the truth of it, according to Van Til, is to light the sun with a candle. Warfield, on the other hand, believed that inspiration rests on the credibility of the revelation Scripture contains. The historical vindication of Christianity as a revelation from God is sufficient to guarantee for us the inspiration of the Holy Scriptures.[38] Van Til, most displeased with this philosophy of Christian apologetics, has continued his attack on this aspect of Warfield's thought, contending he adopted an Arminian view of the defense of Scripture.[39] Warfield believed that the witness of the Spirit terminated upon the *indicia* of truthfulness which the revelation contained, while Van Til holds that the infallibility of Scripture must be presupposed.[40] In our opinion, there are compelling reasons for rejecting Van Til's criticism of Warfield, and a powerful motivation for extending Warfield's thought even further.

THE FIDEISTS

Quite a spectrum of theological opinion today regards any attempt to validate revelation with rational argument as impious, impossible and unnecessary. Some orthodox fideists contend that faith needs no defense, and that to defend it is to slight the Holy Spirit. Neoorthodox spokesmen like Baillie regard all evidence outside their "encounter" superfluous. Orthodox presuppositionalists like Van Til reject empirical epistemology and cling to a system of voluntaristic metaphysics. The liberals deny that revelation has cognitive truth,

37. Warfield, p. 20.
38. Ibid., p. 121.
39. Cornelius Van Til, *The Doctrine of Scripture*, pp. 57-62.
40. L. Gaussen would seem to stand with Warfield, p. 138, in this matter, while Runia and Barth side with Van Til (K. Runia, *Karl Barth's Doctrine of Scripture*, pp. 5-17).

and so have no interest in the project. All in all, the inductive approach faces a thunderous veto![41]

However, the veto is futile since some checking procedure is the only defense we have against horrible self-delusion and a landslide of bigotry and fanaticism. But it is intriguing to observe the extreme diversity of the theologians making it. Fundamentalists, conservative Calvinists, neoorthodox loyalists, and post-Kantian liberals: all agree (more or less) that we should not speak of the objective truthfulness of Christian belief, but wed our case to subjective response. Kant is largely to blame in his denial of the cognitive status of religious beliefs and proposal of a postulational ("upper story") theism; Christian apologetics has only barely survived the tremendous influence of this one man.[42]

No one exceeds Rudolf Bultmann in denying that Christian faith has any objective foundation whatsoever. How do we know that the Christ event was the act of God? He says, "There seems to me to be only one answer: because it is proclaimed as such." He is adamant in refusing to see the resurrection as in any way substantiating the divine claims of Christ and the gospel. Historical events of the past cannot affect faith today. With this in mind it is easy to understand the lack of restraint Bultmann reveals in his critical assault on the historical foundations of the gospel narratives. Nothing really matters except self-authenticating faith. The objectively valid revelation of the New Testament is dissolved into a philosophy of existence. While it is true that Bultmann refuses to demythologize the importance of Jesus completely (as does John Macquarrie, *Scope of Demythologizing*), it would be more in keeping with the logic of his position to do so (as does Schubert M. Ogden, *Christ Without Myth*). At any rate, for Bultmann the validity of the Christian revela-

41. H. J. Paton entitled his third chapter on neoorthodoxy "The Theological Veto" in his *The Modern Predicament*, and F. Ferre picked it up recently in *Basic Modern Philosophy of Religion*, p. 23.

42. F. Ferre, chap. 7-8, has sketched the revolutionary effects of Kant's philosophy of religion with commendable clarity.

tion depends totally upon the decision to believe it, and on nothing else.[43]

In his important work on Christology, *Jesus—God and Man*, Wolfhardt Pannenberg, a leading German theologian, warns against self-delusion. Mere experience of the living Lord cannot add to our knowledge of Jesus. Christian truth is not constructed from the raw materials of experience alone as in Schleiermacher and now Bultmann. Our faith in the living Christ depends in its entirety upon the record of Christ's resurrection and exaltation. "Whatever concerns the certainty of the present life of the exalted Lord is based entirely on what happened in the past."[44] Faith is grounded in the reality and validity of the revelation of God in Jesus. If it is not, there is no reason to call it Christian.

Some examples of fideism applied to the inspiration of Scripture are in order. The decision of the Synod of 1961 of the Christian Reformed Church on the inspiration of the Bible cautions against grounding the doctrine in a historical apologetic.[45] The self-testimony of the Scripture itself is sufficient to establish its inspiration. Infallibility is an article of faith based on the Bible's claim to authority alone. E. J. Young concurs,

> We hold to a high view of inspiration for the simple reason that the Bible teaches a high view.[46]

Calvin supports the same position:

> Let it therefore be held as fixed that those who are in-

43. See especially Walter Schmithals, *An Introduction to the Theology of Rudolf Bultmann*, chaps. 6-8. The situation is identical with Karl Barth. Faith exists without proof. See Montgomery, *Where is History Going?* chap. 5.

44. Pannenberg, p. 28.

45. *Decision of the Synod of 1961 of the Christian Reformed Church on Infallibility and Inspiration in the Light of Scripture and our Creeds*, pp. 74-75.

46. E. J. Young, *Thy Word Is Truth*, p. 31. His paper read at the Wenham seminar on the authority of Scripture concerning Warfield's view of Scripture added: "Our conviction that they are trustworthy teachers, however, rests not upon our own unaided investigation and reason but simply and solely upon the inward testimony of the Holy Spirit" (pp. 29-30).

> wardly taught by the Spirit acquiese implicitly in Scripture; that Scripture, carrying its own evidence along with it, deigns not to submit to proofs and arguments, but owes the full conviction with which we ought to receive it to the testimony of the Spirit.[47]

John Murray agrees:

> The ground of faith emphatically is not our ability to demonstrate all the teachings of the Bible to be self-consistent and true. That is just saying that rational demonstration is not the ground of faith. . . . There is one sphere where self-testimony must be accepted as absolute and final.[48]

Gordon Clark adds:

> Christianity is often repudiated on the ground that it is circular: the Bible is authoritative because the Bible authoritatively says so. But this objection applies no more to Christianity than to any philosophic system or even to geometry.[49]

Herman Bavinck is very frank:

> But if it is then asked: Why do you believe that Holy Scripture is the Word of God?, the Christian has no further answer.[50]

Kuyper does not shrink from such fideism either:

> At no single point of the way is there place, therefore, for a support derived from demonstration or reasoning.[51]

The confessional basis upon which these Reformed men depend is an aspect of the Westminister Confession I.4:

47. Calvin, 1:7:5. "But it is foolish to attempt to prove to infidels that the Scripture is the Word of God. This it cannot be known to be, except by faith" (1:8:13).
48. John Murray, "The Attestation of Scripture," in *The Infallible Word*, pp. 7, 10.
49. Gordon Clark, *Can I Trust My Bible?* p. 28.
50. Herman Bavinck, *Gereformeerde Dogmatiek*, 1:559.
51. A. Kuyper, *Principles of Sacred Theology*, p. 365.

> The authority of the Holy Scripture, for which it ought to be believed and obeyed, dependeth not upon the testimony of any man or Church, but wholly upon God (who is truth itself), the author thereof; and therefore it is to be received, because it is the Word of God.

It cannot have escaped notice that this is precisely Barth's position too with regard to the apprehension of revelation and inspiration. Barth is the great fideist of the twentieth century, and allergic to Christian evidences, even as Kant and Kierkegaard, his mentors, were before him.[52] Predictably then, Barth speaks of the "logical circle" (more properly "vicious circle") in connection with the self-testimony of Scripture.[53] The Spirit enables believers to *know* religious truth.

In summary, the fideistic approach appears to claim that the Bible is inspired (1) because it says it is, and (2) because the Spirit accredits it subjectively. Two streams of argument run together—a bare authority claim, and a bare religious experience claim—and both are hopelessly vulnerable to criticism. The notion that faith based upon such factors is somehow immune from criticism and beyond falsification is pure fantasy. On the contrary, such a defense of inspiration is no defense at all.

1. First, it is evident that an authority claim is *not* self-validating. There are numerous claims to authority, religious and otherwise. Valid authority must present *credentials* which can identify it. Father Divine was not God, whatever he may have said. The Koran is not the Word of God, whatever it may claim. The credentials of the gospel, its open-to-investigation form, is its beauty. If all we had to go on was the fact that the Bible claimed to be true, we could not consider the claim meaningful.

2. Second, a subjective religious experience is a flimsy foundation for anything. In a day in which religion has

52. See Brand Blanshard, "Critical Reflections on Karl Barth," in *Faith and the Philosophers*, pp. 159-200.
53. Barth, vol. 1, pt. 2, p. 535.

literally gone to "pot," the difficulty of distinguishing one religious experience from another has become impossible. Experience is not an autonomous source of theological truth. If it were, LSD all around would be reasonable.[54]

3. Furthermore, it can scarcely be unnoticed that a religious experience lacks substantive content, and tends to confirm whatever beliefs the experiencing subject had to begin with. Thus the "testimony of the Spirit" allegedly tells a conservative Calvinist to believe in inerrancy, and a Barthian only to believe the Christological parts. As Stevick says, "It cannot establish such things as the factual accuracy of the text or conservative conclusions in criticism."[55]

4. Finally, and most important, religious experience is incapable of assuring us whether its origin is divine, demonic or human. A cursory glance at the history of religions will show how much existential fervor there is among savages who gladly perform atrocities on behalf of fiendish gods. A reflection on present culture will turn up a vast amount of misinformed and misdirected "soul." In addition, a bare religious-experience claim is vulnerable to the implacable hostility of a Freud and Feuerbach for whom all such are the projections of wishful thinking, or something much worse.

It will not do to rest our case for revelation and inspiration on so flimsy a base. It leaves us unable to defend Christianity at all, and opens the door to all manner of superstition and bigotry.[56] We strongly dissent from this part-authoritarian, part-existential solution to the question of credibility. For it seems to discredit the doctrine it seeks to defend. It merely

54. See Alan W. Watts, "Psychedelics and Religious Experience," in *The Religious Situation 1969*, pp. 615-31.

55. Donald B. Stevick, *Beyond Fundamentalism*, p. 85.

56. Harnack had the better of the argument with Barth when he addressed this question to him: "If the person of Jesus Christ stands in the center of the gospel, how can the basis for a reliable and common knowledge of this person be gained other than through critical historical study, lest we exchange the real Christ for one we have imagined?" (*The Beginnings of Dialectical Theology*, ed. James M. Robinson, 1:166). As John W. Montgomery asked Altizer, "Will the real Jesus please stand up?" (*The Altizer-Montgomery Dialogue*, p. 31).

makes Scripture vulnerable from a new direction. Evangelical faith rests upon established principle, not upon existential passion. Theologically, the fideistic approach, while sounding pious, is docetic in tendency. The dialectical notion that revelation becomes valid only in subjective response threatens the reality of revelation itself. The New Testament rather insists that the Christ event bears a universally valid truth claim upon which faith grounds itself. Evangelical theologians need to endorse the emphasis of the *Heilsgeschichte* scholars that revelation is an objective historical reality, and valid irrespective of personal decision or religious experience.[57]

Authority is not self-validating. After the fideist has pointed to his Bible or to his community, the question still remains: Which Bible and whose community? If we are to avoid philosophical solipsism and religious anarchy, we must follow the example of the apostles and point to the revelational *fact*, and proceed to build thereon.[58]

THE REVELATION EMPIRICISTS[59]

Warfield believed that the inspiration of the Bible was a component part of a divine revelation which was well attested historically.[60] Christian *faith* is related to historical *reality*. It is no mere solipsistic *Blik* (Hare). To rest faith upon a bare act of the will is to render it indistinguishable from fanaticism. To require a prior commitment to the gospel

57. O. Cullmann boldly resists the existentialist hostility to objective salvation history and repudiates any attempt to divorce the question of existence from that of God's saving acts in history. See his *Salvation in History*.

58. For a telling and humorous critique to presuppositionalism, see John Warwick Montgomery, "Once upon an A Priori: Van Til's Apologetic Epistemology in the Light of Three Parables," in *Jerusalem and Athens: Critical Discussions on the Philosophy and Apologetics of Cornelius Van Til*, ed. E. R. Geehan (Nutley, N.J.: Presbyterian & Reformed, 1971).

59. The empirical method understands the source of knowledge to be experience of the world of factuality. It involves the assumption that a factual world exists, and that the investigating subject is distinct from the data under study. On the basis of the information received, theories are formed and checked by means of further observation. A "revelation empiricist" is one who studies revelation as an objective reality, and comes to conclusions about its shape and credibility on the basis of the evidence available.

60. Warfield, "Apologetics," in *Studies in Theology*, pp. 3-21.

before the evidence for its truthfulness has been weighed is an apologetic that can never succeed. For if there are no reasons for believing the Christian revelation as such, there are no reasons for believing our experience to be revelation or our presupposition to be true.

Those who repudiate reason in matters of faith fail to make a simple distinction between reason as the arbitrating faculty which tests for consistency of argument and noncontradiction, and reason as an independent organ and source of divine revelation. Warfield claimed (1) that reason *was* competent to test religious claims, but (2) that it was *not* capable of inaugurating revealed truth. To deny the competence of reason in the first case is self-defeating because its very denial requires the use of reason and logic. The writing of a book and the carrying on of a discussion *assume* the validity of logic and the law of noncontradiction. In this limited sense, reason is prior to revelation because, if it were not, we could not think at all.[61]

The inductive-historical approach is based upon a positive evaluation of the relation between history and faith.[62] Scripture is the grammatical residue of a revelation which bears marks of credibility. If the gospel cannot be sustained by historical data, it cannot be sustained at all. Myths and fables may be immune to historical investigation if only because they are in essence a-historical; but the incarnation belongs to the flesh and bone of history. The validity of Christian theism rests on its *historical credentials.* Any disengagement from history is docetic in direction and deeply heretical. Faith is not an existential leap into the dark; it is motivated by strong *preambula fidei.* It is indeed a step into light! There is good

61. Charles Hodge writes: "Reason is necessarily presupposed in every revelation. Revelation is the communication of truth to the mind. But the communication of truth supposes the capacity to receive it. Revelations cannot be made to brutes or to idiots. Truths, to be received as objects of faith, must be intellectually apprehended" (*Systematic Theology,* 1:49).

62. See the author's "Toward a Rational Apologetic Based upon History," *Journal of the Evangelical Theological Society* 11(1968):147-51.

evidence that a divine revelation has been given. It is our task to present this evidence to lost men.[63]

It is sometimes argued against historical evidences for Christianity that they possess only probability and lack certainty. Admittedly, absolute certainty adheres only to assertions of formal logic and not to factual, historical beliefs. This is just to admit that mortals have to make decisions on the basis of probabilities. Factual, empirical knowledge falls somewhat short of absolute certainty. When we enter the realm of fact, we deal in probabilities. Life operates on this basis. Skepticism is a pleasant philosophical game, but one cannot live by it! As I. T. Ramsey has pointed out, moral response is reared upon probabilities.[64] Probability is the guide to life; it is the guide to religious truth too.

In an important essay, Kai Nielsen answers the question, "Can Faith Validate God-Talk?" with a convincing negative.[65] We may not, he insists, *begin* by presupposing all we seek to prove is true. Faith cannot make its way past criticism without an *empirical anchor*. To segregate Christian conviction from all empirical verification is to make nonsense of it and to go against the precise claims of the gospel to be historical.

It was the intractability of the arguments for the deity of Christ which moved C. S. Lewis toward faith.[66] It was the

63. Although Barth holds unambiguously to God's entering into human history in its concrete actuality in Christ, he holds that these salvation events are beyond substantiation and authentication by ordinary historical inquiry. We hold that unverifiable events are not very different from mythical ones, and sympathize with Bultmann's consistency in admitting it. Existential subjectivity in Barth's theology is that which hampers the outworking of his incarnational theology in the field of Christian proclamation.

64. I. T. Ramsey, *Christian Discourse: Some Logical Explorations*, pp. 23-24. E. J. Carnell comments: "In our daily living we *proportion* our inward response to the certainty of the evidences . . ." (*Philosophy of the Christian Religion*, pp. 474-475. See Montgomery, *The Shape of the Past*, pp. 139-40, 143-44. J. O. Buswell, Jr., holds that the theistic arguments also are inductive arguments, which enjoy a high degree of probability (*A Systematic Theology of the Christian Religion*, 1:72-101).

65. Kai Nielsen, "Can Faith Validate God-Talk?" in *New Theology No. 1*, pp. 131-49. See also Jerry H. Gill, "Talk about Religious Talk," in *New Theology No. 4*, pp. 99-123.

66. C. S. Lewis, *Surprised by Joy*, pp. 223-24; and *Mere Christianity*, pp. 52-53.

stubbornness of the facts which compelled Frank Morrison to write a book defending the resurrection of Christ.[67] The overwhelming fact of Christ settled the question of inspiration for James Orr.[68] Reformed theologian John H. Gerstner argues for a historical apologetic on behalf of biblical inspiration. He says the mere fact of the Bible's *claim* to authority does not constitute *proof* of that claim. The witness of the Spirit is not without substantive content, and experience cannot establish inerrancy. Gerstner rests his case on the appearance in history of divinely commissioned and authenticated messengers.[69]

Kantzer also rejects a circular argument from Bible to Bible. Belief in revelation and inspiration rests in part upon a number of historical and logical evidences which validate the truth of the Christian message. Divine revelation by means of events in objective history is verifiable in principle and in fact.[70] This thesis has been strongly supported by Fuller in *Easter Faith and History*.[71] Fuller holds that the evidence for the resurrection of Christ is exceedingly cogent, judged on the basis of criteria acceptable to all men. The facts cannot be otherwise explained than by concluding that Christ did indeed rise from the dead. Inspiration rests upon a previously attested revelation. A most emphatic voice on behalf of a historical apologetic has been Lutheran scholar John Warwick Montgomery, who touches this theme in all that he writes. He is convinced that the evidence for Christ and the gospel is eminently satisfying to heart and mind, and no reasonable person can sidestep the necessity of making a decision in regard to it.[72]

67. Frank Morrison, *Who Moved the Stone?*
68. James Orr, *Revelation and Inspiration,* chap. 7.
69. John H. Gerstner, *A Bible Inerrancy Primer,* pp. 11, 14-15, 18-19, 27-46.
70. Kantzer, "The Authority of the Bible," in *The Word for This Century,* p. 42; and "The Christ-Revelation as Act and Interpretation," in *Jesus of Nazareth,* pp. 258-59.
71. Daniel P. Fuller, *Easter Faith and History.*
72. Montgomery, *History and Christianity; The Shape of the Past,* pp. 138-45; *The 'Is God Dead?' Controversy,* pp. 49-59; "Clark's Philosophy of History," in *The Philosophy of Gordon H. Clark,* pp. 353-90.

A similar position has been espoused by Pannenberg. It is his conviction that historical study is capable of validating the resurrection claim of the New Testament. The death of Christ called all that Jesus stood for into question. The disciples were disillusioned and perplexed. It was the resurrection which galvanized them into evangelistic action. The bodily resurrection is the best explanation of the empty tomb, the appearances of Christ, and the success of the primitive Christian mission. The soundness of the ground of faith is crucial to the Christian message. Pannenberg explains:

> Naturally, in theology there can be no talk of proof in the exact mathematical, scientific sense. It neither has to do with deductions from apparent principles nor is an empirical verification of theological statements possible (or even meaningful) in the sense that they can be explained by recorded statements about intersubjective sensorial perception. That is true for the whole field of the humanities. However, "proof" in a broader sense that has also been adopted by theology since the patristic period can also mean that argument which appeals to a reasonable judgment and makes possible at least a provisional decision between contrasting assertions. Understood in this broader sense, a "proof" for the truth of faith does not need to stand in contradiction to its essence, for not every argument means having its "object" at its disposal. It need not displace the mysterious depth of the subject matter of faith, but it can precisely lead into it. Precisely the openness for what has not yet appeared in the history of Jesus of Nazareth, on which faith depends, could be decisive for the "proof" of the truth of faith.[73]

Faith is not destroyed by having a historical ground, but by *not* having one! A casual reader of the New Testament cannot fail to notice the pains its writers go to in insisting that the revelation in Christ is open to investigation and objectively valid (cf. Ac 17:31; Ro 1:4; 1 Co 15:14). Christianity is noth-

73. Pannenberg, p. 110. Alan Richardson has moved along these lines too in *History Sacred and Profane*, pp. 184-212. See also J. J. Navone, *History and Faith in the Thought of Alan Richardson.*

ing without its history. A defense of Scripture which does not relate itself to the factuality of the gospel revelation is self-impoverished and at odds with the apostolic approach. Christian faith is not autonomous. It is dependent on and subject to the given revelation fact. The notion of Protestant liberalism, enunciated by Lessing and Hegel, that religion (the revelation in Christ) is but a defective form of the pure philosophical idea, must be repudiated. The Christian ontology, theology and philosophy arise out of the Christ event. In Jesus the end for which Hegel speculated in vain is provisionally known. Perspective on life and the world which is impossible to relative man embedded in the flux of history now becomes possible on the basis of this decisive happening. The Christian may speak of the meaning of history without in any way committing himself to the ultimacy of his age or its systems because there is a transcendent reference within time, Jesus Christ and His Word.

Curiously, the line of defending the gospel historically is seldom discussed in books on the philosophy of religion. Instead the space is devoted to the revolution in theistic apologetics brought about by Hume and Kant, a topic well deserving extended reflection. But why is there a silence concerning the most promising of all lines of defense, the historical evidence? Because for various reasons the notion is foreign to the versions of theology affected by Kant and Kierkegaard. One of these is the rise of scientific criticism in biblical studies, which has, it is widely believed, made it impossible to treat the biblical material as reliable historical sources. The reason we believe this conclusion to be unduly pessimistic is explained in full in chapter 5. More important in explaining the reluctance to use historical evidences in the defense of the Christian revelation is the vestigal remnant of nineteenth century historicism, which vitiated a proper inductive approach by entertaining an antisupernaturalistic bias. "Miracles do not happen!" Such a statement is itself unscientific and unverifiable. The "laws" of nature are not laws at all, but rather empirical constructs built up upon observation and testimony, descriptive (what happened) not normative (what may happen). Whether Christ arose from the dead is first of all a historical rather than a philosophical question. On the basis of Hume's argument against miracles, as Montgomery points out, the Lilliputians should properly have refused to acknowledge the existence of Gulliver, the evidence notwithstanding, because their universal experience was against it!

The naturalistic bias has today been immersed in existential thought patterns and is doubly hard to rout out. An existential historiography has subjectivized the historical task, so that man's ability to arrive at objective findings is widely doubted (e.g., Dilthey).[74] Bultmann, for example, is both naturalistic (denies miracles) and existentialistic (denies objectivity) with respect to biblical history. Such a bias is untenable and such a pessimism unwarranted. Granted, there are numerous *possible* interpretations of a given historical datum. There are not, however, as many *probable* ones. While it is possible that Jesus was a Martian, a charlatan, or a madman, it is not probable that He was any of these. The manner in which we ascertain *who* He was is by a measuring and weighing of the pertinent data. A standpoint on anything should be *criticizable* and subject to the constraint of the evidence. A bigger difficulty standing in the way of the interpretation of history is the vast profusion of facts which need to be evaluated. It is not so much the "hiddenness" of facts as their sheer number. This is why the resurrection of Christ is such a beautiful answer to the truth question. Here is *the clue*, the hermeneutical perspective, to all history! The fact that we cannot by ourselves comprehend universal history should not yield the inference that "facts are inscruta-

74. Dilthey's notion that historical events need to be understood from the *inside* (one must be rather like Hitler to understand him!) relegates all history to the mystical "upper story," the neoorthodox *Geschichte*. The result is to eliminate the crucial distinction of subject and object. History means whatever one likes, and a relativistic, solipsistic chaos ensues.

ble," as Van Til and H. Ott maintain, but reveal our total dependence on Christ in this as in everything else.

Mention must be made regarding the testimonium of the Holy Spirit and its relation to the revelation data.[75] Scripture mentions this witness in connection with Christ and the gospel, *not* inspiration per se. He assures our hearts that we are saved (Ro 8:16; Gal 4:6-7; 1 Th 1:6; 2:13). There is no evidence that the testimonium is some sort of mystical proof of inerrancy. The Spirit glorifies *Christ* and should not be used to serve as the *deus ex machina* for fideism.[76] Orr perceived the dangers of putting such a stress here.[77] The testimonium could scarcely settle the question of the canonicity of Esther or Ecclesiastes and, when misused, comes perilously close to accrediting only those scriptures which one finds "inspiring." In actual fact, the witness of the Spirit terminates upon the evidence for the truth of revelation. The Spirit creates faith *through* the indications or evidences. Assurance is an inner persuasion based upon extrasubjective truth, not a blind, ungrounded conviction. There is a perfect balance between subjective and objective factors. Because faith is related to historical verity, it *cannot* and *must not* escape (contra Lessing) involvement in historical probabilities. If Christ be not raised (fact), our faith is vain (experience). Ours is a credible *and* spiritual conviction. The Spirit creates certitude in the heart on the basis of good and sufficient evidence. The Christ who appeared *ephapax* in history is the Christ who now reigns exalted in heaven. Christ is not divided. No dichotomy can be tolerated between the historic and the contemporaneous Christ. Faith is *neither* a grand assumption *nor* an unspiritual syllogism. It is man's response to the Word of God, the good news, as the Spirit attests the Christ event past and the Christ presence now. The testimonium is pointed at the stuff of revelation so that the objective datum becomes a subjective datum in our hearts (1 Pe 1:23).

75. See Ramm, *The Witness of the Spirit.*
76. As Kuyper has a tendency to do, pp. 553-63.
77. Orr, pp. 201-4.

With clear insight Warfield depicts the relation of testimonium and the evidences in this way:

> One might as well say that photography is independent of light, because no light can make an impression unless the plate [film] is prepared to receive it. The Holy Spirit does not work a blind, an ungrounded faith in the heart. What is supplied by his creative energy in working faith is not a ready-made faith, rooted in nothing, and clinging without reason to its object; nor yet new grounds of belief in the object present; but just a new ability of the heart to respond to the grounds of faith, sufficient in themselves, already present to the understanding. We believe in Christ because it is rational to believe in him, not though it be irrational. For the birth of faith in the soul, it is just as essential that grounds of faith should be present to the mind as that the Giver of faith should act creatively upon the heart.[78]

God has made Himself known in the fabric of human history as the God of mercy and grace. In relation to this pattern of redemptive revelation, the fact of biblical inspiration is to be understood. The divine self-disclosure in Christ is the foundation stone underlying all theology, preaching, and the life of faith, and this revelation generates the inspired Word. Revelation is not *simply* the communication of knowledge—it is far more than that. Yet it conveys, in the context of trust and fellowship, truth and doctrine, which conserve and deepen our relationship with God. The crisis in theology today is due to a loss of confidence in special revelation as being objective and meaningful.

78. Introduction in *Apologetics,* by F. R. Beattie, 1:25. William Cunningham believed that even the Reformers themselves, in their eagerness to refute the Romanist charge that evangelical faith was lacking in religious certainty, "went sometimes to the unwarrantable extreme of ascribing to the Holy Spirit not merely a subjective influence upon men's understanding and hearts, but an objective presentation of new and additional grounds and reasons for belief" (*The Reformers and the Theology of the Reformation,* p. 117).

2

THE NATURE OF BIBLICAL INSPIRATION

THE PATTERN OF DIVINE REVELATION makes it possible to answer the question of inspiration. Holy Scripture is a component part of divine revelation, and our view of inspiration is that which revelation requires. The validity and nature of biblical inspiration rests on the credentials and shape of revelation. If we are satisfied that God has indeed revealed Himself in Christ, we may proceed directly to determine what view of Scripture that disclosure demands. No appeal is made to the bare self-attestation of the Bible, *petitio principii* (a begging of the question). The mere claim to authority does not establish anything. The important fact is not that a document pretends to be divinely inspired, but that divinely accredited men claim authority for their words and writings. The value of this testimony is measured in terms of the trustworthiness of those who utter it. Christians, who are convinced that the revelation in history of the God of Scripture is objective and true, are obliged spiritually and logically to heed with all seriousness the teachings of Christ and His apostles with respect to biblical inspiration.

In the early decades of the twentieth century, humanistic, liberal theology was decisively challenged. The assumption that the revelation of God could be subjected to secular norms was repudiated and the finality of God's Word reaffirmed. Had the new theology returned to the biblical concept of revelation and inspiration, no need would exist for a book like this one. However, this was not the case. Liberal biblical criticism was not rejected, and the neoorthodox scholars continued to reduce the Bible to a mass of unrelated bits and pieces. Obviously this created a major crisis for them since now a basis no longer existed for building the theological edifice. Theology requires a true and authoritative Word in Scripture, which would judge, correct and redeem the wayward mind of man and give him grounds for saying things about God and the gospel that his own mind could neither discover nor test. But for our purposes at this juncture in the argument, this fact meant that there have been few major theologians defining and defending the authentically Christian position on inspiration. This is the task we have set out to do. For, while we may be grateful that modern theology allows some place for supernatural revelation, there is little evidence yet that it is prepared to do justice to supernatural *inspiration.*

Some have ventured the opinion that the Bible contains no doctrine of its own inspiration, or at least none which requires infallibility or inerrancy.[1] This is not, however, the problem we face in adducing the evidence for it. Our problem is the superabundance, not the scarcity, of biblical material pertaining to the doctrine. Warfield wryly comments that the effort to silence this evidence text by text is comparable to an effort to stop an avalanche one stone at a time![2] James Orr adds,

> It may surprise those who have not looked into the subject with care to discover how strong, full, and pervasive, the testimony of Scripture to its own inspiration is.[3]

An avalanche is not an inappropriate metaphor to describe the phenomenon we face. The data is so rich, how can it be cataloged and described? With sufficient space it would be

1. Donald B. Stevick, *Beyond Fundamentalism,* pp. 89-93.
2. B. B. Warfield, *The Inspiration and Authority of the Bible,* pp. 119-20.
3. James Orr, *Revelation and Inspiration,* p. 160.

possible to itemize it serially and expound upon the texts.[4] Our procedure is more modest. We have seleceted four texts as *foci* around which the data may be conveniently grouped. These classic texts are referred to in such a discussion time and again because they establish the point so well.[5] They serve as representatives of a vast body of evidence scattered throughout the biblical record. It seems superfluous to duplicate here the extensive research that has been done already in establishing the high doctrine of written Scripture which the Bible contains. For this is scarcely denied, even by its most ardent critics. What *is* needed is a direct facing of this type of question: What does this information amount to? What are we to make of it? How is it to be comprehended and defended? The present volume is far more interested in such questions. Therefore, we restrict our discussion to a generous sampling of this evidence which allows a fair appraisal to be made and a doctrine to be inferred.

2 TIMOTHY 3:16 (BERKELEY)

> All Scripture is inspired by God and is profitable for teaching, for reproof, for correction, for training in righteousness.

In this passage, Paul affirms the divine authorship of all Scripture.[6] What the Scripture says, God says. It is a God-breathed (*theopneustic*) document. For that reason Paul feels free to personify Scripture as God speaking (Gal 3:8, 22; Ro 9:17). This hypostasis of Scripture can only be explained if Paul identified Scripture and God's Word.[7] God is the *Author* of what Scripture records (Ac 13:32-35). The totality of Scripture is a divine oracle (Ro 3:2). In his writings, the apostle draws upon the full extent of Old Testament Scrip-

4. Stewart Custer adopts this procedure in *Does Inspiration Demand Inerrancy?*
5. E.g., Warfield, pp. 133-41.
6. On the question of Pauline authorship of the pastoral epistles, see E. E. Ellis, *Paul and His Recent Interpreters,* pp. 49-57; and D. Guthrie, *New Testament Introduction,* vol. 2: *The Pauline Epistles,* pp. 198-236.
7. *TDNT,* 1:754.

ture, from every category, and almost every book.[8] His argument can turn upon a single word (Gal 3:16). Its divine authorship ensures that authority belongs to every part, so that Scripture provides a solid basis of teaching (Ac 17:2-3; 26:22-23; 28:25). To Felix, Paul testified, "I worship the God of my fathers, believing in everything written in the Law and the Prophets" (Ac 24:14, Berkeley; cf. Ro 15:4). Nowhere does the apostle dissent from any of the teachings of Scripture. Whether he is referring to its history, doctrine, morals or prophecies, it is always as a completely trustworthy record and the doctrine of Scripture Paul enunciates is common to all the New Testament writers and teachers. Peter announced to the brethren before Pentecost, "Brothers, that Scripture had to be fulfilled *which the Holy Spirit uttered* by the mouth of David in the former times about Judas" (Ac 1:16, Williams). Scripture, as the voice of the Spirit, is a commonly expressed conviction (Ac 4:25; Heb 3:7; 10:15). Scripture *is* the Word of God (Heb 1:5-13; 4:12; 8:8). God is the ultimate Author of Scripture. It does not err because He cannot lie. Scripture is to be believed in all that it teaches because of its divine authorship. In rejecting Paul's use of a certain Old Testament text, Pannenberg makes an important admission in saying that such an interpretation could "provide such a basis only for one who accepts all the statements of the Old Testament as an irrevocable and eternally binding authority."[9] It is an incontrovertible historical fact that Paul held to the plenary inspiration of Holy Scripture. His was the doctrine of God speaking in *all* the sacred writings.

2 PETER 1:20-21 (WILLIAMS)

> Because you recognize this truth above all else, that no prophecy in Scripture is to be interpreted by one's own mind, for no prophecy has ever yet originated in man's will, but men who were led by the Holy Spirit spoke from God.

8. Ellis, *Paul's Use of the Old Testament,* pp. 150-87.
9. W. Pannenberg, *Jesus—God and Man,* p. 250. Cf. "The Crisis of the Scripture-Principle in Protestant Theology," *Dialog* 2(1963):307-13.

While Paul stresses the positive ("*all* scripture is inspired"), Peter mentions the negative ("*no* prophecy has ever yet originated in man's will").[10] Each in his way affirms plenary inspiration and divine authorship. Scripture was not initiated by man, the result of human research. It is of divine origin. The Spirit of Christ spoke through the prophets (1 Pe 1:11), as He did also through Paul (2 Pe 3:16). The notion of men energized by the Spirit and compelled to speak God's Word is basically an Old Testament conception. (Mic 3:8; Zec 7:12).[11] Amos can speak for all the rest: "The Lord God has spoken, who can but prophesy?" (3:8) God's prophets are His spokesmen (Ex 4:10-16; 7:1). David said, "The Spirit of the Lord speaks by men, his word is upon my tongue" (2 Sa 23:2; cf. Mk 12:36). Peter does not intend to restrict his meaning to the prophetic portions of Scripture alone. For a Jew, the prophets would not have precedence over law. It is a case of *pars pro tota* (one part standing for the whole). All Scripture is prophetic in that it is a divine Word. It is clear from Peter's epistles and his speeches in Acts that he regarded the whole extent of Scripture to be divinely authoritative.

At the same time, Holy Scripture was written by *men* in the style, vocabulary and modes of their day. The Spirit controlled the human writers but did not obliterate them. Each had a message to deliver. Yet, in the very mentioning of the human side of Scripture, the apostle makes it abundantly clear that the initiative lay with God, and the literary product was divinely authored. Their work has a divine stamp upon it. For they were moved by the Spirit, and their word was endowed with singular power and truthfulness.

MATTHEW 5:17-18 (BERKELEY)

Do not suppose that I came to annul the Law or the

10. For a defense of the Petrine authorship of 2 Peter, see E. M. B. Green, *Second Peter Reconsidered;* and Guthrie, vol. 3: *Hebrews to Revelation,* pp. 143-71.

11. J. Barton Payne, *The Theology of the Older Testament,* pp. 63-70; A. Berkeley Mickelsen, *Interpreting the Bible,* pp. 80-85.

> Prophets. I did not come to abolish but to complete them; for I assure you, while heaven and earth endure not one iota or one projection of a letter will be dropped from the Law until all is accomplished.

In this text, Jesus pronounces upon the indefectible authority of the Old Testament, and the eschatological understanding of His own ministry:[12] "It is easier for heaven and earth to pass away than for the smallest part of a letter of the Law to become invalid" (Lk 16:17, Berkeley). Jesus called Scripture "the word of God" (Mk 7:13). The Scripture in its whole extent and in all its parts, even down to seemingly unimportant details, is God-given. The Sadducees had failed to reckon on one such detail in their thinking on the resurrection (Mt 22:29, 31-32). Because it was the divine commandment (Mt 19:4-5), everything in Scripture *had* to be fulfilled (Mk 14:49). Hence, Christ refused help from the Father in the face of judicial murder on the cross (Mt 26:53-54). His sufferings had been predicted in prophetic Scripture (Lk 24: 45-46). The one who said, "My teaching is not Mine but His who sent Me" (Jn 7:16, Berkeley; cf. 12:48-50), made the same claim for Scripture as He made for His own words: "My words shall not pass away" (Mt 24:35). The significance of this fact is great. He on whom the salvation of men depends, taught with the greatest of force the full inspiration of extant Scripture. He regarded God as its true Author, and bowed to its divine authority. Jesus constituted Christianity a religion of biblical authority; for although He showed tremendous freedom from human convention and tradition, and claimed divine inspiration for His own teachings, yet He bowed to the voice of His Father speaking in the Scriptures. His arguments were clinched by a text, His foes were rebuked for not knowing the Scriptures better, Satan himself was rebuffed by a simple appeal to the written Word of God, His ministry was governed down to the smallest detail by what

12. W. D. Davies defends the pericope as an authentic word of Jesus in *Christian Origins and Judaism*, pp. 31-66.

Scripture predicted the Messiah would be and do. He refused to separate revelation from Scripture, which He used plentifully, confidently and effectively.[13]

In a full critical study of Christ's doctrine of Scripture, of course various factors would have to be considered: the historical setting of each *logion*, the differences in citation between the several gospels, and the Aramaic substratum. The biblical evangelists do not always agree on what the precise introductory formula was (cf. Mt 4:7, "it is written," and Lk 4:12, "it is said"). And, although most of the canon is cited, not all of it is. Furthermore, it is important that we recognize the setting of Jesus' teachings. The Jewish *doctrine* of Scripture was excellent; their *obedience* to it was not. Christ had to break through to their hearing by means of a fresh hermeneutic. This means care must be exercised in ascertaining precisely what Jesus intended by His words. Even in the face of such considerations, however, the fact is unchanged that He regarded the Old Testament as a divine oracle.[14] Indeed, biblical critics whose views are anything but evangelical, freely admit that Jesus believed in the inerrancy of Scripture.[15]

The force of this evidence cannot be dulled or dismissed simply by supposing that Christ "condescended not to know" or accommodated Himself to the presuppositions of His time. For, if this be true, the discussion shifts from inspiration to Christology. Christ's doctrine of Scripture was fundamental to His understanding of revelation and authority. If He was mistaken in this, nothing He says concerning God and salvation may be trusted. His entire career would have been based upon a fallacy of no small magnitude. Christ was never reluctant to criticize the views of His generation when they

13. For a full treatment of Christ's doctrine and use of Scripture, see Robert P. Lightner, *The Saviour and the Scriptures*.

14. See Robert Kraft, "Contributions of Jesus to a Modern Discussion of Inspiration" (Master's thesis, Wheaton College, Ill. 1957).

15. F. C. Grant, *Introduction to New Testament Thought*, p. 75. See Kenneth S. Kantzer, *Christ and Scripture, His* magazine offprint, p. 2; C. H. Pinnock, *A New Reformation*, pp. 6-10.

impeded the true knowledge of God. If Christ was in error in a matter so central to His message, His divine authority is plainly discredited. Christ located the utterance of God in Scripture. No believer dare impeach Him for this. Orthodox theologians agree completely with Kantzer as he writes,

> To accept Christ as Lord and to submit to his teaching regarding the complete authority of Scripture is consistent. Again, to acknowledge the validity of apostolic claims to authority and to receive their teaching as to the complete authority of Scripture is also consistent. To accept Christ's Lordship and the authority of his apostles and prophets and at the same time to reject their unequivocal teaching regarding the inspiration and authority of Scripture is *not* consistent.[16]

It is consistent to reject Christ *and* Scripture, or to accept both; but it is not consistent or honest to accept one and reject the other.[17] Where Christ is Lord and Saviour, the matter of authority is settled: Scripture is divinely authored and absolutely trustworthy.

It is perfectly evident that Jesus rarely appealed to direct revelation for teaching about His mission. Almost invariably He cites the Scripture as divine witness to His ministry (Lk 4:21; 7:22, 27; 18:31). The greatest error of the Sadducees was not to know the Scriptures (Mt 22:29). God's Word cannot fail or be broken (Mt 4:4; 5:18). "His own understanding of the meaning and fate of his message and mission is entirely bound up with his understanding of the Old Testament."[18]

JOHN 10:35

"Scripture cannot be broken."

Our Lord cited Psalm 82:6 for the purpose of repelling

16. Kantzer, "The Authority of the Bible," in *The Word for This Century*, ed. Merrill C. Tenney, p. 50.

17. For a history of the discussion, see H. D. McDonald, *Theories of Revelation*, pp. 137-60.

18. Ellis, "The Authority of Scripture: Critical Judgments in Biblical Perspective," *Evangelical Quarterly* 39 (1967): 198.

the charge that He necessarily blasphemed in claiming to be the Son of God. The Old Testament passage afforded evidence that the term *God* could, under restricted circumstances, be used to refer to human beings, in this case, in their official capacity as judges. Although the hermeneutic involved in this citation is of considerable interest, it is our intention simply to reflect upon the doctrine of Scripture it presupposes. Obviously for Jesus the Old Testament Scripture is a body of sacred literature whose utterances are completely true and divinely authoritative. The Scriptures in their precise verbal form embody and comprise God's written Word, whose binding force cannot be annulled. It has been charged that the entire argument is *ad hominem*, dictated by the stress of a dangerous situation, and one which cannot supply evidence on our subject. Indeed, the argument itself was calculated to refute the charge against Jesus on a biblical technicality. However, the view of inspiration which made such an argument possible underlies Christ's attitude to Scripture on every occasion. "Man shall not live on bread alone but on every command that proceeds from the mouth of God" (Mt 4:4, Berkeley). Jesus' constant attitude to Scripture was that it had legal, binding force, and that its authority could not be broken.

There is not a granule of evidence that Christ on any occasion

> belittled Scripture (as modern critics do), or set it aside (as the Jews had done with their tradition), or criticized it (although he criticized those who misused it), or contradicted it (although he rejected many interpretations of it), or opposed it (although he sometimes was free or interpretive with it), or operated as a higher critic of the Old Testament in any way.[19]

Abundant evidences exist to prove that for Christ and the

19. David P. Livingston, "The Inerrancy of Scripture: A Critique of Dewey Beegle's Book, *The Inspiration of Scripture*" (Master's thesis, Trinity Evangelical Divinity School, Deerfield, Ill., 1969), p. 98. An admirable summary of Christ's view of Scripture follows.

apostles, Scripture in its entire extent was uniquely inspired and normative. By the supernatural influence of the Spirit exercised upon them, the literary products of the biblical writers were preserved from error and were made divinely trustworthy and authoritative.

The Inspiration of the New Testament Scriptures

For reasons of chronology, the New Testament Scriptures could not have been authenticated in quite the same way as the Old Testament was. Christ's doctrine of Scripture establishes the *nature*, though not the full extent, of Scripture, and enunciates clearly the *principle* that written revelation is the product of special revelation. His witness covers the Old Testament retrospectively and the New Testament prospectively. In regard to the New Testament, two factors stand out: (1) the evident analogy between the periods of revelation in the Old and New Testament times with reference to the place of Scripture, and (2) the structure of authority which Christ Himself set in motion in appointing apostles to lead the infant church.

THE BASIS IN ANALOGY

The appearance of New Testament Scriptures surprised no one in the early church. Inspired writings had been the complement of the revelation under the old covenant, and the same factors were at work in the new. Christ had not given even the Old Testament its authority; He simply recognized and received it. What gave it authority was its divine authorship that had impressed itself upon God's people long before. The New Testament finds its validity as the *written complement* and *product* of *new covenant revelation.* Divine revelation calls for and generates inspired Scriptures. The minds of the early Christians were predisposed to receive it, believing as they did in the Christian revelation. The old covenant revelation was prophetic of things to come. It was the prologue of a greater drama. Just as the revelation in the Old Testament called for its fulfillment in the New, so the Old Testament Scriptures called for a written complement in the New.[20] The importance that written revelation had to the prophetic revelation was not lessened when it came to the Christian revelation. Indeed, it would be wrong to suggest that the New Testament teachers enjoyed merely *equal* rank with their Old Testament counterparts, for the splendor of the covenant they were administering meant that they would enjoy even greater dignity (2 Co 3:4-18; Mt 11:11). Theologically, the production of New Testament Scripture was entirely predictable by analogy with the Old Testament experience, and made legitimate by the fresh flow of divine revelation.

THE BASIS IN DELEGATED AUTHORITY

The historical basis for the inspiration of the New Testament Scriptures lies in the authority of Christ and His delegation of that authority to the apostolate.[21] It is apparent that Christ made claim to divine authority for Himself and His teachings (Mt 7:24, 29; Mk 2:10). The word and deed of Christ are *the* fundamental revelation of the New Testament. The disciples were immensely privileged to have access to Him, the fulfillment of the Old Testament promise (Mt 13:16-17). Early in His ministry Jesus called to Himself His *apostles* (Lk 6:12-13), a term which implies the authority of the one sent to act on behalf of the sender.[22] These select men became Jesus' disciples (learners) so that they might become His apostles (emissaries). He taught and prepared them for a coming ministry when He would no longer be with them (Mk 3:14; 4:11). To these men Jesus promised the teaching charisma of the Holy Spirit (Mk 13:11; Mt 10:19-20; Jn 14:25-26; 15:26-27; 16:13-14). Thus He *preauthen-*

20. A. Kuyper, *Principles of Sacred Theology*, p. 466.
21. See J. Norval Geldenhys, *Supreme Authority;* and Herman N. Ridderbos, *The Authority of the New Testament Scriptures*.
22. See the article "apostello" by Karl H. Rengstorf in *TDNT* 1: 398-447.

ticated their teachings for the early church and ensured respect for their authority. The apostles were to play a crucial role in the plan of redemption, in the founding of the church, and in the writing of the New Testament. Christians are bound to the word of the apostles because of their place in the pattern of authority our Lord set in motion (Jn 17:20).

As soon as we encounter the apostles after the events of resurrection and Pentecost, we find them supremely conscious of the authority delegated to them by Christ. They preached and acted with authority, and their ministries were accompanied with supernatural signs (Ac 3:6-7; Heb 2:3-4). Claims of divine authority abound in the New Testament letters because the apostles were conscious of the revelational status of their witness (Ac 10:41-42; 1 Th 2:13). They spoke in Christ's name and acted on His authority. Paul repeatedly makes this plain (Gal 1:1, 11-12; 1 Co 2:13; 14:37; 2 Co 13: 3, 5, 10; 1 Th 5:27; 2 Th 3:14). It is evident that the apostles regarded their teaching as authoritative and binding. This conviction had nothing to do with personal egotism on their part. It is based on their calling to be foundational in the building of the church (Eph 2:20). Their instructions, oral or written, were from God (2 Co 11:4; 2 Jn 10). The epistles were written, as is evident from their tone, as authoritative teachings of divinely authorized apostles of Christ. The letters were a substitute of their personal presence (2 Co 10:11; 2 Th 2:14). They represent the earliest examples of systematic reflection upon the intellectual content of Christian faith, and constitute both the starting point and ruling norm of all subsequent efforts.

Furthermore, there is every indication that the authority they claimed was received readily by the primitive church (Ac 2:42). The dignity of the apostles was everywhere respected. Christ rules His church by the apostles (2 Pe 3:2). Clement of Rome regarded Peter and Paul as "the greatest and most righteous pillars of the Church," and acknowledged their right to rule and regulate the thought and life of the church in the name of the Lord.[23]

Out of this pattern of authority, the New Testament Scriptures naturally flowed. The expansion of the church and the instability of oral tradition left to itself, necessitated the production of written Scripture. Ramm identifies three pressures which accelerated this process: the need to settle controversies in far-flung churches with a stable, written word; the need to bolster up the historical faith in Christ by means of gospels; and the need to check willful distortion of the tradition as was the case in Judaism (Mt 15:3).[24] The danger of tradition smothering the gospel has proved to be a perennial threat, and it underlies the Reformation's insistence on *sola scriptura* (Scripture alone is the basis of authority). Unless a standard exists to correct tradition and church, the gospel may be taken over by alien speculations. Before the apostles died, they left behind a substitute for their oral teaching in the writings which became the foundation of faith. These "memoirs" the early Christians read in their Sunday worship along with the writings of the prophets.[25] Christian faith was received from the apostles and disciples of the Lord.[26] Thus the intention of the apostles to fix the tradition by their writing was successful in the glad acceptance of them by the vast majority of Christians from the beginning. The authority of the message proclaimed by Christ's apostles attached itself to their literary remains. By her acknowledgment of the canon, the church has set herself to live beneath and be ruled perpetually by the word of Christ through the apostles.[27]

Neoorthodoxy performed a valuable service in renouncing liberalism's humanistic conquest of the gospel. But "its

23. Clement of Rome, *To the Corinthians,* paragraphs 5, 42, 44. See also Polycarp, *Philippians,* par. 3.

24. B. Ramm, *Special Revelation and the Word of God,* pp. 172-73.

25. Justin Martyr, *Apology,* 67.

26. Irenaeus, *Adversus Haereses,* i, 10, 1-2.

27. A full discussion regarding the rise of the New Testament canon is to be found in H. E. W. Turner, *The Pattern of Christian Truth,* chap. 5: "Orthodoxy and the Bible."

interpretation of revelation in terms of selective historical events, fallible records, and encounter with God can only end in subjectivism and in a mystical interpretation of Scripture that fails to do justice to the Biblical view of itself as the words and acts of God revealed through a controlled redemptive history and recorded in written form to constitute an authoritative basis for human thought concerning the divine."[28] Scripture itself makes it plain that divine revelation comes clothed in human language, a genuinely *verbal* communication between persons. Revelation is enshrined in written records and is essentially propositional in nature.

The Doctrinal Implications of the Scriptural Testimony

On the basis of the evidence it is possible, and imperative, to construct a doctrinal model of inspiration which is at once adequate (able to do justice to the data) and judicious (cautious not to overstep the bounds of evidence). Our findings are presented in the following *thesis*, divided into thirteen *ektheses* in which it is to be analyzed:

1 *All Scripture is God-breathed,*
2 *and is God's written Word to man,*
3 *infallible and*
4 *inerrant,*
5 *as originally given.*
6 *Divine inspiration is plenary,*
7 *verbal, and*
8 *confluent.*
9 *As the very Word of God, Scripture possesses the properties of authority,*
10 *sufficiency,*
11 *clarity, and*
12 *efficacy.*
13 *The central purpose of Scripture is to present Christ.*

28. R. K. Harrison, *Introduction to the Old Testament*, p. 466.

EKTHESIS ONE: ALL SCRIPTURE IS GOD-BREATHED (2 TI 3:16)

This statement is the basis for all that follows. Paul asserts that the totality of Scripture as a unity is of divine origin and authorship, the product of the divine breath. *All* the high attributes of Scripture rest on this fact. Inspiration does not have reference to the quality of being subjectively "inspiring" to the readers. It represents the idea of God-breathed Scripture.[29] The confession of inspiration is not an explanation of the process whereby Scripture came into existence. Inspiration does not require any special mental or psychological experience on the writers' part. Some wrote in ecstasy (Rev 1:10); some did not (Lk 1:1-4). It is possible Isaiah or Jeremiah were "inspired' (in the secular sense) in their work, but it is unimportant to this usage of the term. For inspiration is here predicated of the writing itself, not of the writers or of the ideas which made it up. It is this language deposit which owes its existence to the power of God. What the Scriptures *record* is God-breathed, not what the writers may have thought, or what we think they thought.

Inspiration is a quality possessed by Holy Scripture. It is *all* God-breathed. Its inspiration is *plenary*. We have no right to disbelieve any of it. All matters in Scripture were placed there by God for our learning. The Bible is authoritative in all that it teaches, in the cognitive-factual assertions as well as the doctrinal and ethical material. Furthermore, inspiration is a *fact* which does not admit of *degrees*. There are detectable levels of revelation but not of inspiration, which is true of all Scripture. To speak of degrees of inspiration is to confuse the secular-artistic with the biblical-theological meaning of the term. All Scripture is of divine authorship. No doubt the Chronicles occupy a humbler place in the body of Scripture than Romans does. The latter has a different *function* to perform. Both, however, belong to the written language revelation inspired of God. It ought to be

29. Warfield, pp. 245-96, did the linguistic spadework on *theopneustos*, proving it to be a passive, not an active, term.

stressed that inspiration does not consist of a vague inspiration of persons or ideas, but specifically of *words*, verbal inspiration. Men *spoke* as they were moved by the Spirit. Their articulated language was God speaking (Heb 3:7). Plenary, verbal inspiration alone is true to the biblical self-attestation. Scripture has God for its Author.

EKTHESIS TWO: GOD'S WRITTEN WORD TO MAN (MK 7:13)

There is a stubborn refusal in modern theology to *identify* the Word of God with Holy Scripture. The virtual equation of revelation with the Bible is said to be the "heresy" of Protestant orthodoxy. Paul Tillich writes,

> Probably nothing has contributed more to the misinterpretation of the biblical doctrine of the Word than the identification of the Word with the Bible.[30]

Even among the Barthians we hear only that the Bible is a *human witness* to revelation. A divorce is made between the Scriptures and the Word of God, a distinction born in liberalism and retained by neoorthodoxy. Fearful warnings are issued against "bibliolatry," and ridicule is directed toward those who idolize their "paper pope." Nels Ferre detects even a demonic motif in the identification, while Brunner refers to "all its disastrous results."[31]

Curiously, the Bible itself is not afraid to identify Scripture with the Word of God but does it repeatedly! The Old Testament is always cited in the New as the *univocal* Word of God: ". . . what the *Lord* had said through the prophet" (Mt 1:22, Berkeley); "The *Holy Spirit* spoke rightly to your fathers through Isaiah the prophet" (Ac 28:25, Berkeley). What Scripture says, God says. Luther had no hesitation in identifying the Word with Scripture: "You are so to deal with the Scriptures that you bear in mind that God himself is saying

30. P. Tillich, *Systematic Theology,* 1:158-59.
31. N. F. S. Ferre, *The Christian Understanding of God,* p. 179. See McDonald, pp. 176-95; Emil Brunner, *The Christian Doctrine of God,* p. 28.

this."[32] *Scripture* and the *Word* are interchangeable terms. Even Brunner reluctantly admits this is often true in the biblical data.[33] The New Testament writers *do* identify the two. Scripture is *God's utterance* (Gal 3:8; Ac 4:24-25). We cannot, therefore, regard this identification as a theological iniquity, as we are asked to do. It is rather the *failure* to make the connection which is a serious error. The Bible is no mere record of revelation, but is itself revelation, mediating an authentic knowing of God because it embodies truth revelation. Our encounter with God is charged with meaning because it occurs within the context of a valid, conceptual revelation. Scripture is that mode of revelation in which the redemptive events are explained and the living Word encountered by faith. Scripture is the culmination of the divine acting and speaking in special revelation. When we speak of the divine authorship of Scripture, of course we mean it in a complex rather than a simple way. God did not write Scripture by Himself! His Word was transmitted by significant human authors, not penmen, in words flavored by their touch. The literary product is nonetheless the very Word of God.

This is not to deny that in certain circumstances the Bible may be only letter (*gramma*, 2 Co 3:6). By their traditional interpretations, the rabbis had invalidated the Word, not merely transgressed it (Mk 7:6-13). When the light breaks through, *revelation* is not too strong a word to use (Lk 10:21). As God's Word, Scripture does not infallibly impart spiritual truth to every reader. Many factors enter into the impression it makes (Lk 8:4-10). The Scripture is not an effective medium of revelation where the Spirit does not speak. Yet that text is a unique medium and contains the freight of revelation to such an extent that the gospel is truly attested where the Spirit is effectually working.

EKTHESIS THREE: INFALLIBLE (PS 19:7)

The term *infallible* as applied to Scripture has a noble vin-

32. Luther as cited by Francis Pieper, *Christian Dogmatics*, 1:216.
33. Brunner, pp. 22-23.

tage. It means "not liable to deceive" or "make a mistake." It was used by the English Reformers, Cranmer and Jewel, as well as by Wycliffe.[34] The Belgic Confession, Article 7, calls Scripture "an infallible rule." The Westminster Confession I.9 says, "The infallible rule of interpretation of Scripture is the Scripture itself." The meaning is clear. Scripture as God's Word is nondeceptive and nonfailing. It does not deceive or mislead, because it is the utterance of the God who cannot lie (Titus 1:2). Complete veracity is the hallmark of His Word. Scripture is clear about the sanctity of truth.[35] Infallibility *is* a necessary deduction from the doctrine of inspiration. God's Word does not and cannot deceive or it would not be *His*. The doctrine of Scripture is hedged about by negative terms, *infallible* and *inerrant*, just as the doctrine of Christ is protected by a set of four other negative terms in the symbol of Chalcedon.[36] They serve to repulse heretical notions *without* reducing the mystery to a formula. John Gill caught the meaning of infallible when he wrote,

> In general there is nothing in them unworthy of God; nothing contrary to his truth and faithfulness, to his purity and holiness, to his wisdom and goodness, or to any of the perfections of his nature; there is no falsehood nor contradiction in them; they may with great propriety be called, as they are, *The Scriptures of Truth*, and the *Word of Truth*.[37]

John Macquarrie has noted that belief in biblical infallibility dies hard in some parts of the Christian world.[38] He need not be surprised. The reason is not difficult to perceive. Not only is it the view espoused by our Lord and His apostles, and endorsed by most theologians until recently, but it is the only secure basis on which an affirmative theology may rest. The current demise of authoritative preaching and teach-

34. J. I. Packer, *'Fundamentalism' and the Word of God*, pp. 94-95.
35. John Murray, *Principles of Conduct*, chap. 6.
36. Namely, "inconfusedly, unchangeably, indivisibly, inseparably."
37. John Gill, *Body of Divinity*, p. 14.
38. John Macquarrie, *Principles of Christian Theology*, p. 9.

ing of theology is sad testimony to the loss of this conviction. The foundation of theology is only as secure as the Bible is trustworthy. *Sola scriptura* and biblical infallibility are inextricable. An erring standard provides no sure measurement of truth and error. Infallible Scripture is the necessary link epistemologically between sinful man and the inscrutable God. The surrender of infallibility is a disastrous mistake, with deadly effects on theology and the church. These effects are even now highly visible in the tragic ambiguity of contemporary Christian thought.

The infallibility of Scripture is not, in one sense, absolute. Its field is restricted to the *intended* assertions of Scripture understood by an ordinary grammatical-historical exegesis of the text. Scripture operates under a normal correspondence idea of truth.[39] When it records a historical fact, we understand a real event to have occurred corresponding to it. Where it speaks of the purposes of God, we assume these are His very intentions. The intentionality of Scripture is identical with its plain and literal sense and is not superimposed arbitrarily upon the text. The divine intention is revealed precisely *in* the text of Scripture. There is no justification for arbitrarily deciding beforehand wherein Scripture may truly speak. Scripture is true in *all* that it *teaches*. *Quidquid docetur a scriptore sacro, docetur a Spiritu Sancto.* (Whatsoever is taught by Holy Scripture, is taught by the Holy Spirit.) The intended sense must neither be artificially restricted (e.g., by Bultmann's anthropocentric bias), nor arbitrarily expanded (e.g., by Rimmer's scientific contraband smuggled into the text). The sense of Scripture is left up to Scripture.[40]

In this connection it is sometimes necessary to distinguish the *subjects* Scripture teaches from the *terms* employed to

39. Robert Preus, "Notes on the Inerrancy of Scripture," in *Crisis in Lutheran Theology*, ed. John W. Montgomery, 2:37-38.

40. The principle is applicable to every branch of Christian scholarship and science, that wherever Scripture enunciates a truth unequivocally, contrary hypotheses are, strictly speaking, irrelevant (e.g., who Jesus' father was, or how man evolved by chance from nothing). The Christian scholar is the minister of God, directed in all his endeavors by the biblical revelation data.

discuss them. For example, the biblical writers pictured the natural order of the world in modes of expression current in their day. Paul was caught up to the "third heaven," and the earth stands secure on pillars (2 Co 12:2; 1 Sa 2:8). Such expressions stand in contexts where there is no intention to teach cosmology.[41] Infallibility does not update the writers' view of the physical cosmos where this is unnecessary. A man need not be an astronomer to marvel at the glory of the heavens. Inspiration did not make Paul a physicist nor David a physician. These matters do not affect biblical infallibility. In such passages we may gain a hint of what some writer believed about cosmology, but it is an exaggeration to say Scripture *teaches* an outdated theory of the structure of the world. Such references are *incidental* to the teachings intended. We need to ask what is being *asserted* in this passage.[42] We can hardly object to the biblical writers describing the world as they saw it in popular terminology when we do the same thing ourselves (e.g., the four corners of the earth, the sun rises). The phrase "heaven above, . . . earth beneath, and . . . water under the earth" (Ex 20:4) is a Hebrew expression of *totality*. Communication of meaning was no problem in Moses' day nor is it in ours. Certainly the biblical writers employed expressions drawn from the culture of their own day, but this does not negate infallibility. The language adopted in the second commandment serves perfectly well to convey the total scope and exclusiveness of the divine claim. Infallibility is relative to the intended scope of scriptural assertions. On occasion, form must be distinguished from content. An infallible judgment may be made which makes use of allusions or concepts which are time-conditioned.[43] To admit that the

41. Mascall and most moderns believe Scripture never touches on scientific matters. See E. L. Mascall, *Christian Theology and Natural Science*, pp. 11-12. We do not believe this principle can be supported exegetically.
42. See Packer, pp. 96-99. Charles Hodge, *Systematic Theology*, 1:170, distinguished between what the biblical writers thought and what they taught.
43. *Veritas est in judicio, non in simplici apprehensione* (Truth lies not in a simple first reading, but in considered judgment). For example, it may be

writers used modes of speech common to their day is only to say they wrote to be understood. In the case of the washing of the feet or the wearing of the veil, we are capable of distinguishing the concrete cultural act from its absolute, religious principle. God's Word is given in a particular social and cultural situation and is colored by it. The task of interpretation is to penetrate the form of Scripture so as to elucidate its matter, in the conviction that the biblical teaching is infallibly true on the subjects it claims to treat.[44, 45]

EKTHESIS FOUR: INERRANT

> I, the LORD, speak the truth and declare what is right (Is 45:19, Berkeley).
> Every word of God has proven true . . . add not to His words, lest He reprove you, and you be found a liar (Pr 30:5-6, Berkeley).

Inerrancy is to be regarded as an essential concomitant of the doctrine of inspiration, a necessary inference drawn from the fact that Scripture is *God's* Word. Hardly a notable theologian failed to draw this conclusion until the time of the great defection, the rise of deistic rationalism in the eighteenth century. Inerrancy is a property of inspired Scripture.[46] As Wesley put it:

> If there be any mistakes in the Bible, there may well be a thousand. If there be one falsehood in that book, it did not come from the God of truth.[47]

If the biblical writers erred in one particular, we have no assurance they did not err in many more. St. Augustine observed,

that Jude in citing the apocryphal book of Enoch (v. 14 f.) *intends* to condemn heretics of his time, and not to teach us that this book is itself authentic. See J. Levie, *The Bible, Word of God in Words of Men,* pp. 216-17.

44. See Klaas Runia, *Karl Barth's Doctrine of Holy Scripture,* pp. 81-90.

45. Runia also has an important article on the nature of biblical infallibility, "The Authority of Scripture," *Calvin Theological Journal* 4 (1969): 165-94.

46. See C. C. Ryrie, "The Importance of Inerrancy," *Bibliotheca Sacra* 120 (1963): 137-44; Preus, p. 37.

47. John Wesley, *Journal,* Wednesday, July 24, 1776.

> In an authority so high, admit but one officious lie, and there will not remain a single passage of those apparently difficult to practise or to believe, which on the same most pernicious rule may not be explained as a lie uttered by the author willfully and to serve some higher end.[48]

If one believes the Scripture to be God's Word, he cannot fail to believe it inerrant. Inerrancy has been the constant teaching of the Fathers, Protestant and Catholic theologians, and recent popes, because it is a necessary conclusion from the fact of divine authorship.[49] In *Providentissimus Deus*, Leo XIII states that inerrancy is the inescapable corollary of divine inspiration.

> For all the books . . . are written wholly and entirely, with all their parts, at the dictation of the Holy Spirit; and so far is it from being possible that any error can coexist with inspiration, that inspiration not only is essentially incompatible with error, but excludes and rejects it as it is impossible that God himself, the supreme Truth, can utter that which is not true.[50]

Inerrancy is even more urgent for Protestants because the *sola scriptura* principle cannot be maintained without it. An erring authority cannot serve as the only source and judge of Christian theology.[51]

Inerrancy is not, as some charge, a claim for Scripture which is constructed more rationalistically than biblically. It is the conclusion reached by inductive examination of the doctrine of Scripture taught by Christ and the biblical writers. This, and not an assortment of problem passages, is the

48. Augustine, *Epistle*, 28, c. 3.
49. See *New Catholic Encyclopedia*, pp. 384-85, 513-18.
50. Papal encyclical 3292 in Heinrich Denzinger, *Sources of Catholic Dogma*.
51. Vatican II in its *Constitution on Divine Revelation* qualifies inerrancy in an earlier draft with the adjective *salutaris*, and in the final text with "that truth which God wanted put into the sacred writings *for the sake of our salvation*." This subtle qualification is indicative of the swing in the new Catholicism toward the existential, neo-Protestant frame of reference.

truly relevant data for our knowledge of what Scripture is. Montgomery remarks,

> A doctrine of limited biblical authority derived from passages manifesting difficulties is as false an induction and as flagrant a denial of the analogy of Scripture as is a morally imperfect Christology derived from questionable acts on Jesus' part. In both cases, proper induction requires that we go to the express biblical teaching on the subject [Jesus' deity; Scripture's authority] and allow this to create the pattern for treating problem passages.[52]

It is when we meet a biblical difficulty that we need most to know what the Bible is and how we should handle it. Because Christ's attitude toward Scripture was one of total trust, we confess inerrancy, even though we cannot yet demonstrate it. But we believe that all difficulties will be resolved and eventually disappear because we are certain our Lord was not deceived. Inerrancy is the standpoint for a Christian to adopt in his examination of Scripture. This *Gestalt* is inductively derived and provides the framework for understanding what kind of book the Bible is.

Inerrancy, like infallibility, is relative to the intentionality of Scripture and an artificial standard must not be imposed.[53] The degree of precision is determined by the cultural milieu. For example, the Hebrew expression for "son" describes a broader field of relationships than does the English word. It may refer to a grandson, a descendant in an indefinite sense, or even an unrelated person. Furthermore, nothing in Scripture requires us to view the Hebrew vowel points as inspired or to demand that the New Testament citations of the Old be verbally exact. Whereas Matthew reads, "Hosanna in the highest" (21:9), Luke substitutes "Glory in the highest" (19:38). At issue is only which word would convey the meaning best to Luke's Gentile readers. Scripture selects the degree of ex-

52. Montgomery, "Inductive Inerrancy," *Christianity Today* (Mar. 3, 1967).

53. See Everett F. Harrison, "Criteria of Biblical Inerrancy," *Christianity Today* (Jan. 20, 1958).

actness it requires. Whereas the principle of inerrancy is derived from Christ, the application of it depends on the proper interpretation of each passage. For instance, the mustard seed was considered the smallest of seeds by Hebrews, and so Jesus used it to illustrate a spiritual truth (Mt 13:31). His parable was not slanted to teach botany![54]

In holding that the infallibility and inerrancy of Scripture are relative to what the text, by objective analysis, intends to teach, we do not mean to restrict biblical authority but, rather, to let it function. We are not free to determine beforehand what God would say to us. By careful and responsible exegesis we are to define the boundaries of teaching binding upon us. It might help to take the narrative of the fall of Adam into sin as an example. A fair reading of the account, standing as it does at the beginning of Old Testament history, absolutely requires that a time-space rebellion against God on the part of the first man is being described. The New Testament treatment of the passage as historical truth confirms this presumption. However, it is far less obvious how the writer intends us to understand various details in the story. Such understanding rests on a determination of the precise literary genre that lies before us. Belief in inerrancy certainly does not close the question, for example, as to whether the serpent really spoke, because it cannot be established without doubt that the writer intends simple literalism. Whether the account is literal description or a graphic depiction of the historical fall is a matter of interpretation, not of inerrancy. We must indeed insist on the basic historicity of the event described, but allow a certain latitude in the understanding of details where it is not possible as yet to ascertain completely the degree of literalness intended.

There is evidence at present, however, of a weakening of

54. But fairness to Scripture compels us to point out that the Greek form is comparative and not superlative ("smaller" not "smallest") and thus the illustration is a perilous one to prove errancy! Moreover, Palestinian mustard is not like North American mustard. Its seeds are similar to the petunia or even smaller in size.

conviction about inerrancy among evangelical scholars. A move is abroad to limit the concept to what is sometimes called "revelational matters." It is held that among the subjects Scripture does teach, there can be distinguished "soteric" doctrines which alone need to be regarded as inerrant.[55] The more liberal view in regard to inerrancy may have begun with James Orr. This British scholar himself had a magnificent view of Scripture. He believed that "the Bible, impartially interpreted and judged, is free from demonstrable error in its statements, and harmonious in its teachings." He was, however, keenly aware of "apparent errors" existing in the text and felt obliged to account for them. Therefore, he proposed a seemingly innocent theory: he suggested (and it is only that) that some of these difficulties might be explained if the sources of information on which some of the historical writers depended were themselves in error.[56] Thus a preoccupation with critical problems led him to accommodate his view of inspiration to them. E. F. Harrison endorsed the idea that errors in the sources might account for difficulties in the text.[57] Subsequently E. J. Carnell translated the theory into an important principle. According to Carnell, the Old Testament contains "infallible" accounts of historical errors which were lifted without correction from the public registers and genealogical lists.[58]

The device is certainly a neat one, and gets us around some

55. D. Masters discusses this difference of opinion among Evangelicals in *The Rise of Evangelicalism*. On the newer view see D. P. Fuller, "Warfield's View of Faith and History," *Journal of the Evangelical Theological Society* 11 (1968): 80-81; A. F. Holmes, "Ordinary Language Analysis and Theological Method," *Journal of the Evangelical Theological Society* 11 (1968): 137-38; Ridderbos, "An Attempt at the Theological Definition of Inerrancy, Infallibility, and Authority," *International Reformed Bulletin* 32/33 (1968): 27-41; Ellis, "The Authority of Scripture: Critical Judgments in Biblical Perspective," *Evangelical Quarterly* 39 (1967): 196-204. For a general discussion, see R. H. Nash, *The New Evangelicalism*, chap 5; Lightner, *Neo-Evangelicalism*, pp. 73-88; Millard Erickson, *The New Evangelical Theology*, pp. 74-81.

56. Orr, pp. 216, 179.

57. Harrison, "The Phenomena of Scripture," in *Revelation and the Bible*, ed. Carl F. H. Henry, p. 249.

58. E. J. Carnell, *The Case for Orthodox Theology*, pp. 102-11. Levie agrees, p. 221.

real difficulties. However, it conceals a hazardous principle. In admitting errors into the text itself, even into the body of teaching that text affords, the point is conceded to the critics of the Bible in every age; namely, that the actual teachings of Scripture may, or may *not,* be true. In his review of Carnell, John B. Cobb was quick to pick up this very point: "Obviously, if such an interpretation of Scripture is accepted, the fact that a statement appears in Scripture is not grounds for believing it to be true."[59] We are convinced that this criticism is well founded. This sort of admission does severely undercut the truth value of the Bible. Little of Scripture was written *ex nihilo,* that is, without the use of some sort of source, whether written or oral. The chronicler mentions twelve himself. It is certain that Moses and Luke were dependent on sources for their work. Therefore, if inspiration cannot guarantee the integrity of what is actually set down in Scripture, what can it guarantee? Surely inspiration refers to the text itself, after all the sources have been used and discarded.

The recorded speeches of liars in the book of Job is a scant parallel. For these "errors" are *recited* rather than *asserted.* The literary form permits us to distinguish between the fact that they said this (the *veritas citationis*) and the truth of what they said (the *veritas rei citatae*). The deliberate literary mode makes it clear that the writer is not trying to put anything over on us here. A less obvious example would be Luke's record of Stephen's apology (Ac 7). Inerrancy in this case would have primary reference to the fact that a speech of this substance was actually delivered on that occasion. Luke is concerned to give us a résumé of the speech itself, not to teach us Old Testament history. This rule would seem to be a safe one: where the sacred writer records data in such a way that it is apparent he regards it to be true and expects us to take it as such, we must assume that it is. Inspiration

59. John B. Cobb, book review of E. J. Carnell's *Case for Orthodox Theology, Interpretation* 14 (1960): 96.

is posited in reference to writing. For that reason, whatsoever it asserts as true and free from error is to be received as such. The charge that Scripture *teaches* error is tantamount to a denial of inspiration. For if God, who does not lie, is the Author of it, the text possesses complete veracity.[60]

Recently the dean of Fuller Theological Seminary, Daniel P. Fuller, published an important paper on "Benjamin B. Warfield's View of Faith and History" in which he proposed a corrective to Warfield's view of inspiration.[61] Warfield believed that inerrancy extended to *all* that Scripture taught, that all Scripture was revelational, and that no grounds existed for limiting its accuracy. Some matters are *soteric* biblical truths, but all are biblical *truths.* Fuller argues that the doctrinal verses teaching inspiration do not require so broad a view, but teach only inerrancy in *revelational matters.*[62] Fuller proposes this as only a "slight corrective" to Warfield, with considerable advantages. It leaves revelational matters (those which for the most part, he claims, lie outside empirical investigation) safe and secure, while difficulties affect only areas where historical control is possible.[63] Here lies the difficulty: The claim that Scripture does *not* err in those places where it may not be tested is meaningless if it *does* err in those places where it can! The extent to which the verifiable portions of Scripture are fallacious is the degree to which the *whole* of Scripture is discredited. Wherever faith and knowledge are opposed like this, faith suffers. The factual assertions of Scripture are bound up with the theological affirmations (e.g., Mt 12:41). The theological truth is discredited to the extent that the factual material is erroneous. Fuller has only made it harder to defend Scripture. Furthermore,

60. For further on this subject, see J. A. Mill, "The Bible and Non-Inspired Sources," *Journal of the Evangelical Theological Society* 3 (1960): 78-81; Payne, "Hermeneutics as a Cloak for the Denial of Scripture," *Journal of the Evangelical Theological Society* 3 (1960): 93-100; P. Woolley, "The Relevancy of Scripture," in *The Infallible Word,* p. 201.
61. Fuller, pp. 75-83.
62. Ibid., pp. 80-81.
63. Ibid., p. 83.

Fuller's (and Dewey M. Beegle's) point that the Bible does not claim for itself complete inerrancy, is false.[64] All Scripture is divine in origin, and truthful in all its cognitive assertions.

Inerrancy is not a new theory created by Protestant orthodoxy. It has always been an implicit if not an explicit belief in the church (see chap. 4). Modern embarrassment with it is not due to the novelty of the idea, but to a shift in the tone of modern theology itself (see chap. 5).[65] Beegle makes a strong plea for recognition that inspiration is not lost when inerrancy is given up. Limited inerrancy, it seems, need not lead to unlimited errancy. He fears the specter of one proven error overthrowing the entire edifice of the Christian faith. *Falsus in uno, falsus in omnibus.* But this is to misrepresent the situation. What is lost in admitting errors in Scripture is *not* necessarily the truth or efficacy of the revelation it contains (though it discredits it), but rather the consistency and stability of the theology which concedes them. The result of denying inerrancy, as skeptics well know, is the loss of a trustworthy Bible. Limited inerrancy is a slope, not a platform. Although we are repeatedly assured that minor errors in unimportant matters would not greatly affect the substance of the Christian faith nor the authority of Scripture, this admission has the effect of leaving us with a Bible which is a compound of truth and error, with no one to tell us which is which. What is lost when errors are admitted is divine *truthfulness*. Evangelicals confess inerrancy because it is biblical to do so. The critic who pontificates on

64. See Dewey M. Beegle, *The Inspiration of Scripture.* Evangelicals and Catholics who deny inerrancy in the face of confessional commitments to the contrary are reduced to pleading that inerrancy does not exclude errors, which is rather like saying a circle does not exclude corners! A. C. Piepkorn of the Lutheran Church–Missouri Synod suggests we just refrain from using the word at all. "What Does Inerrancy Mean?" *Concordia Theological Monthly* 36 (1963): 577-93.

65. A colleague of Piepkorn's, Martin H. Scharlemann boldly states that the Hebraic idea of truth is existentialist, not concerned with factual precision, and that divine revelation is of the I-Thou variety, not a communication of truth. "The Inerrancy of Scripture," paper delivered to the faculty of Concordia Seminary, St. Louis, Feb. 25, 1958.

"errors" in Scripture, which we regard simply as "difficulties," has usurped for himself the infallibility which he has denied the Bible.[66]

We walk by faith and not by sight. Inerrancy has not been fully demonstrated in the field of biblical studies, and residual difficulties remain. In the midst of the interchange over inerrancy we need to recall that Warfield, the staunch defender of inerrancy, was willing to welcome James Orr for the Stone Lectures at Princeton (1903); and Orr, sensitive to difficulties in the phenomena of Scripture, requested Warfield to prepare key articles on inspiration and revelation for the *International Standard Bible Encyclopaedia* of which he was editor-in-chief. Present-day Evangelicals should manifest the same degree of mutual trust and openness to one another as these two giants did.

EKTHESIS FIVE: AS ORIGINALLY GIVEN (2 PE 1:21)

It is common for Evangelicals to distinguish between the inspired originals or autographs and the uninspired copies or apographs. This distinction is often ridiculed by critics as irrelevant and absurd. After all, if the original text has disappeared, it is impossible to define its character in terms of infallibility. Such a theory has no practical value either, since it refers to no extant text. The appeal to an infallible autograph is surely an escape from the embarrassment caused by the fallibility of copies.

A little reflection, however, reveals that the distinction is quite sound. Few are prepared to claim inspiration for the copyists or translators of Scripture—Philo did so in the case of the Septuagint translation (an example of overbelief)—yet, if this is so, it cannot fail to be of great interest what the sacred penman set down as distinguished from a mistake in copying or translating. There is nothing absurd about an infallible text imperfectly transmitted. Indeed, if this is the case, as Evangelicals insist, the distinction is a necessary one.

66. See Livingston.

If there is good evidence for the trustworthiness of the Bible as it came from the hand of God, and there is (the entire testimony of Christ and the apostles referred to above); and there is no evidence for the inspiration of copyists or translators, and there is none; then it follows quite logically that such a distinction must be made.

Augustine showed good sense when he remarked:

> I have learned to yield such [absolute] respect and honour only to the canonical books of Scripture; of these do I most firmly believe that the authors were completely free from error. And if in these writings I am perplexed by anything which appears to me opposed to truth, I do not hesitate to suppose that either the *manuscript is faulty*, or the translator has not caught the meaning of what was said, or I myself have failed to understand it.[67]

If we are reading Hamlet or Plato, it is of the greatest interest to know, if we are serious students, what the original genius wrote as opposed to such slips of transmission as may have crept in through the vicissitudes of textual transmission. If holy men spoke from God, as the Christian faith claims, then it is the account of their words that will concern us, and not a series of glosses interpolated by a medieval scribe. This is what textual criticism is all about. Because Luther recognized that in places the Scriptures had suffered corruption, he labored diligently in an attempt to recover the original readings.[68]

Divine inspiration, as we have noted, has immediate reference to writing as God gave it. If someone insists that no one has seen the infallible originals, it is just as correct that no one has seen the fallible originals either! It boils down to the question of what Scripture is. God gave His Word in human language. That Word has been entrusted to God's people. The errors they may make in transmission are certainly not to be attributed to God.

67. Augustine, *Letter to Jerome*, 82.3.
68. M. Reu, *Luther and the Scriptures*, pp. 57-59.

Mavrodes has pointed out the complexity involved in a question of the original text.[69] Where secretarial help was employed by the biblical writers, as in 1 Peter 5:12, for example, the "original" would also be in a sense the first "copy," no doubt checked and revised by the author. There *is* a danger of speaking glibly of autographs, because a good deal more is involved in the preparation of Scripture than the putting of pen to paper. The confession of inspiration is not to reduce to clarity the process by which that document was produced.

Interest in the original text was quickened by the rise of textual science, which established a gap between the autographs and available copies. Thus a new question was born which called for reflection. When the New Testament writers allude to Scripture, it is to a particular text type or translation that they refer. They were well aware of diversities in the several text traditions. Informed by the fact of Christ and directed by the Spirit of God, they often selected the reading which best carried the divine meaning. Textual diversity did not cause them anxiety. Belief in God's providence alone was sufficient to assure them that the inspired Word in the copy was quite capable of functioning as a divine utterance. If Scripture was given for the instruction of God's people always, it would not be permitted to become so corrupt as to be unintelligible for that purpose. The character of the Word of God remains unaffected by the minor variants on the borders of Scripture. Perhaps, as Kuyper and Sauer suggest, the autographs—had they been preserved—would have been cherished as relics and worshiped like the serpent of brass![70]

The Westminster Confession speaks of God's providential care of the biblical text in 1.8:

69. G. Mavrodes, "The Inspiration of the Autographs," *Evangelical Quarterly* 41 (1969): 19-29.

70. Kuyper, *Encyclopedia of Sacred Theology*, 3:67; E. Sauer, *From Eternity to Eternity*, p. 110.

> The Old Testament in Hebrew . . . and the New Testament in Greek . . . being immediately inspired by God, and by his singular care and providence kept pure in all ages, are therefore authentical; so as in all controversies of religion the Church is finally to appeal unto them.

A controversy surrounds the interpretation of this article. Warfield understood there to be in the minds of the Westminster divines a distinction between autographs and apographs. More recently, however, it has been forcefully argued by Rogers that a different question concerned the assembly. The framers of the confession were concerned to affirm that the Hebrew and Greek texts rather than the Latin Vulgate were to be the manuscripts appealed to in any question of religion. It was not a question of a change in that Hebrew or Greek text over the ages since its inception, but rather the precedence to be respected in a copy in the original language over a copy of a mere translation, the Latin.[71] Although the confession does assert the inspiration of the autographs, it does not appear to reflect upon the importance which textual errors in the Hebrew or Greek manuscripts might have for our doctrine. Had this been the question, and it is not inconceivable that it might have been raised, there is every reason to suppose the confession would have made the kind of distinction we must make today. The necessity of answering this question did not become urgent until the results of textual criticism became better known. Then the question of the impurities in the extant text has to be faced.

Before going further it should be noted that in reality the dimensions of the problem are not very great. Textual criticism is the science dedicated to restoring intact the original pristine text of Scripture. Unlike higher criticism, which is often influenced by philosophical assumptions, textual work is quite an objective attempt to determine what Scripture actually is. It accomplishes its task by sifting and evaluating the variant readings which occur in the manuscript evidence.

71. Jack Rogers, *Scripture in the Westminster Confession*, pp. 391-98.

The results are quite reliable and encouraging. Textual criticism has contributed much to our understanding of the Bible. Theological presuppositions seldom vitiate its results, and there is now substantial agreement about the integrity of the text we possess.[72]

If it were the case that the distance was great between the original text and the present copies, we would have a real difficulty. But the fact of the matter is that textual variants effect not a single item of evangelical belief. The vast majority concern minor aspects which scarcely affect the meaning of the passage in question. The high degree of purity in our present text is a demonstrated fact. Textual corruption is slight and inconsequential. There is simply no room for pessimism. Although critics of biblical faith in the past have found it useful in their polemics to allege that the damage was considerable, the charge is quite contrary to fact. A. T. Robertson estimated that hardly one thousandth part of the New Testament was affected. In that case, the problem is removed for Evangelicals when they insist on the distinction between original and copy. A copy which is substantially like the original can function like the original itself.[73]

Quite evidently God is willing to use an imperfect copy or translation of Scripture in the work of saving sinners. The King James Version, although it is based on an inferior Greek text and contains some quite erroneous renderings, has contributed to the salvation and edification of millions. The truth and power of Scripture are not annulled by the presence of a degree of textual corruption. This fact, however, does not give grounds for complacency. An imperfect text should be replaced by a superior one where available, and a poor translation by a better. Christian scholars are called

72. See B. M. Metzger, *The Text of the New Testament;* G. E. Ladd, *The New Testament and Criticism,* chap. 3; John H. Skilton, "The Transmission of the Scriptures," in *The Infallible Word,* pp. 137-87; Norman Geisler and William Nix, *A General Introduction to the Bible,* pp. 365-66.

73. See R. Laird Harris, "How Reliable Is the Old Testament Text?" and A. Berkeley Mickelsen, "Is the Text of the New Testament Reliable?" in *Can I Trust My Bible?*

upon to remove textual corruption where possible and improve the level of translation by more refined linguistic techniques. Behind every human rendering shines the bright light of God's own Word. But it is part of our stewardship to recover the best text possible and provide the clearest translation in our power.

Because in the last analysis the autographs represent the purest form of God's Word to man, priority is to be given to the original-tongues text over the translation text made from them, and to the best text over the lesser. Scripture has been entrusted to our keeping. What God has said has not and must not be forgotten. The message deposited in the Bible needs to be expressed eventually in all the languages of earth. The modern missionary movement has proven that the biblical message has universal appeal even among the remotest cultures. Obviously the inspired content of Scripture has not been lost by its transmission and translation. Yet, because none of our copies and translations is a perfect mirroring of the original, the challenge remains to strive after the highest standard possible to us.

The issue may be put in this way: Evangelicals hold with good reason that the Bible they possess is substantially identical, apart from minor transcriptional variations, with the inspired originals, while their critics prefer to believe that the authenticity of the Bible is discredited in both copy and original. We hold that this latter view is contrary to textual science and to the high doctrine of inspiration enjoined on us by our Lord. Our Bibles are the Word of God to the extent that they reflect the Scripture as originally given; and because it is clear that they are virtually identical to it, it is also correct to regard them as virtually infallible themselves.

EKTHESIS SIX: DIVINE INSPIRATION IS PLENARY (RO 15:4)

Scripture is an organism, inspired in the whole, not merely in its parts. It is truthful in the soteric and nonsoteric, in the doctrinal and the historical, in the primary and the secondary features. Inspiration guarantees *all* that Scripture teaches. It is a seamless garment, an indivisible body. Jesus Christ accepted no dichotomy or dualism in Scripture between true and false, revealed and unrevealed, matters. His attitude was one of *total trust*. For example, He obviously regarded the entire Old Testament history as factually correct: the gospels record at least twenty allusions to incidents from the creation of Adam to Daniel's prophecies and Jonah's preaching.[74] He regarded the *entire* Scripture as trustworthy, the commonplace as well as the extraordinary. Criticism is often leveled at the Bible for the trivialities (*levicula*) it is said to contain. Inspiration should not be blamed for nonessential details which seem unworthy of the Spirit's breath. Scripture does not, however, recognize this dichotomy either. No doubt some things in Scripture are more essential than others, but this fact does not justify critical surgery and the discarding of what *we* deem unimportant. Certainly the New Testament does not recognize trivialities in the Old Testament (Ro 15:4). The Bible is a unitary product. Who is the judge capable of differentiating between matters of great weight and those of *none* at all? The effort to rid Scripture of trivial minutiae is an unwarranted endeavor. Recall the encouragement Erasmus received for his scholarly labors from the mention of Paul's parchments (2 Ti 4:13)! The objection to *levicula* suggests an irreverent attitude to Scripture, for it calls into question the divine wisdom in willing Scripture to take the form it does.[75] Certainly Luther would have nothing to do with any criticism of trivialities beneath the dignity of the Spirit! When we take offense at the *levicula* in Scripture, this is proof positive that we do not grasp the indignity suffered by the Son of God in becoming man.[76]

The words of the evangelical Anglican bishop J. C. Ryle are worth recording in full:

74. Lightner tabulates all twenty-two in *The Saviour . . .*, p. 98.
75. See L. Gaussen, *Theopneustia,* pp. 306-22; T. Engelder, *Scripture Cannot Be Broken*, pp. 249-72.
76. Francis Pieper, *Christian Dogmatics,* 1:251-55; Reu, pp. 51-56.

> We corrupt the Word of God most dangerously, when we throw any doubt on the plenary inspiration of any part of Holy Scripture. This is not merely corrupting the cup, but the whole fountain. This is not merely corrupting the bucket of living water, which we profess to be present to our people, but poisoning the whole well. Once wrong on this point, the whole substance of our religion is in danger. It is a flaw in the foundation. It is a worm at the root of our theology. Once allow the worm to gnaw the root, and we must not be surprised if the branches, the leaves, and the fruit, little by little, decay. The whole subject of inspiration, I am aware, is surrounded with difficulty. All I would say is, notwithstanding some difficulties which we may not be able now to solve, the only safe and tenable ground to maintain is this,—that every chapter, and every verse, and every word in the Bible has been given by inspiration of God. We should never desert a great principle in theology any more than in science, because of apparent difficulties which we are not able at present to remove.[77]

The control exercised by the Spirit was so complete that human proneness to error was overcome and the writers were the perfect mouthpieces of infallible revelation. Against Barth, we must affirm the uniform inspiration (*gleichmässig*) of Scripture. Without plenary inspiration the Bible is an equivocal authority. No biblical text is other than the authentic utterance of God. Plenary inspiration does not, however, rule out cumulative, or progressive, revelation. Certain passages, because they occur at the summit of redemptive revelation, are more familiar to and treasured by Christian people. Plenary inspiration does not imply each text has the same weight or importance as any other. It means only that every text is there because God willed it, and we are to study the entire biblical corpus seriously because it is from God. Theologians deny plenary inspiration in order to free themselves from the controlling influence of Scripture so as to be able to

77. From a sermon on 2 Co 2:17 which J. C. Ryle preached in 1858. It was reprinted in *Warnings to the Churches*, p. 31.

exalt one aspect of biblical teaching over another. By this technique of divide and conquer the Bible may be constrained to teach anything whatever.

EKTHESIS SEVEN: VERBAL (MT 4:4)

Although many still denounce verbal inspiration as a detestable theory, it is the only scriptural and meaningful one. Precisely because inspiration has to do with *graphe,* it has to do with words and language. Truth incapable of being expressed in language is a contradiction in terms. If inspiration were not verbal, it would be irrelevant. William Sanday, Bampton Lectures of 1893 on *Inspiration* sought to shift the locus of inspiration from the writings to the writers. In this way he would allow for errors in Scripture. The new theory caught the mood of the nineteenth century. Authority rested in the warm, living experience of men, and interpreters were free to admit all the mistakes they wished to. It is, however, unsound and unbiblical to contrast a *suggestio rerum* (a supplying of the matter) with a *suggestio verborum* (a supplying of the words). There is an inseparable connection between thought and word. Words are the conventional symbols of thought, and necessary to its communication. Inspired thoughts not properly expressed are not revelation. The matter *and* the form are given by inspiration of God. Scripture was efficaciously willed by God as the means for conveying the divine message, and revelation is mediated in these words. All of the rich functions of language are called upon to convey the divine message: to *inform* us of fact, doctrine, idea; to *express* to us the inner feelings and experiences of faith; to *impress* upon us the radical power of its theme.

Surprisingly, verbal inspiration is admitted by many critics of evangelical doctrine. James Smart contends that man encounters divine revelation in the *text* of Scripture: "It is through these words and no others that God intends to speak to us, and, when he does, we know that there is no other kind of inspiration than verbal inspiration."[78] John Baillie rejects *plenary* inspiration, but affirms without hesitation "that inspiration extended not only to the thoughts of the writers, but to the very words they employed in the expression of these thoughts." Baillie considers it safe to affirm verbal inspiration so long as plenary inspiration is denied![79] Evidently these men employ the term *verbal inspiration* in a watered-down sense. It is a dramatic way they have of saying the text is important but they do not intend to suggest that God spoke all these words.

Verbal inspiration is the recognition that the Bible, *as a language deposit,* is God's Word. Scripture is the extension of the modality of the divine speaking. The impact of this word deposit is always veracious, and conveys the freight of divine revelation effectively to the human mind. "If the words were not wholly God's then their teaching would not be wholly God's."[80] The very fact of divine truth revelation calls for the creation of *graphe* to preserve and conserve it. Verbal inspiration assures us that God's truth has been correctly and properly communicated. The attack on verbal inspiration is really directed against the biblical truth revelation, the citadel of Christianity.

In an effort to discredit verbal inspiration, appeal is often made to the nature of language. Human language is supposed to be incapable of communicating revealed truth, and unfit to be the vehicle of divine revelation.[81] The American theologian Horace Bushnell regarded language as decrepit, and words as faded, indistinct metaphors tied to their history, so that, at best, language could only be a poetic attempt to

78. James Smart, *The Interpretation of Scripture*, pp. 195-96. His remark is not orthodox, of course, because the "revelation" we encounter does not involve propositional truth, and the Scripture we read is not perspicuous, but "interpreted in the context of the church." But it is a truth he has grasped, even though he proceeds at once to bury it.

79. John Baillie, *The Idea of Revelation in Recent Thought,* pp. 115-16.

80. Packer, p. 90.

81. See M. E. Taber, "Fundamentalist Logic," *Christian Century* 84 (1957): 817-18; Gordon H. Clark, *Religion, Reason, and Revelation,* pp. 119-50.

express the inexpressible.[82] It is, of course, *not* any inability of language which is bothering Bushnell, for he never had any difficulty communicating his own views. (Skepticism toward language has no future as an argument, because it casts doubt on the sentences of the one proposing it!) His real hang-up is a form of metaphysical dualism he holds to which denies the possibility of God revealing Himself in finite language. *Finitum non est capax infiniti.* This is not a problem a Christian should have, however, because the incarnation cleared it up once and for all. The absolute has appeared in the phenomenal realm where He may be met (1 Jn 1:1-3), and Scripture is a veracious language revelation. This is not to say that verbal inspiration implies either a mechanical mode of inspiration or an atomistic hermeneutic. The words were not doled out one by one from a heavenly computer. Verbal inspiration does not nullify the significant human authorship of the writers of Scripture. It simply affirms that the words written in Scripture are the words of God. It means we may trust *this verbal form* as the trustworthy and sufficient vehicle of divine revelation. Words signify and safeguard meaning. We get at the meaning of the inspired writers by means of the words they employ. Each jot and tittle plays a part and influences the total impact of Scripture. This fact calls for the science of careful hermeneutics because we are committed to a serious and exacting study of its language.[83]

Existential theologians denigrate biblical language in a different way. They consider the subject matter of revelation to be quite different than can be expressed in human language. Revelation is an ecstatic experience of the holy and unconditioned. This theory leads away from any notion of truth revelation or verbal inspiration. But, as we have seen, the neo-Protestant view of revelation cannot be biblically sup-

82. See Sydney E. Ahlstrom, "Theology in America," in *The Shaping of American Religion*, eds. James Ward Smith and A. Leland Jamison, 1:281-82.

83. Ladd, chap. 4.

ported. The divine speaking is a central motif in biblical revelation, and written revelation is a component part of redemption. Faith is directed and guided by the light of God's language revelation. The fact that we enjoy a personal relation with God through Christ makes a language revelation *more,* not less, important. Grace has made us speech partners with God Himself. Language revelation supplies the cognitive environment in which the divine-human encounter is created and nurtured. The precepts of the Lord rejoice the heart and enlighten the eyes (Ps 19:8). Divine revelation calls language into service in all of its rich and diversified functions—to inform, rebuke, summon, correct, praise. Verbal inspiration is at the heart of what inspiration is, and underlines the fact that God has spoken to us in our language.

EKTHESIS EIGHT: CONFLUENT (2 SA 23:2)

By confluency is meant the dual authorship of Scripture, the fact that the Bible is at one and the same time the product of the divine breath and a human pen. The miracle of inspiration is analogus to the union in one person of the two natures of Christ; the Word of God in the words of men. This is a mystery we can only confess and not explain. It is a subject to raise when heaven's school begins its classes, and one about which we dare not claim to know more than we do.

The context in which the concept of confluent authorship is intelligible is that of *biblical theism.* God and man can both be significant agents simultaneously in the same historical (Ac 2:23) or literary (2 Pe 1:21) event. The Spirit of God worked concursively alongside the activity of the writers, Himself being the principal cause and they the free instrumental cause. The result of this concursive operation was "that their thinking and writing were both free and spontaneous on their part and divinely elicited and controlled, and what they wrote was not only their own work, but also God's work."[84] There is a monotonous chorus of protest against the

84. Packer, p. 80.

biblical concept of inspiration on the grounds that it involves mechanical dictation. The only way to explain the repetition of this false charge is to recognize the sad eclipse of biblical theism today. Men seem unable to conceive of a divine providence which can infallibly reach its ends without dehumanizing the human agents it employs. According to the Bible, the sovereignty of God does not nullify the significance of man.[85] As Warfield put it,

> If God wished to give his people a series of letters like Paul's, he prepared a Paul to write them, and the Paul he brought to the task was a Paul who *spontaneously* would write just such letters.[86]

Against the biblical concept of confluence only a deist would object! The biblical God is no passive onlooker, but actively works all things after the counsel of His own will (Eph 1:11). It is a tiresome necessity for Evangelicals to state that "mechanical dictation" is not now, and never has been, their view.[87] Where "dictation" has been spoken of, as for example by Calvin, it refers to the *extent*, not the mode, of inspiration. It means that every detail of what the writers wrote was divinely willed by God. Even the orthodox Lutheran dogmaticians of the seventeenth century did not intend to imply that the Spirit controlled the biblical writers as lifeless automata. They wished only to say that the resulting *text* consisted of the words God actually willed.[88] We can only conclude that the purpose behind the attempt to smear the evangelical doctrine is to deny the divinity of the scriptural word and identify it totally with the word of man.

Justice must be done to the *dual* authorship of Scripture.

1. Because it is a human word, we recognize human factors.

85. Packer, *Evangelism and the Sovereignty of God.*
86. Warfield, p. 155.
87. T. Engelder, pp. 301-30; Harris, *Inspiration and Canonicity of the Bible,* pp. 21-22. There have of course been exceptions, for example, the Consensus Helvetica (1675).
88. For Calvin, see Kantzer, "Calvin and the Holy Scriptures," in *Inspiration and Interpretation,* ed. J. F. Walvoord, pp. 137-42; for the dogmaticians, see Preus, *The Inspiration of Scripture,* pp. 71-73.

The sacred writers retain their individuality. The personality of Paul shines lucidly through his letters. The Spirit plays upon many keyboards, and a rich diversity of sound results. The prophet "cries out" and "boldly speaks" (Ro 9:27; 10:20). The Spirit accommodates Himself to the manner of men's speaking. The human *auctores secundarii* were authors, not penmen. They made use of the full range of their human capacities.[89] No single psychological experience was common to all the sacred writers. To the prophets the divine impetus came like a fire (Jeremiah), or like the roaring of a lion (Amos). To the historians of Israel and the writers of wisdom, no supernatural impulse is claimed. It is the fact of inspiration, not the mode of it, that matters. At the same time it must be strenuously denied that, in order to be human, Scripture must be fallible and errant. Error is no more a requisite of the Bible's humanity than sin is native to Christ's human nature! Christ was truly human and free from sin; Scripture is truly human and free from error. In their effort to divorce the human element of Scripture from the divine Word, modern theologians reveal their "Nestorian" tendencies in the field of inspiration.[90] Evangelicals are simply trying to appreciate the authentic human character of the divine Word written. It is not the humanity of Scripture we are reluctant to believe, but its alleged errant "sinful" humanity. Critical theories which propose deceitful literary forms and historical blunders do indeed manifest belief in the humanity of Scripture, but explicitly repudiate its divine authorship.

2. Because Scripture is a divine Word, "The Holy Spirit spoke by David," we insist on its *truthfulness* in all that it teaches. Scripture is a perfect union of the divine and human speakers. Inspiration can be plenary and verbal without

89. See an important passage in Karl Barth, *Church Dogmatics,* vol. 1, pt. 2, pp. 503-26. See Gaussen, pp. 38-52.

90. Nestorius was condemned at the ecumenical council of Ephesus (431) for dividing the one Christ into two persons. Critics often jeopardize the *unity* of divine and human in Scripture.

being mechanical because of the mystery of *confluence.* In an inscrutable way, the Spirit employed an imperfect human instrument in order to give His church the written Word of God.

Properties of Holy Scripture

Because it is the kind of book it is, the Bible possesses certain properties which enable it to function as a standard for the church. These divine attributes are: authority, sufficiency, clarity and efficacy. Any attempt to limit inspiration inevitably leads to the loss of these attributes. The Bible of modern theology does not manifest these high qualities.

ekthesis nine: authority (is 1:2)

Scripture has the exclusive right to command our *obedience* because it alone is the Word of God. More than merely an article of faith, the doctrine of inspiration is fundamental, the epistemological foundation of sacred theology, the basis of every article. Scripture is the *causa media* (mediating instrument) of our knowledge of God, the *principium cognoscendi* (first principle of knowing). The doctrine of Scripture is perennially at the heart of the theological discussion. Our decision about inspiration will affect everything else we do. Scripture must be our judge, norm, standard, control, canon. We are authorized to accept no other, and conscience-bound to believe and obey all its declarations. "The Holy Scriptures are the rule of our faith and life; therefore, also, the judge of theological controversies," says Gerhard.[91]

Karl Barth devotes a considerable section to the exclusive authority of the Bible.[92] He sees a similarity in Roman Catholicism and Protestant Liberalism, both of which tend to deify a human word and disregard the final authority of Scripture. The divine principle is replaced by an egoistic one, re-

91. For a catena of statements by Lutheran theologians, see Heinrich Schmid, *The Doctrinal Theology of the Evangelical Lutheran Church,* pp. 51-64.

92. Barth, vol. 1, pt. 2, pp. 538-85.

flecting the desire for autonomy and self-defined limits. Barth opts for the exclusive, *not* inclusive, authority of the Bible.[93] He deserves great credit for defending the sole authority of Scripture as witness *in* and *to* the church. Criticism of Barth must not muffle the gratitude we feel. Like Luther, we boast of being nothing other than "catachumens and pupils of the prophets."

Nothing but Scripture can claim our obedience, because *it* is God's Word. Rejection of Scripture amounts to an affront to the divine majesty. He is no disciple of Christ who rejects His doctrine of inspiration. Scripture may not be adulterated (by adding to it churchly tradition) nor emasculated (by diminishing it according to the supposed dictates of reason). It stands above everything else and judges it.

EKTHESIS TEN: SUFFICIENCY (2 TI 3:15)

To confess sufficiency and clarity is just to affirm that Scripture contains *enough light* to save sinners and direct the church. If it were not clear or not sufficient, it could *not* function as *sola scriptura.* For it would require another font of revelation to lighten or complement it. For this cause, the sufficiency and clarity of Scripture have been attacked by Roman Catholics and liberal Protestants.

The sufficiency of Scripture means that everything a believer *needs* to know about salvation and the Christian walk is contained therein. Scripture contains enough truth to lead men to Jesus Christ, and enough to ensure the doctrinal, spiritual and ethical welfare of the people of God (2 Ti 3:15; Lk 24:25-27). Our guides are the noble Bereans who searched the Scriptures daily to see if certain teachings were so (Ac 17:11). The Scriptures proved sufficient for Christ and *His* apostles, for they had recourse to no other authority. They thoroughly furnish the man of God for good works (2 Ti 3:17). "Nor is there any afflictive circumstance a good man can come into, but there is a promise in the word of God

93. Ibid., p. 546.

suitable to him," says Gill.[94] This is not to say that Scripture exhausts all possible or even all actual revelation (Jn 21:25), or that a total theological system may be induced from its teachings (1 Co 13:12). There are historical and doctrinal lacuna therein. But our rule of faith *is* a sufficient guide. It makes wise the simple. Congar demonstrates that for the early Fathers, the Holy Scriptures were the *only* source of truth, and that they suffice for the defense and exposition of the faith.[95]

If Scripture were not sufficient for its end, informing us of the saving purposes of God, it could not stand as our sole authority. It would have to be amplified and supplemented by a "Bible to the second power," namely, a human *ego*, whether a collective ego (tradition) or an individual one (the pope's or my own). If sufficiency is surrendered, the deficiency in Scripture has to be made up by some outside source, inevitably a human authority. Although other sources of theological truth have been proposed, we do not believe any can justify its legitimacy theoretically or practically.[96] The Bible must have the last word because it is the deposit of apostolic doctrine, the life-giving and truthful Word by which many have come to faith (Jn 17:20). Calvin remarks, "For Scripture is the school of the Holy Spirit, in which as nothing useful and necessary to be known has been omitted, so nothing is taught but what it is of importance to know."[97]

EKTHESIS ELEVEN: CLARITY (PS 119:105)

It is necessary for Scripture, if it is to be our authority, to be clear so that we can read and understand it. If it were not,

94. J. Gill, *Body of Divinity*, p. 20.
95. Yves M.-J. Congar, *Tradition and Traditions*, pp. 107-11. Congar himself, a leading Catholic ecclesiologist, accepts the material sufficiency of Scripture as containing in one way or another all truths necessary to salvation. He insists that the Bible is the primary objective standard of judgment for theology, the datum against which all postapostolic experience is to be measured. He denies, however, its formal sufficiency, and invokes the rich tradition and teaching authority of the Roman Church.
96. Ibid, pp. 142-56.
97. John Calvin, *Institutes*, 3.21.3.

a further light would be needed to enlighten it. *All* Scripture is not equally clear. "All things in Scripture are not alike plain in themselves, nor alike clear unto all," says the Westminster Confession 1.7. Yet, as Augustine puts it, "In the *clear* passages of Scripture everything is found that pertains to faith and life." Or, as the confession goes on to say:

> . . . yet those things which are necessary to be known, believed, and observed for salvation, are so clearly propounded and opened in some place of Scripture or other, that not only the learned, but the unlearned, in a due use of ordinary means, may attain unto a sufficient understanding of them.

As Peter said concerning Paul's letters,"There are *some* things in them hard to be understood" (2 Pe 3:16), which the "unstable and ignorant twist" to their own detriment. Such difficulties as do appear are to be resolved by the analogy of Scripture. Because God is its Author, the Bible is a unity, and one part sheds light upon another part. This is the proper hermeneutical circle. John Knox remarked,

> If there appear any obscurity in one place, the Holy Ghost, who is never contrary to himself, explains the same more clearly in other places: so that there can remain no doubt, but to such as obstinately remain ignorant.

Scripture is a "light shining in a dark place" (2 Pe 1:19). The "Father of lights" has given His Word to be a lamp to our feet and a light to our path (Ps 119:105). It is not inaccessible and hidden from us (Deu 30:11-14). We are commanded to read and search it (Jn 5:39; Ac 17:11). It makes wise the simple, revives the soul, rejoices the heart, enlightens the eyes (Ps 19:7-8). Scripture is clear because it is *God's*. If it were not clear, it would fail in its intention. Everything necessary to be known is clearly taught therein. Obscure passages do not affect the clarity of the essential doctrines of salvation. Luther wrote, "It is a pestilent dictum of the Sophists, that the Scriptures are obscure and equivocal."[98] He

98. Martin Luther, *Bondage of the Will*, p. 125.

countered the charge by an appeal to the counterclaims of Scripture itself. If it were obscure, why did God give it? The theological issue runs deep. Laymen cannot read the Bible if it is a dark, hidden, churchly book. Another doctrinal guide would be required. An obscure book could not perform the functions Scripture would perform . A denial of perspicuity is a denial of the *sola scriptura* principle itself.[99]

The clarity of Scripture is denied by every man-centered theology in interest of promoting another source of "clearer revelation." The Bible is supposedly clarified by papal utterances in the Roman tradition, and by inner light in the liberal one. It is often claimed that the interpretation of any text is a matter of personal opinion, and that certain knowledge of what the Bible says is impossible. The argument is fallacious and self-defeating. If the Bible is by definition inscrutable, how is it that the papal utterance or inner light escapes obscurity? If the "Bible to the first power" requires an interpreter, the "Bible to the second or third power" needs one too, and so on, ad infinitum. On purely logical grounds, if a person's interpretation is invalid simply because it is *his* interpretation, then the objector's opinion is wrong because it is *his* opinion. Granted, there *is* a danger of confusing our ideas with biblical teachings. But the solution is not to declare this vice a virtue (as in the New Hermeneutic), but to check our ideas continually by Scripture's. Personal opinions and prejudices can be criticized and corrected *if* the biblical data is allowed to operate upon them. The text of Scripture must *not* be fused with the mind of the interpreter, whether that of church or individual. It is to stand over us. Denial of clarity reflects a refusal to be bound by Scripture and a determination to follow one's own inclinations. Whenever a church or a theologian takes it upon himself to define truth without reference to the objective authority of God's Word, he becomes demonically solipsistic. The Roman Catholic

99. See Ralph Bohlmann, *Principles of Biblical Interpretation in the Lutheran Confessions*, pp. 57-68; cf. U. Duchrow, "Die Klarheit der Schrift und die Vernunft," *Kerygma und Dogma* 15 (1969): 1-17.

and liberal Protestant theologies are not so far apart as they seem at first glance. In one case the papal ego and, in the other, the theologian's are the lights which lighten Scripture. In each case something *human* is placed above Scripture. It is vital, therefore, for them to hold to the obscurity of Scripture, lest its truth should break forth and challenge the interposed human authority. We have no right at all to place anything above God's Word.[100] These "Bibles to the second power" do not exist.

There are, however, serious disagreements between Christians as to the meaning of Scripture at certain points. As Clement of Alexandria put it, "I do not think there is any Scripture so happy as to be contradicted by none." As a description of a state of affairs, this is true. But it is not normative of what *ought* to be the case. Scripture is capable of yielding norms for theological theory construction, and data for their correction. No doubt many systems of interpretation have existed (Tillich's, Mary Baker Eddy's, Marcion's), and Scripture has judged them to be false. But as to the Christocentric and redemptive focus of Scripture, there can be no doubt; and those who claim obscurity do so to evade the clear teaching of Scripture (e.g., the liberal denial of the vicarious atonement of Christ in the face of overwhelming evidence). On the other hand, some differences between Christians in biblical interpretation may be surface fissures only and trace back to deeper theological motifs not at all in contradiction. It often seems, for example, in reading Wesleyan literature on the grand significance of man, and Calvinistic material extolling the glorious sovereignty of God, that in each case an authentic biblical teaching is being represented, and that what is needed is a higher formula which would do more jus-

100. The theory of Petrine supremacy in a Roman papal succession is biblically and historically indefensible, and proving an increasing embarrassment at the present time to scholarly Roman Catholics. See, for example, Francis Simons, *Infallibility and the Evidence*. In chap. 3 the other candidates for religious authority are discussed also.

tice to the fullness of biblical teaching. Sub-Christian polemics have led the proponents of evangelical parties to emphasize some and suppress other scriptural evidence. The need is not a call for conversion, but a profounder settlement, based upon a profounder reading of God's Word. Is it not also the case that the Baptist insistence upon the conversion of believer's children, and the paedobaptist emphasis on the spiritual oneness of the home are frequently argued as though each side was not prepared to grant the importance of the other's affirmation? So often in evangelical division biblical truths are well represented on all sides, and all that is lacking is the humility to admit it. Truth comes before unity, but let us take care not to confuse shallow partisan convictions with biblical doctrine. Evangelical unity is marred by a sectarian spirit. The road to reunion of true believers lies in the interrelation of those genuinely biblical motifs in the thinking of all, and the construction of a profounder doctrinal map on which to plot our course.[101] Only Scripture is the standard of measurement in deciding doctrinal controversies. The point at issue needs to be carefully defined, and the Scripture pertinent to that point patiently expounded. *Deus dixit: causa finita est* (God has spoken: the matter is closed). If Scripture were not clear, it would not be sufficient. Because it is both, we are commanded to read and obey it.

EKTHESIS TWELVE: EFFICACY (HEB 4:12)

As the Word of God, Scripture possesses the capability of convicting and converting sinners. The Word does not return void (Is 55:11). It is a sharp, two-edged sword (Heb 4:12). Time and again it has proven its potency to overcome disbelief and promote saving faith. In the preface to *Letters to*

101. See Montgomery, *Ecumenicity, Evangelicals, and Rome*, pp. 21-25. Edmund Schlink has developed a "morphological" approach to the structure of dogmatic statements, and concluded that very often two doctrinal expressions of genuine evangelical faith are closer in the depth than on the surface. See his *Der kommende Christus und die kirchlichen Traditionen.*

Young Churches, J. B. Phillips remarks how in translation he felt like an electrician rewiring an old house, and his recent *Ring of Truth* testifies to a growing conviction concerning the divine authority of Scripture.

This divine power (*vis vere divina*) does not lie in the letter apart from the operations of the Spirit. For *graphe* can be nothing but *gramma* (letter, 2 Co 3:6). Both Word and sacrament are nothing *sine fide* (without faith). Where disbelief converts gospel to law, or blindness turns from the light of the world, Scripture lies dormant. The power of revelation-present has no effect, even though it will judge all men on the last day (Jn 12:48). The efficacy of Scripture to work spiritual effects derives from the determination of the Spirit to employ it as His instrument in the conversion of sinners. Vivid metaphors are applied to the Word: a hammer (Jer 23:29), rain, snow and seed (Is 55:10), fire in the bones (Jer 20:9), and milk (1 Pe 2:2). Lutheran theologians have ventured even to speak of the efficacy of the Word *ante et extra usum* (prior to and apart from use) in order to stress its potency. By this they sought to do justice to the crucial role Scripture *always* plays in theology and evangelism. They did not mean, however, to deny the operation of the Spirit, but rather to affirm its continual reality. Because the Spirit wills to act alongside His own inspired transcript of the gospel perpetually, the Scripture is a means of grace, the sacramental vehicle of Christ. The Word by the Spirit and the Spirit in the Word are always effective, even though the effect is not always the same. They may justify or condemn, quicken or judge. The truth of the Bible is there by inspiration; the power of the Bible is there by a union with the Spirit. The reason the Spirit is pleased to go on using Scripture in a unique way is because Scripture is a unique product of revelation. It is more than a sermon about Christ; it is written revelation. Therefore, the Spirit is present wherever Scripture is read and preached, and willing to bless wherever faith is found.

EKTHESIS THIRTEEN: THE CENTRAL PURPOSE OF SCRIPTURE IS TO PRESENT CHRIST (LK 24:27)

Historically, Protestant theology has had no difficulty in recognizing that the focus, end and center of Scripture are Jesus Christ. He is the key to unlock the whole treasury, the hermeneutical guideline grasping the true meaning of the Bible. The core of Scripture is what God has done *propter Christum* (through Christ) in grace for His people. The New Testament interprets the Old according to a *Christocentric* principle. In the written Word we encounter the living Word (2 Ti 3:15). The promise and fulfillment motif dominates Scripture. Christ is the axis of the Testaments. The promises of the Old come to fruition in the New. The whole New Testament concerns messianic fulfillment. Scripture has been fulfilled.[102]

The Christocentric principle has been distorted recently in *two* ways. By some it has been taken to imply a *critical* principle: as if we are bound only to accept that which seems to belong to the central purpose or Christological material in Scripture. In this case, "Christ" (usually the theologian's own pious subjectivity) is a critical scalpel with which biblical teachings are pared away. By others, the scope of Scripture is limited to its "religious" themes, and its infallibility denied in nonrevelational matters. G. C. Berkouwer, formerly a staunch defender of plenary inspiration, seems now to have shifted to a view of infallibility of reduced scope.[103] His denial of the truthfulness of matters not directly concerned with the central doctrines of Scripture is to be resisted.[104] The Christocentric unity of Scripture is *not* a reductive principle for censoring the Bible! It is the main theme we should always keep in mind. Christ is the hermeneutical clue to all the mysteries of revelation. The dominant intent of Scripture

102. See *TDNT* 1:758-61.

103. G. C. Berkouwer, *De Heilige Schrift,* 1:91, 93, 176.

104. See pp. 77-80, 171-72 of the present volume. Contrary to popular opinion, Luther did not have a "canon within the canon." He did not set Christ in opposition to Scripture. His conviction that Scripture must preach Christ is against the perversion of Scripture which would make it teach works.

is to preach Christ, and it achieves this end by speaking *truly* at every point. If it did not, its witness to Christ would be discredited to that extent.

The Spirit and the Word are the witnesses to and the servants of the living Word. The fact that they are servants does not reflect on their divinity, only upon their function. The Bible is second to Christ in redemptive importance, but second to nothing in epistemological importance. Like John the Baptist, who said, "I am not that light, but came to bear witness to the light," Holy Scripture points away to a revelation greater than itself. And also like John, Scripture is a prophetic voice whose authority is from heaven and whose utterance is truth.

The Question of Canonicity

Thus far we have noticed the good pleasure of God in giving to the church divinely inspired oracles, but we have not approached the question of the canon. It must be asked where the circumference of the circle of inspired books falls and how it is recognized. The question is of considerable intricacy and importance, and one which calls for fuller treatment by evangelical scholars.[105] The Spirit did not reveal a list of inspired books, but left their recognition to a historical process in which He was active. God's people learned to distinguish wheat from chaff, and gold from gravel, as He worked in their hearts.

Theologically speaking, the canon exists as soon as the inspired Scripture does. As Packer remarks,

> The Church no more gave us the New Testament canon than Sir Isaac Newton gave us the force of gravity. God gave us gravity, by his work of creation, and similarly he gave us the New Testament canon, by inspiring the individual books that make it up.[106]

105. See Harris; *New Bible Dictionary*, pp. 186-99; Geisler and Nix, pp. 127-207.

106. Packer, *God Speaks to Man*, p. 81.

Scientists do not create facts of nature, and the church does not invent Scripture; they are both divine gifts to be *recognized.* The church did not *authorize* Scripture; she searched it out according to certain principles and submitted to what she found. She is the *minister,* not the master, of the canon and does not constitute this or that Holy Writ. The church did not give the canon to herself, but she submits herself obediently to the inspired canon given by God. We must not think of the canon as accidentally arising, for the recognition of inspired books alone fulfills the purpose for which Scripture was given—to rule the believing church. The Spirit was active in the process of recognizing the canon in pursuance of the divine purpose.[107]

Without entering into a detailed study of how the Old Testament canon came to be settled, it is instructive to note that Christ and the apostles accepted the Palestinian Jewish canon without hesitation.[108] This placid reception, duplicated for the most part in the case of the New Testament, received by the early church, speaks of a deep confidence in the providence of God who caused His people to recognize His Word. In the case of the New Testament, the criteria of canonicity are quite plain. These consisted of the historical and traditional tests: Was the work apostolic or sanctioned by apostles? And had the book proven itself in Christian worship and devotion to be divinely inspired? The church did not ask herself, "What books shall *I authorize?*" But rather, "Which are the inspired books which I must recognize?" She is the child of the divine Word, not its mother.[109]

Luther is variously criticized and commended for his atti-

107. The question of *how* the canon was formed receives little attention from the Protestant confessions. The Westminster statement lists the books but gives no hint how the list was made up. The thirty-nine Articles likewise. The Formula of Concord mentions neither the books nor the marks of canonicity, perhaps that the central emphasis on soteriology be not disturbed.

108. See Geisler and Nix, pp. 148-61; E. J. Young, "The Authority of the Old Testament," in *The Infallible Word,* pp. 53-87.

109. See F. F. Bruce, *Are the New Testament Documents Reliable?* Chap. 3.

tude to the canon, for it is thought that he stands with the critics in their denial of the plenary inspiration of the Bible because he was hesitant in admitting the canonicity of certain books. The fact of inspiration and the extent of the canonical list are, however, *two different* things. Luther had no doubt *whatsoever* about the inerrancy of the undoubtedly canonical books of Scripture. He did share the hesitancy concerning the canonicity of certain antilegomena (e.g., James, Jude, Revelation), as did the early church.[110] Blind faith cannot improve the historical credentials of a book. If those close to the New Testament expressed doubt about certain books, we would be impudent to be surer than they! Luther's attitude is a tribute to his candid honesty in admitting an uncertainty which expediency would cover up. The Council of Trent pretended to be certain about the canonicity of apocryphal books whose credentials were doubted and denied by most in the primitive church, and we recognize her arrogance in it. But it is equally arrogant for us to criticize Luther for his integrity to keep to the facts as he had them. Nothing can be concluded from this to prove Luther was a liberal in his attitude to Scripture. His view of the canonical books is that of strict inerrancy.[111]

The results for a doctrine of inspiration from the materials of special revelation are rich indeed. They enable us to speak confidently of the plenary, verbal inspiration, and of the absolute authority of the Holy Scriptures. And they permit concrete decisions as to the nature and character of Christian theology.

110. See Eusebius, *Church History* 3.25.

111. See Pieper, 1:291-92; T. J. Mueller, "Luther's Canon Within the Canon," *Christianity Today* (Oct. 27, 1961). See also pp. 153-54 of the present volume.

3

THE CHARACTER OF CHRISTIAN THEOLOGY

THEOLOGY IS THE ART of articulating the cognitive substance of divine revelation of which Scripture is the medium. With the shape of revelation and the nature of Scripture in view, the character of Christian theology can be discussed. Theology or God-talk is an activity which human beings can engage in because God has spoken to us clearly in Christ. Eternity will solve many of our theological problems, and our most carefully contrived theories will appear childish in the light of His awesome presence. But theology must be constructed so that the life of faith may be nourished and the work of ministry grounded in truth.

THE CRISIS IN CONTEMPORARY THEOLOGY

The reason for the current crisis in dogmatics is as plain as the fact of it: men deny the existence of an adequate foundation on which such a structure could be reared.[1] "When the foundations are torn down, what can the righteous do?" (Ps 11:3). In earlier times, each side in a theological dispute acknowledged the reality of revealed truth and differed only in the interpretation of it. Today there is widespread skepticism as to whether a revelation deposit exists at all. The crisis runs very deep. The chasm between the Reformation and the papacy begins to look narrow when compared with the divide between those who affirm and those who deny the

1. J. Orr, *Progress of Dogma*, p. 358.

existence of divine revelation. This disagreement goes to the heart of everything. The alignments with real significance in modern theology seldom run along traditional denominational or confessional lines at all. The continental divide today falls between those who accept the finality of the incarnation and the normative authority of the Scriptures only, and those who reduce all theological concerns to human ones and locate God's Word in the words of universal man. It is a very old controversy between law and gospel. Does God save man, or does man save himself? Are the work and word of Christ final and decisive, or need they be augmented by a human contribution? Other questions pale in the shadow of these fundamental issues. The revolt against infallible Scripture is a phase in the revolt against evangelical truth. Revelation for modern theology boils down to a nonconceptual experience whose significance is a matter of personal conviction. The Word of God is lost, and with it the liberating gospel message.[2]

The church faces the gravest crisis in her history. It is not one particular doctrine which is under attack, but the *foundation* of all doctrine. At stake is not an incidental belief of part of Christendom, but the gospel itself. The rejection of biblical infallibility is not only responsible for the *chaos* of modern theology, whose methodology is bewildering and whose utterances inarticulate, but for the most serious *apostasy* in the history of doctrine. Salvation is bound up with revealed truth (Gal 1:9; 1 Ti 1:19; Titus 1:9). In the dispute over Scripture we literally face the loss of *all* theology. The loss of a reliable Bible means the loss of revealed truth and valid knowledge of redemption. It is ultimately destructive

2. B. Ramm, "The Continental Divide in Contemporary Theology," *Christianity Today* (Oct. 8, 1965). For acute analyses of current theological trends, see Carl F. H. Henry, *Frontiers in Modern Theology;* and William Hordern, *A Layman's Guide to Protestant Theology.* This fundamental divergence in theology may be described in terms of the priority accorded to the "giveness" of revelation or man's personal understanding of existence. It is ontology vs. personalism. Does theology deal with the objective nature and activity of God, the ontological reality disclosed in Christ, or is its concern limited to the existential concerns of men and their authentic experience?

of Christianity. Every article of faith is based on Scripture. *No* question is more decisive at this time than the epistemological one, because a faulty answer to it will be disastrous to untold generations. At stake is the very possibility of knowing and preaching the gospel. The stance we adopt toward Scripture determines the status of all the beliefs we hold. Revelation itself is the issue which faces every Christian. The crisis is ecumenical and worldwide. Modern theology is disreputable and chaotic today because its proper epistemological truth-base has been shoved aside. The church languishes, and the world does not hear the good news.[3]

Traditional theology sought to be "normative"; that is, it believed it could on the basis of divine revelation articulate solid truth regarding God and man. Contemporary theology has become almost entirely "descriptive." It makes no more claim to validity than (1) to be a fair presentation of what Christians have believed, and (2) to establish some sort of relevance with modern secular experience. The notion that theology might actually speak for God is practically never entertained anymore. The line found in Tillich, Macquarrie, Kaufman or Gilkey goes something like this: *revelation* is the word given to the various symbolic languages which men from time to time have adopted in an attempt to qualify their experience of being and existence; *theology* consists of systematic reflection upon such symbolization, usually by a person participating in this ethos; *truth* happens when a given symbol of human origin meshes with what we feel today and renders intelligible for us our experience in the world. In short, the Christian faith can make no claim to eternal truth in the manner she has sought traditionally to do, and must rest content to be one human projection among many whose ultimate value is pragmatic. This vision of theology arises from the belief that the God of the biblical revelation does

3. Herman Otten presents the theological crisis we face with force and clarity in *Baal or God*. The whole culture is in an autonomous phase, in a state of revolt against all form and law. The crisis in Christian authority is an aspect of the broader revolution against all established order.

not exist, except in a pantheon of earth-bound gods which man has chosen to create from time immemorial.

> There can be no more momentous subject and no more important one for theological debate than that which is enshrined in the question: "Can we be sure of a real self-disclosure of God?"[4]

Even Thielicke, for all his genuine warmth toward conservative Christians, really fails to grasp the deep seriousness of the first question posed to him ("Are there errors in the Bible?"), and in his lengthy answer misses the issue of greatest significance.[5] The crucial question in theology today concerns the *truth claim* implicit in the doctrine of inspiration. Are theological propositions merely mundane objectifying representations, ideas from within the rim of human genius, set forth in response to an ecstatic revelation experience? Salvation presupposes revealed truth, and revealed truth the scriptural deposit. Though it seemed for a time that neoorthodoxy could stem the tide of the liberal assault on the substance of the Christian revelation and provide a bulwark for its defense, it was not able to do so. In its refusal to recognize that revelation *is* objectively communicated in historical occurrences and intelligible propositions, neoorthodox theology was incapable of coherently describing the content of revelation which, it believed, was at bottom paradoxical and, in principle, indescribable.[6]

The denial of the final authority of the propositional, divine revelation in Scripture is deeply nihilistic for theology. Few people seem to realize what a small step it is from a "hidden God" to "no God." The "death of God" spokesmen simply *consistently* applied the neoorthodox doctrine of revelation

4. H. D. McDonald, *Theories of Revelation*, p. 7.
5. Helmut Thielicke, *Between Heaven and Earth*.
6. Historic Christian theology has employed the term *propositional revelation* to describe the cognitive truth-content of Scripture. The expression is not intended to deny that Scripture contains a rich multiplicity of literary forms in conveying its message. It merely points to the valid conceptual side of divine revelation.

and inspiration. If no verbal text or concept can unequivocally be identified with God's Word, then perhaps there is no "Word of God" or even "God of the Word." A theology without truth content must remain speechless. When Bultmann says, "What then has been revealed? Nothing at all, so far as the question concerning revelation asks for doctrines,"[7] he simply fails to recognize the absurdity of his position. It will not do to protest that God does not need to justify Himself. Jaspers has the answer to that: "It is not a matter of God justifying himself—but of a 'word' or 'revelation' that claims to come from God justifying itself." The new mentality cannot align itself with any stream of historic Christian faith. J. M. Creed writes,

> Had any Christian of any church between the end of the second century and the closing decades of the eighteenth been asked a question as to the content of the Christian religion, his answer could scarcely have failed to be to the general effect that the truths of the Christian religion were contained and conveyed in the inspired books of holy Scripture.[8]

In the present climate the Bible provides some themes for theology, but no norms. Its true canonicity is broken. Theology drifts unchecked on the surface of the reigning philosophical consensus. Wherever the content of Scripture is displeasing or fails to satisfy, it can be bypassed in favor of present experience. The result is the death of Christian theology. The loss of the *sola scriptura* leads to a new sacerdotalism (the church is the matrix of the tradition), a new clericalism (the scholar applies his existential gnosis to the text on our behalf), and a new mystical agnosticism (a faith tailored to survive even if God is not there).

7. Rudolf Bultmann, *Existence and Faith,* ed. S. M. Ogden, p. 85. Cf. Günther Bornkamm: "There is also a recognition of the paradoxical character of a revelation that can never be authenticated in the historical-empirical realm but can only be encountered in the Word event and grasped by faith" (*The Theology of Rudolf Bultmann,* ed. C. W. Kegley, p. 5). A theology whose fact and truth claim are exempt from critical verification is non-sense.

8. J. M. Creed, *The Divinity of Jesus Christ,* p. 105.

The great ecumenical creeds of the early church sought *truth* even at the price of unity. Modern statements of faith strive for *unity* before truth. A recent confessional document of the United Church of Canada managed to summarize the Christian faith without alluding to the transcendent majesty of God, the sinfulness of man, or the finished work of Christ. The "1967 Confession" of the Presbyterian denomination is filled with generalizations, and is less a statement of burning conviction than a door of accommodation to liberalism and Romanism.[9] The basis of so much ecumenical "snuggling up" today is the absence, rather than the presence, of strong Christian convictions. In 1956 there was scarcely a ripple when Adlai Stevenson joined a Presbyterian church while keeping membership in a Unitarian one. The pastors all agreed that his membership in both groups was perfectly consistent! Bipartisan politics calls for nondenominational religion. The truth question is quite secondary to the demands of the human situation. Theology has taken a humanistic turning. To confess Christ as Lord now means to acknowledge "the serious importance of human existence."[10] Neither theology nor prayer has any transcendent referent. Christianity and humanism both have an open position on truth which permits unlimited dialogue and syncretism. "What's best in your theology should freely interact with what's best in my theology, to produce a new set of beliefs not yet discernible to either of us, a synthesis superior to either of our present positions." The courtesy of this stance blinds us to the fact that the entire project operates within a human egocentricity divorced from the normative rule of God's Word. The ark of God would not stand alongside Dagan's statue in the temple of the Philistines, and God's truth will not blend with

9. G. W. Bromiley points out that the confession moves away from the more orthodox features of Barth's theology and follows the weaker, less biblical, elements. See "The '1967 Confession' and Karl Barth," *Christianity Today* (Mar. 4, 1966).

10. For the secular directon modern theology is taking, see Robert Kysar, "Toward a Christian Humanism," *Christian Century* (May 21, 1969); Robert McAfee Brown, *The Religious Situation 1969*, pp. 395-422.

human speculations. It is our duty to be faithful to truth and intolerant of error.

The confusion in modern theology and its hostility to orthodoxy cannot be interpreted as a guileless missing of the way. The desire to be free of Scripture is rooted in the desire to *postulate* a religion of one's own. A postulated theism (a self-defined *Blik*) is a *modifiable* theism! A theology subject to no objective controls may be altered and adopted at will to suit the taste. At its deepest level, objective certainty is sacrificed for the sake of personal divinity! The human ego occupies the throne of the deposed divine oracle. For Frederick Ferre, Christian faith is a model he finds useful to fit the facts of his experience of life.[11] But because it *is* a model, it can be reformed and adapted. This plasticity he calls the quality of a "living religion." It is, in fact, the mark of an egocentric one. Both Frederick and Nels F. S. Ferre proceed to reform the Christian model in the direction of what both conceive to be an *agape* theology.[12] Their revision detached from biblical norms illustrates the solipsistic separation of modern theology from revelation data. Stripped of its piosity, the Ferre *agape* standard turns out to be the inner light of the theologizing subject. In this fashion the theologian is free to bend revelational reality to his liking, and relativize the biblical absolutes, dissolving the gospel in the acid of radical subjectivity. The Christian faith is "living," not because it is plastic, but because it is the true Word of Him that lives forevermore. The ferment in contemporary theology is not a sign of healthy vitality, but the death rattle of a Christian theism being transmuted into a mystical humanism.

The Sola Scriptura: A Proper Method for Theology

In contrast to theological anarchy, orthodox Protestantism holds to *sola scriptura*, the conviction that Scripture is God's infallible Word and the *only* source of revealed theology. Any

11. See Frederick Ferre, *Basic Modern Philosophy of Religion*, pp. 408-39.
12. See Nels F. S. Ferre, *The Universal Word* .

theology which relies on an alternate source or appeals to multiple norms is humanistic because it elevates the human ego above the oracles of God. The authority of Scripture is the watershed of theological conviction, the basis of all decision-making. Having discarded the orthodox method of building theology, that is, a careful synthesizing of the statements of Scripture, modern theology has been hard put to discover an alternative method, and until now has failed in its search.[13] Orthodoxy holds that only Scripture constitutes revelation data and, therefore, theology is to be relative to Scripture alone. "Where the Scriptures speak, we speak; where the Scriptures are silent, we are silent," said Thomas Campbell.[14] In the words of the Westminster Confession,

> The whole counsel of God, concerning all things necessary for His own glory, man's salvation, faith, and life, is either expressly set down in Scripture, or by good and necessary consequence may be deduced from Scripture: unto which nothing at any time is to be added, whether by new revelations of the Spirit, or traditions of men.[15]
>
> The supreme judge, by which all controversies of religion are to be determined, and all decrees of councils, opinions of ancient writers, doctrines of men, and private spirits, are to be examined, and in whose sentence we are to rest, can be no other but by the Holy Spirit speaking in the Scripture.[16]

Sola scriptura is the Protestant principle. Scripture consti-

13. See Alan Richardson, *The Bible in the Age of Science*, pp. 77-99.

14. Cf. Ludwig Wittgenstein's famous dictum in philosophy: "Wovon man nicht sprechen kann, darüber muss man schweigen" (One should remain silent regarding matters whereof he is unable to speak), *Tractatus Logico-Philosophicus*, p. 7. His wish that philosophers would stop talking about matters for which they had not a granule of verifiable information applies to theologians also.

15. Westminster Confession, 1.6.

16. Ibid., 1.10. Karl Barth also insists on the *sola scriptura*. The Bible is the authoritative witness to Jesus Christ, "the source and guiding principle of all Christian doctrine and exposition." (*Against the Stream*, p. 220). Scripture is self-interpreting and requires no magisterium outside itself. He opposes Rome and Bultmann alike because alien presuppositions control their hermeneutic. We must concentrate on the text itself to hear God's voice (*Church Dogmatics*, vol. 4, pt. 2, pp. 38-39, 122-23, 149-50).

tutes, determines and rules the entire theological endeavor. What it does not determine is no part of Christian truth. Extrabiblical claims to knowledge of ultimate reality are dreams and fancies (Jer 23:16). As the *Formula of Concord* puts it in the Epitome,

> We believe, teach and confess that the prophetic and apostolic writings of the Old and New Testaments are the only rule and norm according to which all doctrines and teachers alike must be appraised and judged.

Our source of authority is the Holy Spirit speaking by Scripture, the product of His own creative breath: *Deus locutus* and *Deus loquens* (God has spoken; God is speaking). The Protestant principle is not *scriptura prima.* For, although it goes without saying that Scripture is the primordial witness to revelation, it is a good deal more than that. Scripture is itself the divine utterance, and stands above everything before and after it in determining revealed truth.

According to Paul Tillich, the *sola scriptura* is the Protestant *pitfall!*[17] In its place he proposes a different principle, namely, a refusal to identify the absolute in any way at all. If God were in any way characterized, He would be less than ultimate. Altizer took Tillich seriously and refused even to identify ultimacy with being. Tillich's widow connects his death with the shock of this suggestion. Tillich's Protestant principle means that being cannot be qualified, is compatible with any state of affairs whatsoever, and hence meaningless.[18]

17. Paul Tillich, *Systematic Theology,* 1:157. Since the rise of liberal theology, it has been fashionable to regard as the principles of the Reformation the right of free enquiry and private judgment. More profoundly, however, the Reformation deserves our gratitude for holding fast to the evangelical truths of Holy Scripture against the perversion of them by the Roman church.

18. "Tillich never once understands the word [Protestantism] in its historical sense of a protestation or confession of the Gospel. Instead he takes it abstractly as a concept signifying 'the attitude of protest against form.' By means of such an interpretation—a drastic *re*interpretation, of course—he bends it to support his idealistic dogma that the eternal may appear in the temporal but can never be identified with anything found there" (Kenneth Hamilton, *The System and the Gospel,* p. 232). See also Paul Edwards, "Professor Tillich's Confusions," *Mind* 74 (1965): 192-214, and John W. Montgomery, "Tillich's Philosophy of History," *Gordon Review* 10 (1967): 130-49.

For Tillich all symbols fall short of adequately defining the nature of ultimate reality. Theology is without content, and religion alone remains. Tillich's principle is, however, the exact *opposite* of the biblical one. We do not worship such a version of the "unknown God," but the God who reveals Himself. Idolatry is not to *name* God, but to name Him wrongly! The best defense against idolatry is Jesus Christ (1 Jn 5:19-21). It is not a question of avoiding symbolic expressions, but of finding *legitimate* predicates for God. God's revelation in Christ is the standard of valid theological models, and the Scripture is His Word. Tillich gives us no way to distinguish proper from improper ultimate concerns. Therefore, there is no reason to think Christianity is true or reliable as a source of the knowledge of God.

In a sense, Tillich agreed with Wittgenstein who taught that the limits of language are the limits of the world, and so it would not be possible to speak of God. Yet, talk about God Tillich did, teaching that "God" refers to "that which is unconditionally beyond the conceptual sphere." Why use a *word* to refer to something which transcends our conceptual world? We may not speak of "knowing" God if God refers to that which is unknowable! But the answer to Wittgenstein (and Tillich)is nothing but the gospel: God entered into cosmic reality in Christ and left His footprints (as it were), as signals of transcendence, behind. We may speak of God because He has revealed Himself in flesh and spoken of Himself in human language. "Give Scripture its due as the verbally inspired, infallible Word of God; give Christ his due as the sole and entire source of our salvation, and you have a truly sound theology and saving religion," said Albrecht.

The evangelical church lives by the *sola scriptura*. It is her check against demonic self-delusion. Scripture is the objective standard by which all subjective opinion is to be measured. The peril of Romanism and liberalism is their *uncriticizability*. There is nothing to jolt and correct them when they go wrong. The meaning of the *canon* of Scripture is its *critical* role. There is a norm of true Christianity embodied in written (and fixed) documents, and therefore a resource for self-correction. At the present time, the modern Protestant who has given up Scripture, and the Catholic who has added pope and tradition to it, are in a very similar plight. Sasse asks,

> One wonders which tragedy is greater: to add another source of revelation to the inspired Scriptures, as in Roman Catholicism; or to lose the Scripture as the inspired Word of God, as in modern Protestantism? Which is worse: to add a mediatrix of all graces to the only true Mediator between God and man; or to lose Christ as the Mediator entirely?[19]

It will not do to dismiss the *principium* with the charge that it makes Scripture a paper pope or treats it as a legal code book. The linguistic *form* of Scripture is indeed complex and many-sided. It contains all manner of poetry, proverb, parable and history. Furthermore, it is a cumulative revelation, not all given at once, but organic and growing throughout the history of its formation. Nevertheless, the teachings of this book, when ascertained by careful interpretation, are in fact binding. To submit to Scripture is part of our Christian servitude. "Give us liberty" is not our cry. Freedom from Scripture is darkness, not light. It is a freedom no Christian should seek (Jn 8:31; 2 Pe 2:19). As Paul put it, "Whoever teaches differently and does not adhere to the wholesome sayings of our Lord Jesus Christ and to the teaching that is according to our faith, is conceited and without understanding" (1 Ti 6:3-4, Berkeley). Not only theology, but all our knowledge, should be scriptually normed. In many respects, the Reformation which took place in theology during the sixteenth century has yet to be carried through with regard to the other sciences. Genuine perspective in the entire cultural spectrum

19. Herman Sasse, "The Inspiration of Holy Scripture," in *Crisis in Lutheran Theology*, ed. Montgomery, 2:17.

cannot be gained apart from the written Word of the transcendent God. Much ground remains to be possessed.

While Scripture indeed has a normative authority shared by nothing else, it is not true that reason, tradition and conscience play no role in the *exercise* of that authority. We read as intelligent men in a modern society. That is, we do not come to Scripture *de novo*. We stand on the shoulders of Christians before our time who reflected long upon God's Word. Peter Berger points out:

> The fundamental questions of theology have been passionately considered for at least three thousand years. It is not only insufferable arrogance to think that one can begin theology in sovereign disregard of this history, it is also extremely uneconomical. It seems rather a waste of time to spend, say, five years working out a position, only to find that it has already been done by a Syrian monk in the fifth century.[20]

To neglect tradition is often to fall prey to sectarian errors. He who ignores history is compelled to repeat history's mistakes. Tradition is an important commentary on the Bible. The *sola scriptura* principle does *not* exclude a respectful listening to the wisdom of the past. For we stand in a community of faith and cannot leap over two thousand years of Christian history in disregard of the prodigious labors already done. A careful, though critical, hearing is due the testimony of tradition because, despite heresies and declensions, there is a real doctrinal continuity in her history.

Biblicism is an antitraditional preoccupation with the Bible. It limits its interests to the Bible alone and does not seek nor accept the guidance and correction which the history of exegesis affords. There is something audacious about such a leap from the twentieth century back into the first century without even a glance at the ways in which Scripture has hitherto been understood. Indeed, in such a case there is the real danger that the interpreter will bring the Bible under

20. Peter Berger, *Rumor of Angels*, p. 98.

his own control. Every explicit denial of tradition involves a hidden commitment to a personal brand of tradition. We cannot stand apart from the spirit of our age and time altogether, but we stand in need of the chastening of two millennia of biblical study. The Holy Spirit has been teaching Christians these hundreds of years, and we should listen to what they have learned. At the same time, however, what we hear from tradition does *not* stand on the same level with canonical Scripture. For the Bible is a *critical authority* confronting the church, and the church and tradition are guided and corrected by the canon of Scripture. If the church were directed by tradition alone, she would engage in dialogue with herself. As it is, Scripture stands in judgment upon her, and her tradition is tested by it.[21] Therefore, though we all stand in the flow of historical theology—in a cause-and-effect relation with what goes before and what follows—the result is *not* theological *relativism.* For Scripture is capable of checking opinions born merely out of cultural finitude and of speaking a sure word from one beyond the flux.

Does the *sola scriptura* principle lead to a narrow position theologically? Not at all! In actuality, no man-made theology, or one created out of a mere selection of biblical topics, is capable of conceiving so *broad* a system as the Scriptures contain. Where a high doctrine of inspiration is not held, the constant temptation in hermeneutics, is to eliminate biblical ideas which are *prematurely* considered incompatible by the interpreter. We might say of studies in the atonement of Christ that in a real sense the classical, the Anselmian and the moral-influence theories *all* enshrine actual biblical teaching, and must *not* be counterposed. Any valid biblical model would have to reflect the victory, the judicial, and the exemplary motifs, for the doctrine of the cross is many-sided and will not be boxed up in a narrow hypothesis. Scripture can support all three, and a valid doctrinal model may not exclude

21. See Barth, *Church Dogmatics,* vol. 1, pt. 1, pp. 117-18. For his remarks on the biblicism of Gottfried Menken, see vol. 1, pt. 2, pp. 607-9.

any. The inference is plain. One Scripture teaching should not be used to discredit another scriptural teaching because, when we look closely, the one contains aspects which the other does not. One good idea need not be pitted against another! If the Bible is *not* our standard, we run the danger of one-sidedness because our inclinations (or strong denominational loyalties) tend to limit the *breadth* of biblical doctrine.[22]

The *sola scriptura* is the Protestant answer to the problem of authority. Theology without valid authority is like art with all freedom and no form, or a ship without a rudder. An authority is simply that which has a recognized right to rule us. Divine revelation itself structures authority for us. Scripture alone has a right to command our compliance and obedience. "My conscience is subject to the Word of God," said Luther. This single fact renders a truly affirmative theology possible. Mystical theology has held that the truth of revelation is so wholly other, beyond mundane beliefs, that no one can really say what it is, or what it is not. Since Kant, Protestant theology has moved in this direction. The universal validity and univocal content of theological utterances were virtually denied. Theology shifted its interest exclusively to experienced truth. Dogmatics became "the science that systematizes the doctrine prevalent in a Christian church at any given time," as Schleiermacher defines it. Such a denial of the univocal element is fatal to theology. Revelation no longer *reveals*. Neoorthodoxy did not really resolve the theological crisis because its own existential view of revelation also excludes rational, affirmative theology.

H. M. Kuitert has written an important book on the antimetaphysical trend in modern theology.[23] Although his analysis of movements in modern theology is thorough and perti-

22. See Montgomery, *Chytraeus on Sacrifice*, pp. 139-46; Leon Morris, *The Apostolic Preaching of the Cross*, 3d ed., and *The Cross in the New Testament*.

23. H. M. Kuitert, *The Reality of Faith*. Kuitert represents the new evangelical viewpoint at the Free University of Amsterdam.

nent, he plots a dangerous course for orthodox Protestants. In failing to appreciate that the liberal attack upon Protestant orthodoxy was in reality an attack on evangelical faith in the interests of humanistic religion, Kuitert concludes that there is no way back to orthodoxy![24] Instead he points us to tradition.[25] Thus an anthropological conquest of theology (liberalism) is countered by a conquest by tradition. Kuitert does not give us the answer. The key to an affirmative theology is the *sola scriptura,* the conviction that divine truth is explicit and implicit in Scripture and can be presented in language which is not merely static and sterile. Theology is a science. Revelation data exists on the basis of which it is proper to speak of our world in relation to invisible reality. Not that God Himself is in any way dissected and objectified by critical thought; rather, it is the revelation data which is subjected to careful examination, and the living God who is known thereby.

MULTIPLE-SOURCE THEORIES

Few modern theologians limit themselves to Scripture in the formulation of their thought. Most seek to appeal to many "formative factors" (Macquarrie lists six, and says there are probably more!)[26] and seek to develop a calculus to handle them. All these sources are supposed to contribute material from which theology is drawn. In actual fact, such multiple-source theories generally reduce to single-source theories as soon as conflict between the sources arises and a decision has to be made. When that happens, *one* source rises to the top and is given preference. Macquarrie has not been altogether frank with us, for he has not told us what his *final* authority is. Upon closer examination it becomes apparent that he does not do complete justice to all six formative factors but only to one: namely, the theologian's pious

24. Ibid., p. 141.
25. Ibid., pp. 144 ff.
26. They are: experience, revelation, Scripture, tradition, culture, reason. John Macquarrie, *Principles of Christian Theology,* pp. 4-17. See also Tillich, 1:34-40.

self-awareness of truth. To him Scripture is only the community's memory bank and not infallible, and tradition is certainly not perspicuous. That leaves us, the living faithful, with the task of developing theological categories to suit ourselves. Macquarrie heavily qualifies the "objective" factors but fails to criticize the "subjective" ones.[27] His procedure is a paradigm for many others. Multiple-source theories tend to break down under pressure to single-source theories, which stand in competition with *sola scriptura*.[28] Either something is exalted *over* Scripture or something is added *to* it. Whether it be by substitution or adulteration, the Word of God is silenced. Each in its way enthrones the human ego as teacher of Christians. There are not many ways of doing theology; there are only *two*: that which appeals to genuine revelation data in Holy Scripture, and that which appeals to nonrevelation data originating in the human ego.[29] We wish to examine three claims to extrabiblical revelation material: reason, tradition, and Christian experience.

Reason. Because the term *reason* has a bewildering number of senses and uses, a good deal of the controversy over revelation and reason is based on the failure to define terms. The elemental fallacy of much theological discussion on the relationship is the failure to distinguish reason as the logical, discriminating faculty charged with detecting logical contradictions, and reason as the actual source of revelation data. We wish to *defend* vigorously the competence of reason to test religious claims, but we dispute its ability to inaugurate revealed truth. In a limited sense, reason is prior to revelation, for unless it were we could not know a true revelation

27. "In every assumedly scientific theology there is a point where individual experience, traditional valuation, and personal commitment must decide the issue" (Tillich, 1:8). G. D. Kaufman admits that as a theologian his own understanding may lead him to reinterpret and amend the portrayal of Christ he finds in Scripture (*Systematic Theology: A Historicist Perspective*, p. 71).

28. See Montgomery, "The Theologian's Craft: A Discussion of Theory Formation and Theory Testing in Theology," *Concordia Theological Monthly* 37(1966): 78-79.

29. Francis Pieper, *Christian Dogmatics*, 1:196-213.

when we encountered it. If reason, presupposing the law of noncontradiction, were not valid, it would be impossible to understand a revelation, much less distinguish a true from a false one. A revolt against reason in this sense will get precisely nowhere. Revelation must be examined to be received and believed.[30] For there is no lack of existential passion among savages! Tillich comments, "Theology is as dependent on formal logic as any other science."[31]

Reason has, however, been incorrectly related to revelation by Unitarians and rationalists. The theologians call it the *magisterial* use. By it one is supposed to be able to formulate the final truths of religion. However, formal reason, like pure logic, deals in inference and deduction, and orders our mental universe; but it is unable to inform us as to the content of the world. It is incapable of rising above tautologies to give us information about what is in *fact* the case. Christianity is a historical religion, and reason can neither add to nor diminish from our knowledge of what it is. This can arise only as we test the data available describing it. The "I" receives data but does not create it. When elements of Christian faith are rejected as unreasonable, it is because they do not square with other data which has been accepted from another source. Reason itself cannot be that source. When it is claimed it is, reason is a surrogate term, standing in for the unadmitted actual source, usually the current humanistic consensus.

When Lessing came out with the famous dictum, "Accidental truths of history can never become the proof of necessary truths of reason," and concluded that certain biblical concepts were those "against which my reason rebels," he was not being quite honest with us. What he should have said was that these were notions against which his aprioristic metaphysic rebelled. It was the specific view of God which

30. C. A. Campbell, *On Selfhood and Godhood*, p. 18; Charles Hodge, *Systematic Theology*, 1:49-50; F. H. Cleobury, *Christian Rationalism and Philosophical Analysis*, pp. 18-19.

31. Tillich, 1:56.

he already held (Spinozistic) which informed him in advance that the biblical fact revelation could not be so. *Reason* had nothing to do with it.

Human reason has no power to initiate truth. It is rather an instrument which organizes and draws inferences from sources of data outside of itself. As such it is an honorable minister of the gospel.

Tradition. This confession is required of the faithful Roman Catholic:

> I also admit the holy Scriptures, according to that sense which our holy mother Church has held and does hold, to which it belongs to judge of the true sense and interpretation of the Scriptures; neither will I ever take and interpret them otherwise than according to the unanimous consent of the Fathers.[32]

In the Roman communion, truth becomes fossilized in an ecclesiological form. Scripture and the teaching office of the church are assimilated. The oral unwritten tradition deserves equally devout reverence, as do the books of the Bible (cf. "The decree concerning the Canonical Scriptures," Fourth Session, Council of Trent). However, because the tradition is vast in compass and less than perspicuous in nature, it became necessary for the tradition itself to have an interpreter. This the first Vatican Council (1870) provided in its dogmatic constitution on the church, in which the primacy, perpetuity and infallibility of the Roman pontiff was defined. The pope, speaking *ex cathedra* in the discharge of his apostolic office, legislates for and binds the conscience of the universal church. Since none can know with assurance what the teaching of the tradition is, it falls to the church's magisterium to render a verdict. Thus the principle of authority in Rome is Rome itself.[33] Authority becomes the opinion of holy church in motion as it is articulated by papal decree.

32. *Professio Fidei Tridentinae,* 3.
33. See V. Subilia, *The Problem of Catholicism,* pp. 125-44.

There is at present a moving together of the new Catholic and radical Protestant positions.[34] On the one hand, the Roman Catholic theologians are interpreting dogma in an evolutionary, existential way; and, on the other hand, Protestants are adopting a historicist view of truth. In both cases, Scripture and tradition are drawn together organically, and the subject-object distinction of church-Scripture is dissolved. The result is a wholly *situational* theology, which is the faith of the community, and the core reality of revelation is the sociological group itself. The one side (Tavard, Rahner, Congar)[35] stresses the unity of Scripture and tradition, with the magisterium acting as referee, and the other side (Barth, Macquarrie, Kaufman)[36] insists the Bible is always interpreted in the light of the church's ongoing tradition. The hermeneutical circle from Bible to tradition is thus a vicious one, so that the meaning of the text depends on the context of the interpreting community. This was Rome's position in opposition to the Reformation; now it is Rome's *and* radical Protestantism's in opposition to orthodox Evangelicalism. In essence the community becomes the final arbiter of truth, and her evolving thought is subject to no correction save the vicissitudes of process itself. Kaufman puts it baldly:

> The ultimate arbiter of theological validity is not reason or experience or the Bible or the Church, but the movement of history itself—understood theologically: the providence of God. It is this movement which in actual fact sorts out

34. See Robert H. Bryant, *The Bible's Authority Today*, pp. 82-113. The orthodox, Catholic, and Protestant theologians are all playing variations on the theme that canonical Scripture is to be understood in the context of the ongoing, living tradition. It fits into the dynamic, existentialist concept of the evolving truth, and is a step away from the Reformation insistence that the church stand beneath Scripture. Instead, Scripture is sucked into her tradition, and the Word of God identified with a fallible human society. Cf. E. G. Jay, "The Church as the Locus and Medium of Revelation," *Canadian Journal of Theology* 11 (1965): 94-105.

35. See George H. Tavard, *Holy Writ or Holy Church;* Karl Rahner and Joseph Ratzinger, *The Episcopate and the Primacy;* Y. M.-J. Congar, *Tradition and Traditions.*

36. See Barth, *Church Dogmatics*, vol. 1, pt. 2, pp. 606-12; Albert C. Outler, "Scripture, Tradition and Ecumenism," in *Scripture and Ecumenism*, ed. L. J. Swidler; Macquarrie, pp. 10-12.

> the valid from the invalid, the significant from the insignificant.[37]

His principle is dangerous and unworkable. A process tells us nothing of right and wrong, true and false. Mere movement may be divine or demonic. It gives us no clue at all to what we are to preach or believe. Process philosophy applied to theology does not help a bit toward solving the truth question. The *critical* role of Scripture must be stressed as an objective authority confronting the church if this trend toward deifying the consensus of opinion is to be checked.

It would be wrong, however, to conclude that what we see here is a return to pre-Reformation Catholicism. For when the new theologians speak of "truth" known to the church, they mean *existential* and *relativistic* "truth." In Catholicism, this emerges in the new view of the history of doctrine. As Pope John XXIII put it: "The substance of the ancient doctrine, contained in the 'deposit of faith' is one thing; its formulation is quite another." Granted, John's words could be read in such a way as to imply nothing startling. But it gives, in fact, the green light and open door to the liberal Catholic theologians to radically alter traditional beliefs. This is accomplished by the application of evolutionary theory to the development of dogma. Newman was not converted to Rome; Rome was converted to Newman. His theory of dogma, not as a fixed deposit of unchangeable concepts, but as an organism which evolves and matures, has had momentous effects. His biological analogy prepared the way for an existential understanding. Truth is what grips the mind of the community in a particular age. Thus any foreign branch grafted on the vine (e.g., Mariology) is claimed for the root. Truth is never fixed, and its direction cannot be plotted. It

37. Kaufman, p. xv. For the Catholics, Leslie Dewart presents the concept of truth as constantly evolving in *Future of Belief*. For Gogarten, too, God is the religious name for "mystery," the boundary of man's evolution, which may help to explain his early support for the Nazis in Germany, who, if nothing else, were "moving."

just evolves and unfolds.[38] The Chalcedonian symbol, for example, represents a beginning, not an end, and its formulation is *historical* (meaning: relative to its day). The formula can be an obstruction if taken too literally, and not according to its inner "meaning." Our thoughts develop through confrontation with our subject matter out of the past. For the radical exponents of this theory, dogmatic expressions have reference, not to timeless truths, but to the existential concerns motivating the church at that time. We are not obliged to bow to the terminology or thought in which the pronouncement was couched, but only to empathize with its existential tone.

The new Catholic modernism has attractions for liberal Protestants too, for it offers them the comfort of a historical creed and community without the liability of having to believe anything literally! Liberals who feel estranged from traditional Christianity can by this means get their toe back into history, and enjoy the comforts of "orthodoxy" without its demands. Protestants can interpret their own confessions "historically" too, analyzing the occasion which gave rise to this or that formulation, and escaping the need of believing them strictly. The secret is to regard "the truth known and knowable to be always relative to the historical situation of the knower" and to leave that which transcends our situation as unqualified and unconditioned.[39] Thus theology is relative, time-conditioned, and unbinding. Even Kuitert, in his repeated insistence on the "historicality" of all man's verbal formulations, borders on this grievous error.[40] Admittedly, theology is "ectypal" (a copy), and not "architypal" (the original), in its knowledge of God, but what knowledge we

38. Karl Rahner, *Theological Investigations,* 1:41. See J. Seynaev, *Cardinal Newman's Doctrine on Holy Scripture.*

39. Kaufman, p. 14. Neoorthodox theologians all ought to read Radhakrishnan, modern apologist for Hinduism. His view of religion as experience, God as man's limit, truth as existential, and dogma as relative is almost identical to the view of neoorthodox thought. Western theology has been Easternized to its own detriment. See Sarvepalli Radhakrishnan, *The Hindu View of Life.*

40. Kuitert, p. 187.

have in Scripture *is* knowledge of *God.* Sociology has shown, as Kaufman and Kuitert are so aware, that human knowledge is relative to the culture in which it exists, and that religions are historically conditioned.[41] *However,* this observation damages all but the Christian position. If the scriptural revelation were just another man-made religion, it would be characterized by "historicality" at every point; as it is, it makes an explicit claim *not* to be. The finality of Jesus Christ and the inspiration of Scripture provide an Archimedian point in the flux of the human situation against which the flow of history may be measured and evaluated. The radical theology ends in speechlessness because of unbelief with respect to the divine authority of Christ and the gospel. It is naturalism dressed in existential garb. We do not claim to know the nature of God as triune through the ontic capacity of our minds. We know it on the basis of valid ectypal revelation.

The new view of truth held in Catholic and Protestant circles corresponds remarkably to an age-old motif in the Eastern Orthodox Church. From earliest times Orthodox theology has stressed mystical experience, and rested authority with the Spirit moving in the church.[42] A broad ecumenical consensus has developed as the mysticism of the East has met the existentialism of the West. The canonical Scriptures are not to be understood except in the context of the tradition. Truth is closely identified with the evolving consciousness of the church. The problem of how to recognize theological truth remains—the consciousness of which church, and at what stage in its evolution. Truth evaporates in a mystical cloud of unknowing. Church and tradition stand in great need of the critical voice of Scripture to prevent them

41. H. Meyerhoff, *The Philosophy of History in Our Time,* p. 10; I. M. Bochenski, *Contemporary European Philosophy,* pp. 122-24.

42. See Montgomery, *Ecumenicity . . .,* pp. 25-44; P. I. Bratsiotis, "An Orthodox Contribution," in *Biblical Authority for Today,* eds. A. Richardson and W. Schweitzer, pp. 20-22; John Meyendorff, "The Meaning of Tradition," in *Scripture and Ecumenism;* Ernst Benz, *The Eastern Orthodox Church,* pp. 48-53.

from teaching error. A magisterium not subject to the external controls of God's Word could prove to be demonic.

The Roman Catholic solution to the problem of authority fails at several crucial points. For one thing, the pretensions of the Roman magisterium cannot be justified biblically or historically. Scripture does not commit supreme jurisdiction to the succession of Roman pontiffs.[43] Furthermore, if it be argued that an infallible Bible requires an infallible interpreter (a Bible to the second power), this interpreter also requires another, and so on in an infinite regress. No doubt the message of the Bible is encountered within the life of the church. However, her collective experience is not the *norm* for theology. On the contrary, the biblical message is the norm, judge and criterion of that experience.[44] The church is the handmaiden, not the mistress, of Scripture, and her life is to be continually reformed by her teachings (*ecclesia semper reformanda*). The *sola scriptura* is an indispensable check against the church's deifying herself and the boundary of reflection within which her thought should circulate. Existential Protestant theology is not free from the same danger in its stress upon *Christus praesens,* the up-to-the-minute Christ who goes on acting and revealing Himself today, and turns out to be a striking resemblance to the reigning philosophical mood of modernity.[45]

Increasingly we are being confronted with a theology in motion. A doctrine is "true" for one generation, not for the next. Yesterday's error becomes today's truth. Harnack held that while it was wrong for Marcion to reject the Old Testament, it is right for us to do so. All human knowledge, even theological concepts, is relative to the knower caught in the process of flux and change. "Whirl is king, having driven out Zeus," said Aristophanes. The key question becomes what role a notion played in the process of evolving self-awareness.

43. See Montgomery, *The Shape of the Past,* pp. 351-57.
44. Tillich, 1:52.
45. See Dietrich Ritschl, *Memory and Hope: An Inquiry Concerning the Presence of Christ.*

Everything revolves in the sphere of relativity. In the name of history, the uniqueness and finality of the Christian revelation are denied. The community is divine, and the process itself truth.[46] This view of the liberal Protestant, and now, increasingly, the new Catholic as well, is diametrically opposed to the biblical claim that God has spoken. There is indeed no possible way for finite man in the process of historical becoming to gain an absolute perspective upon his life. But there is a solution to that dilemma in the coming into history of Jesus Christ and the infallibility of His written Word.

Christian Experience. Protestants, and increasingly, Catholics as well, frequently revert to Christian experience when seeking to determine correct theological results. Religious experience itself is thought to yield guidelines to meet the needs of contemporary man. The criterion of truth is feelings, and theology "first person." Rather than attempt to write theology impersonally, the theologians report on their inner life and how that helped them shape their beliefs. Church alumnus James A. Pike was traveling this road when it took him into pure humanism. But, whether it be the "I" of the rationalist or the "I" of the pietist, the human ego is permitted to pass judgment upon the teachings of Scripture. Personal opinion and sentimentality become the true canon. The biblical revelation is accepted or rejected at will. Since Kant's repudiation of rational religion the focus has turned within. Revelation was regarded as an indwelling light. What began as an essentially Quaker doctrine became the hallmark of liberal theology: revelation within the immediacy of religious experience. The reality of religion lay beyond reason. The doctrine appeared both in Schleiermacher's idea of utter dependence being the presupposition of all religion, and in Otto's theory of the numinous.[47] At its heart, religion is

46. See Kaufman, *Relativism, Knowledge and Faith.*

47. Schleiermacher, the father of liberal theology, strongly repudiated the cognitive dimension of divine revelation. Instead, he relied on religious self-consciousness as a variety of *feeling.* The current revival of interest in his

thought to be mysticism. Religion as dogma, church, ritual and Scripture—all this comes later, and counts for less than the religious vision itself. Religions start, as Frost said, with a lump in the throat. A theology based on religious experience is subjectivity posing as Christianity. Both the older Liberalism and the newer existential theologies are basically pietistic, experience theologies. Their concern is with man's self-understanding and current situation in life, not with the objective biblical message.

A good illustration of this is found in Kaufman's treatment of the concept of divine wrath. If theology were bound to the express words of Christ and Scripture, he admits, then the idea could not be omitted from our doctrine of God. But this is not the case. The norm is the event of "revelation" subjectively received, and employed to correct the biblical language and ideology itself. For Kaufman, theology must take the course required by the standpoint of the theologian himself.[48] Thus he is free to construct it to suit his fancy. Even Brunner, whose theology is generally true to Scripture, finds it necessary to observe that the authority of the Bible is conditioned by his idea of Christ.[49] Wherever it appears, the idea is unmistakable. "Truth" comes in the form of an inner revelation from beyond without external controls. The theologians are following the ethicists into situationalism. Unfortunately the situation does not supply the truth necessary for a decision, and thus the theologian himself ends up providing it. *Schwärmerei* (blind enthusiasm) is not dead!

theology reveals the fundamental similarity of the liberal and neoorthodox theologies at root. See F. D. E. Schleiermacher, *The Christian Faith.* The modern revolt against the competence of language to depict truth, the ability of reason to grasp it, and the legitimacy of all external authority to bind the conscience, is characteristic of Zen-Buddhism. Absolute faith is placed in man's own inner being. See Lit-sen Chang, *Zen-Existentialism, The Spiritual Decline of the West,* pp. 32-34.

48. Kaufman, *Systematic Theology . . .*, p. 154. The theoretical base of his relativistic and solipsistic theology is laid down in another work, *Relativism, Knowledge and Faith.*

49. Emil Brunner, *The Christian Doctrine of God,* p. 81. For a discussion of the Anabaptistic view of Scripture which this sort of thing resembles, see William Klassen, "Anabaptist Hermeneutics: The Letter and the Spirit," *Mennonite Quarterly Review* 40 (1966): 83-96.

The refusal to allow private revelation to be normative over inscripturated truth is a basic Christian attitude. It is a way of indicating the absolute supremacy and permanently normative character of the Christ disclosure. It does not carry with it the necessary implication that any and all claims to private revelation are ingenuine. We simply refuse to regard such revelations as regulative or obligatory for belief, and demand that they be placed under the judgment of biblical truth. To deny the very possibility of private revelation would be to imply that God is now silent. However, a check there must be on such things. Religious experience or private revelation more often than not corresponds to the mind-set of the recipient. Rather than introducing new truth, it very often confirms values already held by the experiencing subject. A theology which rests on personal experience is incurably relative to the belief system already held, with little to indicate the proper objects of faith. Tillich wisely noted, "Insight into the human situation destroys every theology which makes experience an independent source instead of a dependent medium of systematic theology."[50] Furthermore, progress in the science of psychology warns us against trusting in the transparent purity of man's existential life! Christianity is rooted in historical divine disclosure, by which its faith is to be informed and controlled. Subjective experience ought to be subject to the controls of the objective revelation data adhering to the Christ event (1 Co 15:1-19). It is almost idolatry to worship the "Christ" of experience alone because it may represent merely the projections of our own impulses. Experience needs the checks and guidance which Scripture can provide.

C. S. Lewis put the matter well:

> The human mind has no more power of inventing a new value than of planting a new sun in the sky or a new primary colour in the spectrum. Every attempt to do so consists in arbitrarily selecting some one maxim of traditional morality,

50. Tillich, 1:46.

> isolating it from the rest, and erecting it into an *unum necessarium.*[51]

The present turning in theology from the objective standard of God's Word to mystical experience as a source of revelation is deplorable. Mysticism, like drug experience in our culture, leads directly to the destruction of intellectual discrimination and the rational ordering of reality. It represents a retreat to a primitive mode of consciousness similar to that which a newborn baby must experience confronted by an undifferentiated sea of images. For theology to turn to mysticism is to replace the sharp intelligible relationship between God and man which the Bible calls salvation with a sloppy, amorphous religion uninformed and uncorrected by special revelation.

None of these three candidates—reason, tradition or experience—separately or together is capable of supplying reliable revelation data for Christian theology. Each needs to be checked and measured by Scripture, which alone has been validated as a genuine source. These are not sources at all, and the attempt to develop a "calculus" for handling several together will not succeed. The simple fact of the matter is that none of these deserves our unquestioned obedience. Only Scripture possesses final authority.

PROPER THEOLOGICAL METHODOLOGY

Once it has been established that Scripture is the inspired Word of God, the character of Christian theology is fairly easy to define. Scripture is the "shoe" which theological theories must fit! [*Quod non est Biblicum, non est theologicum.*] The theologian is a believer whose task it is to reflect on the revelation data of Scripture, to form and test doctrinal theories concerning divine truth in accord with and under the supervision of this standard of faith. The method is, therefore, *exegetical-synthetic.* Scripture is the source both of the norms and of the data for theological theorizing. John Gill first com-

51. C. S. Lewis, *Christian Reflections,* p. 75.

pleted an exposition of the entire Bible before proceeding to lay before his congregation a "scheme of doctrinal and practical divinity." Theology is charged with the organization of the results of exegetical science, a methodical elaboration of the truth of divine revelation deposited in Scripture.

As an example of the modern approach, John Macquarrie offers this definition of theology:

> Theology may be defined as the study which, through participation in and reflection upon a religious faith, seeks to express the content of this faith in the clearest and most coherent language available.[52]

Undoubtedly the theologian ought to be a believer, since there are levels of understanding inaccessible to a detached observer. However, the definition is silent on the subject of valid sources proper to theology, and implies theology is the phenomenological description of faith consciousness. Theology *must* be related to objective revelation data. It flounders when it is isolated from it. Neoorthodoxy fails *apologetically* because of its refusal to relate faith to fact, and *theologically* because of its refusal to link faith to objective Scripture.

Theology is the inductive science which catalogs, interprets and relates the revealed data. Just as natural science is the technical expression of the data discovered in nature, theology is the expression of the truths of divine revelation. "It is the province of theology to examine all the spiritual facts of revelation, to estimate their value, and to arrange them into a body of teaching."[53] Theology renders explicit in orderly doctrines the truth implicit in the Word of God. It expresses logically the truths which are set forth chronologically in the Bible. Christian theology treats Holy Scripture thematically, and seeks to exhibit the relation of one truth to another. All the data of Scripture are relevant data, the

52. Macquarrie, p. 1. See also his essay, "How Is Theology Possible?" in *Studies in Christian Existentialism*, pp. 3-16.

53. W. H. Griffith Thomas, *The Holy Spirit of God*, pp. 121-22. See Hodge, 1:1-17.

raw material of theological models. There is no place for originality as such in theology, for "its whole materials are contained in the actual statements of God's Word; and he is the greatest and best theologian, who has most accurately apprehended the meaning of the statements of Scripture."[54] In theology, as in art and music, novelty is not necessarily a virtue. Criteria that are timeless are to be applied. The precondition of theological stability and advance is faithfulness to the revelation in Scripture. The conservative theologian sustains a healthy skepticism of theological fads, and a willingness to espouse, if need be, positions at the moment unpopular. Heresies are always novel, at least in appearance.

The theologian does not *create* his data. He is like a cartographer who does not first conceive a mountain range in his mind and then draft a map according to his dream, but who explores the range as it is found to exist and then drafts a map corresponding to the geography. The scientist does not *determine* the nature and qualities of the objects of his investigation. He seeks to discover what they are, and to extrapolate models to fit the data. The exegesis of Scripture thus has *absolute priority* over all systems. Systems which fail to fit the data are to be dismantled. A faulty theological system is one which cannot satisfy the biblical evidence, whether by omitting some of it, or by upsetting the balance of the biblical emphases. Scripture is capable of disciplining her theologians and correcting their work. This is not to deny that we approach Scripture from a standpoint within a Christian community of faith. It only underlines the necessity of having an objective, and perspicuous Bible to criticize that stance (Heb 4:12).

The preacher is subject to the same norms. Because Scripture is God's Word, it is his *duty* to expound all of it to his people regularly, devoutly and profoundly. Sermons which merely exhibit the preacher's intelligence or special interests

54. William Cunningham, *The Reformers and the Theology of the Reformation*, p. 296.

are a sin against Scripture, which is being used as a pretext. The *sola scriptura* will make men expository preachers. It is God's Word people need to hear, not the contrived wisdom we may conjure up. For preaching of the profound biblical type, systematic method in study is required. We study not for the next Lord's day, but for a lifetime of preaching. A homiletical garden is planted, and messages are preached as the fruit becomes ripe. Modern preaching is empty and powerless because modern preachers are not devoted to scholarly digging in God's Word.

No one has defined the nature of theological theorizing more clearly than John W. Montgomery. It operates by a process of induction from biblical data on the basis of which conceptual models are created and continually checked.[55] Theology and science form and test their hypotheses in the same way. The scientist endeavors to render nature intelligible, and the theologian to explain the Holy Scriptures. By a process of induction from the relevant data, each formulates hypotheses with differing degrees of certainty. Theological doctrines are empirical constructs entirely dependent on biblical data for their truth value. Because they are empirical constructs, the evidence is more abundant for some than for others, and hence a varying level of certainty. Just as in science certain hypotheses are very firmly established while others are more tentative proposals, so in theology. It follows, therefore, that firmly established biblical truths (the Trinity, the vicarious atonement, the resurrection) should be tests of fellowship and cooperation, while other theological proposals (pretribulation rapture of the church, the baptism of infants) should not divide the body of Christ. Christian churches should exercise great care in drawing up tests of fellowship to avoid laxity (in which fundamental doctrines are optional) and bigotry (by which unnecessary schism results).

Plenary theological knowledge remains future. Now "we know in part" (1 Co 13:12). While we await the appearing

55. Montgomery, "The Theologian's Craft," pp. 67-98.

of Christ (1 Co 1:7), we reflect on a divine revelation which is valid, but not exhaustive, sufficient but not complete. There exist, therefore, in Scripture genuine mysteries which are more than merely puzzles. Puzzles await solution by the application of sharper hermeneutical insight. But mysteries may not be solved on the basis of what we now know. The Trinity and predestination are examples of mysteries we may not solve, and if we try to do so, we shall undoubtedly find ourselves hopelessly tangled. It is better in such cases to affirm all that Scripture affirms and leave it at that; there is an art of postponing certain questions until heaven's school begins its classes. C. S. Lewis explains why:

> Heaven will solve our problems, but not, I think, by showing us subtle reconciliations between all our apparently contradictory notions. The notions will all be knocked from under our feet. We shall see that there never was a problem.[56]

The purpose of Christian theology is to translate the content of inexhaustible divine revelation into the most intelligible, coherent terms possible. It proposes to go beyond mere description of what the church has believed, and to declare in an orderly, topical manner what the divine truth actually is. The task is not and cannot be finished. The possibility of stating in a fresh, vital manner the essentials of our faith always exists. The method is to reflect with reverence and discernment upon Scripture, to engage the searching questions involved in its comprehension, and to correlate all that we learn from holy writ to contemporary moods and attitudes.

Scripture is the authentic map of the spiritual order. In its teachings we encounter the gracious God in His revelation, a meeting and a knowing. Theological God-talk becomes possible and meaningful because it is grounded in verifiable and ascertainable revelation data.

56. Lewis, *A Grief Observed,* chap. 4. If the hazard of neoorthodox theology is that it leaves open some questions Scripture has closed, the hazard of orthodoxy is that it tries to answer questions Scripture leaves open.

DOCTRINAL THEOLOGY

Doctrinal or systematic theology has its origin in the New Testament epistles, as in the fullness of postresurrection revelation light, the apostles began to reflect upon the intellectual content of faith. They had no choice. Doctrines are road signs to the content of revelation, and fences around truth to exclude heresies. Disorder must not prevail in our understanding of the gospel. The results of special revelation must not be left a mass of undigested facts, but correlated for the stability and welfare of the church. The effectiveness of some cults is testimony to their diligence in systematizing and catechizing. As Hordern says,

> There is no escaping theological questions. We simply do not have the alternative of theology or no theology. Our alternatives are either to have a well thought out theology, a theology which has passed the test of critical thought, or to have a hodgepodge theology of unexamined concepts, prejudices, and feelings. One of the weaknesses of Protestantism today is that so few Protestants know what they believe or why.[57]

The tendency of a modern emphasis on faith as personal trust has been the deprecation of Christian doctrine. The importance of sound doctrine needs to be given fresh emphasis. The intellectual implications of faith are not arbitrary absolutes contrived by men, but belong to the heart of religion. The New Testament is adamant in its insistence that the *object* of our faith be worthy and true (Gal 1:8-9; 1 Jn 5:20). It warns against the dire results of false teaching (2 Co 11:3; 1 Ti 4:1; 2 Ti 4:3-4; 2 Pe 2:1). Faith can take a wrong turn. True doctrine keeps it on the track and nurtures it. Heresy in doctrine reflects perversion in faith. The modern demand for a nondoctrinal, creedless religion is a veiled attack on the content of the gospel, and an attempt to reduce

57. William Hordern, *A Layman's Guide to Protestant Theology*, p. 15. Brunner, pp. 9-10, lists the three factors which make dogmatics essential as (1) the struggle against false doctrine (2) the need for catechetical instruction and (3) the necessity of ordering the *disjecta membra* of exegesis.

it to a contentless (and harmless) experience.[58] Contrary to liberalism, to which the text is pertinent: "Ye worship ye know not what," the Christian gospel has necessary factual and doctrinal content, which it is the duty of the theologian to expound. Luther expressed the polemical and didactic roles of theology in this fashion:

> A preacher must not only feed the sheep so as to instruct them how they are to be good Christians, but he must also keep the wolves from attacking the sheep and leading them astray with false doctrine and error; for the devil is never idle. Nowadays there are many people who are quite ready to tolerate our preaching of the gospel as long as we do not cry out against the wolves and preach against the prelates. But though I preach the truth, feed the sheep well, and give them good instruction, this is still not enough unless the sheep are also guarded and protected so that the wolves do not come and carry them off. For what sort of building is it if I throw away stones and then watch another throw them back in. The wolf can readily tolerate a good pasture for the sheep; he likes them the better for their fatness. But what he cannot endure is the hostile bark of the dogs. Therefore it is of vital importance to set our hearts on truly feeding the flock as God has commanded it.

To discount systematic views of evangelical truth can only lead the church back into the confusion and obscurity of the Dark Ages. The true greatness of the Reformation was the sturdy resolve of its leaders not to surrender firm evangelical principles based upon Scripture. Theologians of today seem resolved to gain distinction by extinguishing the light gained at such great cost.

Doctrinal theology has never been very popular. John Gill noted in 1770 that

> Systematical divinity, I am sensible, is now become very un-

58. Dorothy Sayers has some good things to say for creedal religion in *The Mind of the Maker,* and *Creed or Chaos.* See R. J. Rushdoony, *Foundations of the Social Order,* p. 96.

> popular. Formulas, and articles of faith, creeds, and confessions, catechisms and summaries of divine truths, are greatly decried in our age; and yet, what art or science is there but has been reduced to a system?[59]

In the modern church, differences in doctrine are not given much attention, and the concept of heresy is almost dead. But this is not due to a flood of love and tolerance so much as agnosticism regarding truth itself. As Stalker put it,

> Excessive aversion to controversy may be an indication that a Church has no keen sense of possessing truth which is of any great worth, and that it has lost appreciation for the infinite difference in value between truth and error.

The ecumenical spirit of cooperation between the churches today is a move toward unity in the dark. True Christian unity is grounded in a vital union with Jesus Christ, in the context of divine truth revelation. Creeds and confessions of faith originate when false teachers attempt to give the faith an improper intellectual content. They do not exist to inaugurate new truth but to safeguard the old. Like Timothy, we are charged with keeping "the commandment stainless and irreproachable until the appearance of our Lord Jesus Christ" (1 Ti 6:14, Berkeley).

Adolf von Harnack believed that the development of orthodox dogma was a hellenization of primitive Christian truth and a degeneration of the gospel. Undoubtedly the ecumenical creeds sought to express the biblical faith in the Greek language and thought, and the formulas which resulted represented prolonged reflection upon divine revelation. The development in understanding was, however, entirely necessary, and in keeping with genuine faith. Faith is compelled to clarify intellectually its underlying ideas, and not only for proclamation, but for *worship*. The creedal symbols belong to the liturgical life of the church. They are hymns of adoration and praise, the expression of wondering love toward God.

59. John Gill, *Body of Divinity,* p. xxiii.

Dogma is the component of living worship. It promotes Christian growth by keeping the facts of redemption ever before our eyes. In Western Christianity, doctrine is often too abstract and theoretical. It becomes detached from the life of faith, to be the plaything of the experts. But theology is too important to be left to the theologians, for it regulates and nurtures our mystical union with Christ. True theology should always be doxology. The dogma of the Trinity, for example, arose because the Scriptures taught and the people of God experienced the overwhelming reality of God in threefold form. Trinitarian dogma is the attempt to do justice to the oneness of God's essence and the triplicity of His being. Similarly, Christological dogma sought to accommodate the actual humanity and incarnate deity of Jesus the Christ. In neither case was dogma the result of abstract speculation, but sprang from the wellsprings of faith and love.

The term *system* may be used in theology if by it is understood the harmonious exhibition of biblical teaching. Scripture retains the freedom to determine, criticize and correct the shape of any system claiming to be Christian. The system in the theology of Paul Tillich, on the contrary, is the organization of selected biblical symbols around an extra- and anti-biblical ontology which is more Platonic than Christian. Hamilton bluntly states that "to see Tillich's system as a whole is to see that it is incompatible with the Christian gospel."[60] Texts are not to be manipulated, wrenched out of context, and twisted to say what they do not. The genuine diversity within the unity of biblical religion should not be suppressed or overpowered. Rather we inquire after the finest bouquet that can be gathered from so luxurious a garden. With our gaze fixed on Jesus Christ, by whom God is reconciling the world, we proceed to expound the doctrines, with due respect for emphasis and weight given to them by Scripture.

60. Hamilton, p. 227. See also R. Allen Killan, *The Ontological Theology of Paul Tillich.*

Traditionally Christians have expressed their faith in numerous creeds and confessions which were intended to be elaborations of biblical truth. *Credo, ergo confiteor* (Belief prompts confession). It became imperative for the defense and propagation of the gospel to summarize the principal teachings of the Bible. These statements of faith were the result of patient biblical study, and served as a defense against error, as a catechetical instrument, and as a basis of unity and concord. Even Baptists, who pride themselves in being people of the "Bible only," have issued numerous confessions of faith, recognizing the need of fidelity to the contents of Scripture.[61] The formation of creedal statements follows from plenary inspiration, for if Scripture is our authority and is perspicuous, it is capable of yielding doctrinal principles. Subscription to these cardinal tenets of biblical religion should be judged a test of fidelity to the teachings of the Bible.

> The great Creeds and Confessions of the Church are reminders of prolonged struggles in the past to preserve the wholeness of the kerygma against attempts to make Christianity meaningful at the cost of ignoring or suppressing those parts of it which did not fit readily into the contemporary world-view.[62]

Liberalism is essentially the mentality which seeks to conform the Christian faith to the dominant spirit of the times. Besides being contrary to the final revelation in Christ, the founding of a theology on a philosophy relevant to this age has a serious disadvantage—it is bound to become irrelevant in the next! Marriage to the spirit of this age will leave one a widow in the next.

Often disdain for precise doctrinal formulations is explained by a reverence for the Word of God itself, as if such

61. See W. L. Lumpkin, *Baptist Confessions of Faith.* The slogan, "No creed but the Bible," is seen to be inadequate when it is asked "Who is this Christ?" and "What is this Bible?" Not the slogan, "Only the Bible," but the content of it is the proper test of orthodoxy and fellowship.

62. Hamilton, *Revolt Against Heaven,* pp. 23-24.

tenets were inferior human concepts over against the ineffable Word itself. Far more frequently it is due to a dislike for the controlling influence of Scripture, "from a desire to escape, as far as possible without denying its authority, from the trammels of its regulating power as an infallible rule of faith and duty."[63]

The concept of "freedom" as it has developed in Protestant modernism, which implies every man's right to hold and teach any and all doctrinal views he may please, is incompatible with belief in the authority of the Bible. It amounts to a theology of "inner light" and results in doctrinal anarchy and agnosticism. *Christian* freedom does not include the liberty to disobey Christ! A man is responsible to heed God's Word and obey it. But he is not free to call whatever belief he happens to hold Christian, nor to teach publicly in a church that which contradicts Scripture. "*If* you abide in My word, *then* you are truly disciples of mine" (Jn 8:31, NASB).

There is a center of gravity in Christian theology. All that is in Scripture is not of equal weight. Those truths which touch upon the person and work of the Redeemer and how men appropriate His saving grace are the most important. This is not for a moment to suggest that secondary matters, not directly soteric, need not be believed. Christian discipleship requires that we believe *all* that Scripture teaches. Yet Scripture itself focuses on Christ as the center of its interest, and our theology ought to reflect a balance in its treatment of themes.[64] We need to ask ourselves not only whether our exposition of Christian doctrine corresponds to biblical teaching in detail, but whether it strikes the same chords and plays the same melody.

63. Cunningham, p. 525.

64. Calvin remarks, "All points of the doctrine of God are not of the same order. There are some, the knowledge of which is so necessary that no man may question them, for they are fundamental pronouncements and principles of Christianity. . . . But there are others which are disputed among the churches, and yet do not break their unity" (*Institutes* 4.1.12).

THE CHRISTIAN THEOLOGIAN

In a sense every believer is a theologian, taught of God (Jn 6:45), anointed by the holy One (1 Jn 2:20, 27). There is, however, a divine calling to the teaching office (Ro 12:7; 1 Co 12:8; Eph 4:11), and a theological aptitude which enables some to attain a deeper comprehension of spiritual truth for the good of the whole body (1 Ti 3:2). It is both a noble task (1 Ti 3:1; 4:16) and a dangerous one (Ja 3:1); the standards are high and the judgment strict. The qualifications of the Christian theologian are considerable. In addition to spiritual insight, he must command many natural gifts of language and logic, so that he may be "able to encourage by his wholesome teaching, as well as to refute those who raise objections" (Titus 1:9, Berkeley). But the prime requirement is *faithfulness* as a steward of the mysteries of God (1 Co 4:1-2), not a peddler of God's Word, but a man of sincerity, commissioned by God, in the sight of God speaking in Christ (2 Co 2:17).

> We have renounced underhanded ways of which one should be ashamed. We do not behave craftily, nor do we falsify the word of God, but by clear announcement of the truth we commend ourselves in the presence of God to every human conscience (2 Co 4:2, Berkeley).

Timothy was instructed to entrust the truth of the gospel to faithful men who would be able to teach others also (2 Ti 2:2). Theologians and ministers of the gospel are called upon to remain true to the oracles of God and resist every effort to pervert the gospel.

Familiarity with and faithfulness to the teachings of Scripture are basic to all genuine Christian theology, but there is more to it than that. The theologian must be a man of deep faith and evangelical experience. Spiritual truth will not be grasped simply by an analysis of biblical texts. Orthodoxy which does not rise from its labors and desire to enter into His presence to worship is dead. The theologian must be personally involved with the divine subject of his craft. From the realm of biblical facts we ascend into the realm of the sacred and worship in the presence of God. In fellowship with God, truths are "noticed" which were missed before. The material of theology needs both to be intellectually grasped and spiritually experienced in the community of the faithful. Let the Trinity serve as an example.[65] The biblical evidence for the unity of God, and for the co-equal deity of Father, Son and Spirit, is rich and clear. Trinitarian dogma is truer to the biblical data than the modalistic, Arian, or Unitarian alternative theories. The doctrine can be comprehended on this level as a profound scriptural teaching. But it is impossible for a theologian to treat it as an impersonal concept when it stands for the intense, personal reality of the living God. He is compelled, if he is a believer, to reflect on the fact that this God is *his* God. Starting in the realm of scientific induction, he rises up in wonder and adoration to the realm of the holy, where his words fail him, and the brightness of God's glory stuns him into silence. The activity by which the theologian seeks to communicate his findings to the church requires first the long meditation and contemplation of God. Theology is rooted in the life of faith.[66]

THE TASK OF ORTHODOX THEOLOGY

"There never was anything so perilous or so exciting as orthodoxy," Chesterton said. This excitement is not the giddiness of liberal faddism. It has to do with strenuous effort, wrestling with the profundities of divine revelation and seeing their solidity in an era of relativism and flux. The reason men prefer the new theologies is partly because they never took the time to understand the old. Yet how often orthodox theology is sonorous, repetitious and dull, so that the well of its ideas seems dry, and its empty language hardly a zone of

65. See Montgomery, "The Theologian's Craft," pp. 96-98.

66. Cunningham, chap. 11, observes that the Reformers were characterized by three traits: the extent of their acquired learning; unwearied activity and industry; and the time and attention they devoted to the study of the Word of God.

truth, when even Scripture is "remembered" rather than "heard." We have not placed the value on a scholarly defense and exposition of the faith and have not linked this to a deep evangelical faith as we ought to have. The task lies before us to demonstrate the soundness and vigor of the biblical faith in a renaissance of evangelical scholarship, and it will have to be performed in a day when the theological consensus considers us foolish, even insidious, when an ecclesiastical syndrome resists any effort at reform of its power structure, and when a secular society falls into a deeper and deeper coma. Isaiah faced this kind of difficulty; the people would not heed his message. So he turned to the remnant and committed his teaching to his disciples (8:16), a small band of men capable of understanding what God was saying and willing to put the principles into practice. The prophet did not reduce the profundity of his message in order to gain a hearing, nor whittle it down or adulterate it with trivialities to make it more acceptable. Instead he invested time and effort in the training of a remnant capable of receiving the word and in whose minds the truth would lodge and germinate until the new day when the power of the message would rise above vain humanistic pretensions and assert itself again in the culture. Orthodox theology can be nothing more than the perpetuation of an antiquated language. Its authentic role is to declare ancient verities so that they speak again with force and tremble with vitality. On the success of its prophetic calling depends the promise of a better day for theology and the church. But whatever the outcome in the immediate future, at least in Richard Hooker's words, "Posterity may know that we have not loosely, through silence, permitted things to pass away as in a dream." It may be by God's grace that men will sicken of endless novelty and turn to ancient principles, finding in them the hearty satisfaction of religious certainty.

4

INSPIRATION IN THE CHRISTIAN TRADITION

PART ONE: THE HISTORIC DOCTRINE

DEFENDERS OF THE PLENARY, verbal inspiration of the canonical Scriptures stand in the midst of a mighty stream of historic Christian opinion. The high view of inspiration has without doubt been the majority opinion of Christian theologians, despite the concerted effort to deny it by neo-Protestant thinkers, who have a bad conscience on the subject. The fact needs to be brought out in order to expose the novelty and humanistic root of much modern theology. Traditionally the church has received the Bible as an oracular, God-breathed book, and held the conviction almost unanimously until the great defection of modern times. If she erred in any direction, it was in being too zealous for biblical authority and too open to superstitious opinions regarding it. Broadly, however, the church has been untroubled by rebellions against this cardinal truth until quite recently, and able to reflect on its truths without nagging skepticism. At the Reformation, both sides, Catholic and Protestant, held to Scripture as "a compendium of inerrant oracles dictated by the Spirit. Only in the 19th century did a succession of empirical disciplines newly come of age begin to put a succession of inconvenient queries to exegetes."[1]

Historically, Christian theologians have held that every affirmation of Scripture when interpreted in its natural and intended sense is errorless. As E. A. Litton puts it,

1. James T. Burtchaell, *Catholic Theories of Biblical Inspiration Since 1810,* p. 2.

> If there ever was a general consent of the Church Catholic on any question, it exists on this. East and West, from the earliest to the latest times, concurred in assigning to Scripture a pre-eminence which consisted in its being—as no other collection of writings is—the Word of God.[2]

From the second century to the eighteenth, verbal inspiration was accepted as true.[3] Kirsop Lake makes a telling observation:

> It is a mistake often made by educated persons who happen to have but little knowledge of historical theology, to suppose that fundamentalism is a new and strange form of thought. It is nothing of the kind; it is the partial and uneducated survival of a theology which was once universally held by all Christians. How many were there, for instance, in Christian churches in the eighteenth century who doubted the infallible inspiration of all Scripture? A few, perhaps, but very few. No, the fundamentalist may be wrong; I think that he is. But it is we who have departed from the tradition, not he, and I am sorry for the fate of anyone who tries to argue with a fundamentalist on the basis of authority. The Bible and the *corpus theologicum* of the Church is on the fundamentalist side.[4]

Neo-Protestants have developed myopia when it comes to seeing that conservative Evangelicalism today is organically and ideologically related to orthodox Christian faith as it existed for centuries. The high view of Scripture is neither new nor eccentric, but is simply the mainline view to which the Roman Church and the major Protestant denominations have committed themselves. It is only natural that they should, because Christianity, based on the divine redemptive activity in history, is a religion of biblical authority. The theologians have always found it easier to believe in the plenary inspiration of Scripture, despite isolated difficulties, than to believe

2. E. A. Litton, *Introduction to Dogmatic Theology*, p. 19.
3. See Alan Richardson, *Preface to Bible Study*, p. 25.
4. Kirsop Lake, *The Religion of Yesterday and Tomorrow*, p. 61.

that Christ, His apostles, and the entire church from the beginning had erred in their teaching.[5]

Surprisingly, the doctrine of Scripture was never explicitly defined in the ecumenical creeds of Christendom. The reason is not hard to find. Creeds are called into existence by burning questions and serious challenges confronting the church. The divine authority of Scripture was never a disputed question. Controversies raged over what it *taught,* but not over what it *was.* In those happy days, denials of scriptural infallibility still came from *outside* the Christian community! Cadoux comments,

> The fact that Biblical inerrancy was not incorporated in any formal creed was due, not to any doubt as to its being an essential item of belief, but to the fact that no one challenged it.[6]

What refreshing honesty to admit that the new views of Scripture are a deliberate break with historic Christian opinion. The high view of inspiration reveals itself in numerous ways: in the explicit testimonies of eminent theologians in every period of church history, in the laboriously constructed creeds and confessions whose purpose was only the exposition and preservation of biblical truth, and in the painstaking care exercised in the elucidation of Scripture found in innumerable commentaries on every biblical book. Even latitude in exegesis, so frequently cited as proof of a lower view of inspiration, represents not a denial of infallibility, but an attempt to observe it in difficult places. In every conceivable way the church has confessed her confidence in Holy Scripture as being divine in origin, and consequently infallible and inerrant.

THE EARLY CHURCH

Gaussen sums up the view of Scripture as it existed in the early church:

5. B. B. Warfield, *The Inspiration and Authority of the Bible,* p. 128.
6. C. J. Cadoux, *The Case For Evangelical Modernism,* p. 66.

> With the single exception of Theodore of Mopsuestia, it has been found impossible to produce, in the long course of the eight first centuries of Christianity, a single doctor who has disowned the plenary inspiration of the Scriptures, unless it be in the bosom of the most violent heresies that have tormented the Christian Church.[7]

Indeed, this attitude and unanimity continued right up until the age of negative criticism.[8] The early Fathers and apologists believed without hesitation in the divine inspiration of Scripture, and apparently considered it self-evident and incontrovertible.[9] The fact of inspiration was never in doubt.

Barnabas (1st century) cites Scripture as "the Spirit of the Lord proclaims."[10] Clement of Rome (1st century) calls Scripture "the true utterances of the Holy Spirit."[11] Justin Martyr (2d century) affirmed, "We believe God's voice spoken by the apostles."[12] Athenagoras (2d century) said, "The Spirit using them [the biblical writers] as his instruments, as a flute player might blow a flute."[13] Irenaeus (2d century) says the Scriptures are "divine" and "perfect," being uttered by God.[14] His view of plenary, verbal inspiration is impeccable. Tertullian (c. 200) equates scriptural teaching and true doctrine: "For it is better to be ignorant when God has not spoken, than to acquire knowledge from man and be dependent upon his conjectures."[15] Clement of Alexandria (*c.* 200) says that all Scripture was spoken by the mouth of the Lord.[16] Origen (3d century) refused to accept "a third scrip-

7. L. Gaussen, *Theopneustia*, pp. 139-40.
8. The adjective *negative* must be used because theologians have always employed the critical faculty in assiduously expounding Scripture; but before the rise of negative criticism they had not felt free to charge the Bible with error. This boldness has been only recently attained.
9. J. N. D. Kelly, *Early Christian Doctrines*, p. 42; G. W. Bromiley, "The Church Doctrine of Inspiration," in *Revelation and the Bible*, pp. 207-8.
10. Barnabas, *Epist* 9.
11. Clement of Rome, *Epist* 1.45.
12. Justin Martyr, *Dial* 119.
13. Athenagoras, *Leg pro. Christ.* 9.
14. Irenaeus, *Against Heresies*, 2:41.1; 2.28.2.
15. Tertullian, *De Anima* 1.
16. Clement of Alexandria, *Protrepticus* 9.82.1.

ture" (in addition to the two Testaments) because it would not be "divine" like them.[17] God himself is the Author of Scripture. Cyprian (3d century) too held to the divine authorship of Scripture (*magisteria divina et dominica*). Athanasius (4th century) said, "The sacred and inspired Scriptures suffice for the defense of the truth."[18] St. Cyril of Jerusalem (4th century) said: "The certitude of our faith does not depend on reasoning based on whim, but on the teaching drawn from the Scriptures."[19] Jerome (4th century): "Ignoratio Scripturarum ignoratio Christi est (Ignorance of the Scripture is ignorance of Christ)."[20] Theophilus of Alexandria: "It would be acting according to demoniac inspiration to follow the thinking of the human mind and to think that there could be anything divine apart from the authority of the Scriptures."[21] Augustine (5th century) refers Scripture to "the revered pen of the Spirit."[22] In a letter to Jerome he says, "For I confess to your charity that I have learned to defer this respect and honour to those Scriptural books only which are now called canonical, that I believe most firmly that no one of these authors has erred in any respect in writing."[23]

THE MEDIEVAL CHURCH

The theologians of the medieval period affirm with equal force their faith in the full authority and material sufficiency of Holy Scripture. For men of this period all theological truth flowed from the Bible. The whole of Christian truth is re-

17. Origen, *In Lev nom* 5.
18. Athanasius, *Orat I contra gent.*, 1.
19. St. Cyril of Jerusalem, Catech. 1V *De Spiritu Sancto,* n. 17.
20. Jerome, *In Isaiah prologue.*
21. Theophilus of Alexandria as cited by Jerome, *Epist.* 96.6.
22. Augustine, *Confessions* 7.21.23.
23. Augustine, *Epist.* 82.1.3. See Y. M.-J. Congar, *Tradition and Traditions,* pp. 107-11; J. Barton Payne, "The Biblical Interpretation of Irenaeus," and David W. Kerr, "Augustine of Hippo," in *Inspiration and Interpretation;* A. S. Wood, *The Principles of Biblical Interpretation as Enunciated by Ireaneus, Origen, Augustine, Luther and Calvin;* A. D. R. Polman, *The Word of God According to St. Augustine;* C. J. Costello, *St. Augustine's Doctrine on the Inspiration and Canonicity of Scripture.*

vealed in the Scriptures. St. Anslem (14th century) confessed that he would preach nothing other than what Scripture, produced by a miracle of the Spirit, contained.[24] Rupert of Deutz (8th century) said, "Let us search for wisdom, let us consult sacred Scripture itself, apart from which nothing can be found, nothing said which is solid or certain."[25] Or St. Bonaventure (13th century): "Unde omnis nostra cognitio in cognitione sacrae Scripturae debet habere statum" ("Whence all our knowledge ought to have its basis in the knowledge of Holy Scripture").[26] For Thomas Aquinas (13th century), nothing could be added to or deleted from Scripture. If something was not attested by Scripture, it was not necessary for salvation.[27] Gerson (15th century): "Nihil audendum dicere de divinis, nisi quae nobis a Scriptura Sacra tradita sunt" ("Nothing ought to be heard spoken concerning divine matters unless it be those matters which are handed down to us from Holy Scriptures").[28] Even John Driedo, an erudite opponent of Luther's *sola scriptura*, writes: "Concedamus quod doctrina Christi et apostolorum in libris canonicis expressa sufficienter nos doceat, continens omnia dogmata ad salutem humani generis necessaria" ("We admit that the express doctrine of Christ and the Apostles in the canonical books teaches us sufficiently all the dogmas necessary for man's salvation").[28a]

We are far from claiming that these medieval theologians were crypto-Protestants. Their grasp of evangelical truth was sadly lacking, and their use of Scripture often superstitious. Nonetheless, the record is clear that they regarded Scripture as the very Word of God in which God infallibly communicates divine truths.[29]

24. St. Anselm, *De concordia praescientiae Dei cum lib. arb.*, q. 3, c. 6.
25. Rupert of Deutz, *In Apoc.*
26. St. Bonaventura, *Breviloquium prol.*
27. Thomas Aquinas, *De ver.*, q. 14, a. 10, ad 11.
28. Gerson, *De Exam. doctr.*, II.
28a. John Driedo, *De Eccles. scr. et Dogm., lib.* IV, c. 6.
29. For the evidence, see Congar, pp. 111-16.

THE PROTESTANT REFORMATION

Neo-Protestants today are quite prepared to grant that the pre-Reformation church held to the high doctrine of biblical infallibility. It would be to fly in the face of the evidence to deny it. However, they are far more reluctant to admit that the Reformers, Luther and Calvin, also did. This reluctance is rooted in a certain reverence for the Reformers, which leads neoorthodox scholars to seek to relieve them of their doctrine of inspiration. It is as though between the medieval period and the age of Protestant orthodoxy there were a brief neoorthodox paradise in which such views were for a moment grasped, only to be quickly lost again, and rediscovered by Barth! It would surely be an amazing historical anomaly if the Reformers differed from their predecessors and successors in this respect, and prove to have anticipated neoorthodoxy in their thought! To lessen the shock, it is often allowed that Luther and Calvin did in fact hold to verbal inspiration, but by a felicitous inconsistency on occasion rose above it to *a personalistic*, "Christocentric" conception.[30] The fact is, however, that a Christocentric hermeneutic is not one whit incompatible with verbal inspiration, but is required by it. The Reformers identified the words of the Bible with the Word of God. The notion that they did not, is a product of neoorthodox wishful thinking. Certainly their concern in the sixteenth century lay elsewhere than in establishing the inspiration of the Bible, which no one doubted. But it cannot be disputed that for them the Bible was inspired and authorized by God.[31]

In Luther's case, statements supporting complete inerrancy are so numerous and so uncompromising that the only conceivable way to make him teach anything else is to charge

30. Karl Barth, *Church Dogmatics,* vol. 1, pt. 2, pp. 520-26; Emil Brunner, *Revelation and Reason,* pp. 275-76; James Smart, *The Interpretation of Scripture,* pp. 194-95; J. K. S. Reid, *The Authority of Scripture.* Rheinhold Seeberg was one of the first to try to modernize Luther.

31. Bromiley, pp. 210-212.

him with gross inconsistency.[32] Pieper goes so far as to claim that

> the real difference between Luther and the dogmaticians is this, that the dogmaticians but weakly stammer and echo what Luther taught much more powerfully about Scripture from Scripture itself.[33]

It is a futile task to try and make Luther a neoorthodox prophet. His existential life was kept firmly *under* the rule of infallible Scripture (let the New Hermeneutic note well!): "I am bound by the Scriptures that I have adduced, and my conscience has been taken captive by the Word of God."[34] Phrases like this recur: "The Scriptures cannot err," and "It is impossible that Scripture should contradict itself," and "The entire Scriptures are assigned to the Holy Ghost." Any relation of the historic Luther to the modern existential theologians is purely coincidental. Between Luther's view of a noncontradictory and perspicuous Scripture and the modern view of a fallible, demythologized, and existentially interpreted Bible, there is a great chasm fixed.

Calvin has not escaped these attempts at modernization either, for there are many neoorthodox theologians who would dearly love to claim him for their own ranks.[35] The technique employed is the citing of examples from Calvin which are irrelevant to his doctrine of plenary inspiration, and to conclude from these that had Calvin only lived a little later (after the rise of negative criticism) he too would have espoused a more enlightened view. But it is even less possible to prove this with Calvin than it was with Luther. Calvin's doctrine of verbal inspiration is transparent. Scripture was "dictated" by the Spirit, "commanded by the Lord," and

32. E.g., A. Harnack, *History of Dogma*, 5:235, 246-47.
33. Francis Pieper, *Christian Dogmatics*, 1:277.
34. The full evidence on Luther's doctrine of biblical inerrancy is found in M. Reu, *Luther and the Scriptures;* and Pieper, 1:276-98; cf. H. Bornkamm, *Luther and the Old Testament.*
35. See Richard C. Prust, "Was Calvin a Biblical Literalist?" *Scottish Journal of Theology* 20 (1967): 312-28. H. Heppe initiated the sport of making Calvin anchronistically modern.

"spoken" by God. The writers of Scripture were controlled by God in every detail of what they wrote. Scripture has "come down to us from the very mouth of God."[36] "We owe it therefore the same reverence which we owe to God himself, since it has proceeded from him alone, and there is nothing human mixed with it."[37] "It is God who speaks with us and not mortal men."[38] Warfield, Kantzer and Murray have all listed such evidences of Calvin's view *in extenso*.[39] Nothing could be clearer than that Calvin held to verbal inspiration.

The English Reformers are no exception in this regard, as the Thirty-nine Articles clearly show. The Bible is God's Word written, according to Article 20. Article 6 states:

> Holy Scripture containeth all things necessary to salvation: so that whatsoever is not read therein, nor may be proved thereby, is not to be required of any man, that it should be believed as an article of Faith, or be thought requisite or necessary to salvation.

The only reason the creeds are to be believed is because "they may be proved by most certain warrants of Holy Scripture," according to Article 8. God "caused all Scripture to be written for our learning," says the collect for Advent. Scripture is the foundation of Christian faith, and must, affirms Cranmer, "be taken for a most sure ground and an infallible truth; and whatsoever cannot be grounded on the same, touching our faith, is man's device, changeable and uncertain."[40] James Pilkington writes, "Scripture cometh not first from man, but from God; and therefore God is to be taken for the author of it, and not man."[41] In the words of Bishop Hugh Latimer,

36. John Calvin, *Institutes* 1.7.5.
37. Calvin, commentary on 2 Ti 3:16 in *Commentaries on the Epistles to Timothy, Titus, and Philemon.*
38. Calvin, commentary on 2 Pe 1:20 in *Commentaries on the Catholic Epistles.*
39. Warfield, *Calvin and Augustine*, pp. 48-70; Kenneth S. Kantzer, "Calvin and the Holy Scriptures," in *Inspiration and Interpretation*, pp. 115-55; John Murray, *Calvin on Scripture and Divine Sovereignty*, pp. 11-51.
40. Thomas Cranmer, *Works*, 1:24.
41. James Pilkington, *Works*, pp. 286-87.

> The excellency of this Word is so great, that there is no earthly thing to be compared unto it. The author thereof is so great, that is, God himself, eternal, almighty, everlasting. The Scripture, because of him, is also great, eternal, most mighty and holy.[42]

By these and innumerable other examples it is evident that the Anglicans of the Reformation (as distinct from their Laudian and Tractarian successors) were believers in the sufficiency, authority and infallibility of the whole Bible.[43]

THE AGE OF ORTHODOXY

The magnificent period of Protestant orthodoxy has been much maligned, and its high view of Scripture ridiculed and distorted. While it is scarcely necessary to demonstrate that the Lutheran and Reformed orthodox traditions hold to the plenary, verbal inspiration of the Bible (none would venture to deny it), a word in defense of their integrity and piety is in order. Admittedly, as the Roman Catholic apologists exaggerated inspiration by claiming it for the Vulgate, the orthodox Protestants sometimes erred in claiming it for the Hebrew vowel points. They may be forgiven a little excess. The point is that their view of Scripture did *not* differ materially from the Reformers themselves. These were deeply Christian men, and none should have part in the abuse hurled at them. We may on occasion disagree but should never belittle.[44] The majestic Formula of Concord (1576) rests on the inerrancy of the Bible, a belief which pervades every article. It is the clear, pure fountain of eternal truth, the true norm by which all teachings are to be measured. Scripture is

42. Hugh Latimer, *Works*, 1:85.

43. For further proof, see Philip E. Hughes, *Theology of the English Reformers*, pp. 11-44; R. S. Werrell, "Authority of Scripture for the Anglican Reformers," *Evangelical Quarterly* 35 (1963): 79-88.

44. In addition to his well-known *The Inspiration of Scripture: A Study of the Theology of the Seventeenth Century Lutheran Dogmaticians*, Robert Preus has written a prolegomena to Lutheran dogmatics (*The Theology of Post-Reformation Lutheranism* [St. Louis: Concordia, 1970]), which is the first volume of two on the theology of classical Lutheran orthodoxy. Cf. his "The Word of God in the Theology of Lutheran Orthodoxy," *Concordia Theological Monthly* 33 (1962): 469-83.

God's "pure, infallible, and unalterable Word," according to its preface.[45]

For the similar testimony of Calvinistic orthodoxy, one need only consult the numerous Reformed confessions. The first Helvetic Confession (1536), Article 1 says, "Die heilige, göttliche, biblische Schrift, die da ist das Wort Gottes usw" ("The sacred, divine, biblical Scripture, which is the Word of God, etc.). The Belgic Confession (1561), Articles 3-7, says,

> We confess that this Word of God was not sent nor delivered by the will of man . . . (God) commanded his servants, the prophets and apostles, to commit his revealed Word to writing . . . against which nothing can be alleged . . . believing without any doubt all things contained in them. . . . We believe that these Holy Scriptures fully contain the will of God, and that whatsoever man ought to believe unto salvation, is sufficiently taught therein . . . therefore, we reject with all our hearts whatsoever doth not agree with this infallible rule.

The same emphasis appears in the Work of the Westminster Assembly (1647) and in the writings of the English Puritans (Owen, Goodwin, Henry). It appears in a Baptist Confession most eloquently:

> We believe that the Holy Bible was written by men divinely inspired, and is a perfect treasure of heavenly instruction; that it has God for its author, salvation for its end, and truth without any mixture of error for its matter; that it reveals the principles by which God will judge us; and therefore is, and shall remain to the end of the world, the true center of Christian union, and the supreme standard by

45. Preus, "Biblical Hermeneutics and the Lutheran Church Today," in *Crisis in Lutheran Theology*, 2:83-84; Ralph A. Bohlmann, *Principles of Biblical Interpretation in the Lutheran Confessions;* and Edmund Schlink, *Theology of the Lutheran Confessions*, pp. 1-5. For further *testimonia* from orthodox Lutherans, see Heinroch Schmid, *The Doctrinal Theology of the Evangelical Lutheran Church*, chap. 4.

> which all human conduct, creeds, and opinions should be tried.[46]

John Wesley also held to the full inspiration and inerrancy of the Bible. He writes, "I really believe the Bible to be the Word of God," and, "According to the light *we* have, we cannot but believe the Scripture is of God; and, while we believe this, we dare not turn aside from it, to the right hand or to the left."[47] "I will speak for one, after having sought for truth, with some diligence, for half a century, I am, at this day, hardly sure of anything, but what I learn from the Bible. Nay, I positively affirm, I *know* nothing else for certain, that I would dare to stake my salvation upon it." "If there be one falsehood in that book, it did not come from the God of truth."[48] And, needless to say, verbal inspiration and biblical inerrancy are the official doctrine of the Roman Catholic Church. The fourth session of the Council of Trent declared itself on this matter by stating that Scripture was divinely authored and dictated "either orally by Christ or by the Holy Ghost." The inerrancy of Scripture was later strongly reaffirmed by Pope Pius X in "Lamentabili" on July 3, 1907, and especially "Pascendi Domenici gregis" on September 8, 1907, and Benedict XV in "Spiritus Paraclitus" on September 15, 1920.[49]

Part Two: Dissent and Evasion

In the face of this widespread unanimity, a remarkable reversal has taken place, a great defection. Whereas formerly it was a prime theological virtue to subject oneself to the written Word as final authority, now it is considered an iniquity at odds with true Christianity. Even in traditionally orthodox Protestant groups like the Lutheran Church—Missouri

46. The New Hampshire Baptist Confession (1833), Art. 1.
47. John Wesley, *An Earnest Appeal*, p. 27.
48. See H. D. McDonald. *Ideas of Revelation*, pp. 255-59; George A. Turner, "John Wesley as an Interpreter of Scripture," in *Inspiration and Interpretation.*
49. See Burtchaell.

Synod and the Southern Baptist Convention, there has been a remarkable degree of slippage from faith in a verbally inspired Bible. In the place of the broad consensus regarding inspiration, we now hear a chorus of protest against this "dishonest and harmful belief." Brunner expresses concern at orthodoxy's false identification of Scripture and the Word: "How much genuine Biblical faith was spoiled or hindered or compromised through a false theory of the Bible!"[50] In another place he remarks,

> The orthodox doctrine of verbal inspiration has been finally destroyed. It is clear that there is no connection between it and scientific research and honesty: we are forced to make a decision for or against this view.[51]

His view is shared by many, Millar Burrows has written,

> The Bible is full of things which to an intelligent, educated person of today are either quite incredible, or at best highly questionable.[52]

To which George A. Buttrick adds,

> Literal infallibility of Scripture is a fortress impossible to defend; there is treason in the camp. Probably few people who claim to "believe every word of the Bible" really mean it. That avowal held to its last logic would risk a trip to the insane asylum.[53]

Such views could be multiplied without limit from the writings of leading modern theologians. Often it seems as if all good manners may be suspended when one is engaged in demolishing this doctrine; certainly few make much effort either to understand or to refute it with intelligent argument. Verbal inspiration is just assumed to be an antiquated and harmful superstition, for the destruction of which invective is an excellent substitute for argument. Even Barth has called it

50. Brunner, *Divine-Human Encounter*, p. 171.
51. Brunner, *The Mediator*, p. 104.
52. Burrows, *An Outline of Biblical Theology*, p. 9.
53. George A. Buttrick, *The Christian Faith and Modern Doubt*, p. 162.

a "spook" (Gespenst), while others label it "bibliolatry" (Fosdick), "obscurrantism" (Whale), and even "heresy" (Cotton).[54] In a recent letter to *Christianity Today,* Dr. Willis E. Elliott said, "I consider adherence to the infallibility of Scripture demonic." And he went on to point out, that, although the ecumenical movement was open to all manner of Christian viewpoints, "hatred for the doctrine of the perfect book is very strong in a very large segment of ecumenical leadership, and I can hardly be considered irresponsible and ecumenically inauthentic in voicing this hatred."[55] These are strong words, and indicate that a good deal of ecumenical "progress" in recent times has been realized on the basis of a neoorthodox view of Scripture which allows spiritual fellowship amid serious doctrinal deviations from biblical teaching.[56]

Evangelicals agree that a wrong view of the Bible is a very wicked thing. Christianity is a historical religion, dependent on historical sources. No Christian can be indifferent to anything which might impugn the integrity of our only record of divine revelation. Therefore, we are surprised and dismayed when we see that the neo-Protestant apologists have succumbed to all the empty charges of skeptics of every age, and now plow, as it were, with Paine's heifer! Voltaire and Ingersoll have been installed in chairs of sacred theology! These valiant warriors for the faith, the liberal apologists, sally forth against unbelief only after having conceded all that it demanded and, at the end of the day, return home, proudly announcing that the enemy has disappeared. The liberal contention that a naturalistic version of Christianity requires a naturalistic view of the Bible is understandable, but we are at a loss to comprehend how the supernaturalistic version of Christianity which neoorthodoxy claims to embrace is compatible with a naturalistic view of Scripture. It

54. See T. Engelder, *The Scripture Cannot Be Broken,* pp. 5-29.
55. Willis E. Elliott, Letter to the editor, *Christianity Today.*
56. See David Hedegard, *Ecumenism and the Bible,* p. 47.

is a surprise to find liberal and neoorthodox battalions fighting shoulder to shoulder against Scripture after we had been assured that neoorthodoxy made a clean break with religious humanism. We wonder how clean the break really was.

We are not, of course, unaware that particular objections to the high view of inspiration exist and are advanced against our position. The striking fact is just how antiquated these objections are, how easily answered, and how inconclusive. When we consider that our orthodox predecessors faced problems in Scripture no less perplexing than those we face, without feeling moved to jettison their doctrine of inspiration, we begin to suspect that it is not the pressure of difficulties that has lifted theology from its moorings, but a *shift in the philosophical climate*.[57] The kind of objections advanced against the high view of inspiration is proof enough of the philosophical and not biblical nature of the protest. It is claimed that a mass of *new facts* has accumulated as a result of scientific biblical criticism which renders the traditional view untenable and obsolete. The examination of this claim is the theme of the following chapter. But it is apparent that (1) most of the difficulties proposed are highly archaic and not new at all, (2) others are pseudo-problems created by hypercriticism, and (3) still others are the result of a non-Christian approach to Scripture. In actual fact, the really significant advances in biblical studies have been in the area of languages and archeology, not literary criticism, and the results from these areas have been most hospitable to a very high view of biblical integrity. It is charged that the theory of verbal inspiration is a rationalistic doctrine supraimposed upon an unsuspecting Scripture, which does not arise from its teachings (e.g., the Auburn Affirmation). Brunner contends that

57. John Burnaby admits that, until the nineteenth century, Christian theologians were unprepared when they encountered difficulties in the reading of the Bible to solve them in any way that would cast doubt upon the full veracity of the text. The crumbling of that absolute confidence lately has not been due to fresh critical discoveries but to a general hesitancy to unequivocally affirm the supernatural core of Christianity. See Burnaby, *In What Sense Is the Bible Inspired?* p. 6.

Evangelicals are guilty of the sin of Bible worship.[58] In fact, however, the high view of inspiration was taught by Christ and His apostles and is to be accepted on their high authority. We treasure Scripture as God's Word concerning His Son, and we are no more idolaters for this than they were. It is alleged that the high view of inspiration has the effect of denying the true humanity of the Bible, and reducing the writers to secretaries. A mechanical-dictation theory of inspiration is, however, no necessary concomitant of verbal inspiration. The humanity of the Bible no more necessitates errors in the text than the humanity of Christ requires sin in His life.

The defection from a high view of inspiration has a sad aspect theologically. As Joseph Parker puts it, "Are we to await a communcation from Tubingen, or a telegram from Oxford, before we can read the Bible?" The defection has left theology without a truth base—hesitant, floundering, uncertain. If man is the judge of Scripture, who is his judge? Belief in biblical infallibility is not responsible for modern skepticism as Herbert charges, so much as a century of disbelieving it. The results apologetically have been just as disastrous: modern man, in the spiritual vacuum of the twentieth century, has learned well from the theologians that Scripture is not to be trusted, and has turned away from the message which it conveys. The only truly fruitful direction for theology to take is a return to her only sound basis in the high view of inspiration.

CONTEMPORARY CATEGORIES OF EVASION

The traditional view of the Bible saw a close, intimate relationship between divine revelation and the text of Scripture. Although "revelation" had reference to something broader than Scripture, the Bible constituted written revelation, and was truly and properly God's Word. It was believed to be a deposit of written revelation, divinely authored and

58. "The Bible an idol and me its slave" (*Revelation* . . ., p. 181).

vouchsafed to the church. This understanding of Scripture was derived from the explicit testimony of divinely authenticated teachers, and enjoyed an almost unopposed primacy. At the present time, however, the search is on to discover a safe way to detach revelation and authority from so exclusive a connection with the Bible and attach it to something else, whether divine activity, an I-Thou encounter, or religious experience.[59] The result is the same in every case, namely, the loss of any ascertainable Word from the Lord in human language. Whatever the gains of abandoning verbal inspiration may at first appear to be, the cost is formidable! A number of evasions are proposed as substitutes for the historic Christian view, but all agree on one point: namely, that Scripture is a merely human witness to divine revelation and does not represent infallible divine truth. There is ultimately only *one* evasion; it stems from a disinclination to submit to Scripture as the Word of God. The multiverse evasions represent attempts to justify a refusal to tremble at God's Word (Is 66: 2). The theories aim to liberate their inventors from subjection to the requirements of Scripture so that its literal teachings do not restrict experimentation with the current theological speculations. We call these "low" views of inspiration, not because their proponents do not regard the Bible highly, but because they are lower than the doctrine of inspiration required by special revelation. In every case, the loss to theology and faith incurred by the rejection of the high view is considerable. It becomes impossible to know what revelation is, to distinguish revelation from nonrevelation, or to rescue theology from the never-never land of arbitrary, subjective value judgments.

The categories of evasion we wish to discuss are all generic of a neoorthodox approach to Scripture. However, the liberal attitude to the Bible provided the ideological background

59. Contemporary theologians are well aware that in opposing a simple identification of the Christian revelation with the Bible they are breaking with long-established tradition. They are less aware of the peril of their innovation. See John Baillie, *The Idea of Revelation in Recent Thought*, p. 109.

to it. This liberal view was influenced by rationalistic deism, by Kant's critical philosophy, and by Schleiermacher's pantheistic, man-centered theology, each of which militated against the doctrine of plenary inspiration. Scripture came to be regarded as a merely human testimony, containing a mixture of truth and falsehood, and needing to be sifted by means of the critical intelligence. The liberals felt compelled to reject a good deal of doctrinal and ethical material which could not pass the test of their "scientific" thinking. Any unity the Bible might have was due, not to its unique inspiration, but to a constancy of religious experience and devotion which the writers shared. Fosdick's *The Modern Use of the Bible* is a good illustration of the liberal perspective.[60]

Neoorthodoxy or dialectical theology provided a haven for liberal refugees fleeing from the disenchantment with and devastating consistency of their own optimistic humanism. Ostensibly, it marked a return to classical Protestant orthodoxy and, although the change was noticeable, certain similarities with liberalism remained. This is especially true of its attitude toward Scripture, in which liberal criticism is continued as if it were incidental to and untainted by liberal ideology, and the neo-Kantian denial of objective truth revelation lives on in existential garb.[61] For neoorthodoxy, the Bible is the Word of God only in a restricted and derivative sense; namely, as it becomes the Word by a miracle in the heart, by which its fallible witness mediates an encounter. As witness to revelation, the Bible is an indispensable, though human, document because it occupies a preeminent place chronologically in the Christian faith. The Spirit uses the fallible, human text to induce a dynamic revelation encounter in contemporary man. Whatever the new emphases are which neoorthodoxy has sounded against the older liberalism,

60. Harry Emerson Fosdick, *The Modern Use of the Bible.*

61. Both liberalism (leaning on Kant) and neoorthodoxy (leaning on Kierkegaard) embrace a divided field of knowledge in which religious concepts lack objective validity. See the author's *Set Forth Your Case*, pp. 9-15.

its perspective on the *nature* of Scripture itself is not very different. Henry writes,

> Despite its profession of a higher role for the Bible than liberalism allowed, dialectical theology can retain no decisive significance for Scripture as normative. The Bible is assigned a mere chronological prophetico-apostolic priority as testimony.[62]

Indeed, the difference with the liberal view is *not* what Scripture *is* (a fallible and errant text), but what Scripture is supposed to *do,* namely, mediate a quasi-mystical encounter with the mystery. Language—meaningless one minute—is suddenly charged with meaning the next! God could as well have employed the Dow Jones Industrial Averages, so little do the truthfulness and content of the text seem to matter. It is the neoorthodox view of Scripture which Evangelicals have to face, with its refusal to identify revelation and Scripture, its acceptance of rationalistic biblical criticism, and its fascination for the existential concept of truth. We wish to discuss four categories by which the historic doctrine of inspiration is evaded.

Category one. Scripture, it is said, does not communicate propositional truth, but mediates a personal encounter with God. Revelation is dynamic, not conceptual or dianoetic, and involves a personal confrontation of man by God. It is a subject-to-subject meeting which requires neither truth content nor checking procedures. The fact is, of course, that it needs both desperately.[63] John Baillie is enamored with this precarious approach:

> For the revelation of which the Bible speaks is always such as has place within a personal relationship. It is not the revelation of an object to a subject, but a revelation from a subject to a subject, a revelation of mind to mind.[64]

62. Carl F. H. Henry, "Divine Revelation and the Bible," in *Inspiration and Interpretation,* p. 266.
63. See pp. 23-25 of the present volume.
64. Baillie, p. 24.

Often quoted in this connection is this word of William Temple:

> What is offered to man's apprehension in any specific revelation is not truth concerning God but the living God himself. There is no such thing as revealed truth. There are truths of revelation; but they are not themselves directly revealed.[65]

The point was made earlier by liberal Wilhelm Hermann:

> The thoughts contained in Scripture are not themselves the content of revelation . . . it goes without saying that *God* is the content of revelation.[66]

God, it seems, does not reveal information by communication, but Himself by communion. If any such polarity were legitimate, it is curious how Baillie himself was so singularly able to lead men through his published prayers to communion precisely by communication!

Karl Barth is the primary spokesman for this transcendental, personalist view of revelation and Scripture. Though early in his career he turned away from modernism, owing to the influence of Kierkegaard, he did not return to the orthodox view of Scripture. While he was prepared to grant the Bible a supreme place as witness to revelation, he refused to equate what Scripture said with what God said, and believed the biblical writers were guilty of actual error in their work.[67] Barth arrives at his view of the Bible out of his view of revelation. Revelation is a sovereign, personal meeting of God with man, never a *datum,* always a *dandum* (something to be given). For revelation to be free, it must not be tied to the text of Scripture.[68] Scripture is a human word about God in action, and not a divine word about God Himself. Revelation has to do with Jesus Christ, whereas in the Bible we have to

65. William Temple, *Nature, Man, and God,* pp. 316, 322.
66. Wilhelm Herrmann as cited by Baillie, p. 33.
67. Barth, *Church Dogmatics,* vol. 1, pt. 2, pp. 457-72; vol. 1, pt. 1, pp. 127-28; vol. 1, pt. 2, p. 529.
68. Ibid., vol. 1, pt. 2, pp. 529-30.

do with human attempts to reproduce this Word in particular historic situations. *God said* and *Paul said* are two different things.[69]

Brunner's view of Scripture bears the same characteristics as Barth's, and differs chiefly in being more emotionally charged and antiorthodox. What he is against is somewhat clearer than what he is for. His polemic against the doctrine of verbal inspiration is a sustained, harsh criticism. Orthodoxy, he believes, has become impossible for anyone who knows anything about science.[70] Revelation is Jesus Christ, not a doctrine about Christ. It is Thou-truth, not it-truth. The Bible is a literary fixation of the faith-confessing, faith-creating testimony of the apostles. In their witness to Christ, the biblical writers could and did err. Theology rests, not on the Bible as an infallible authority, but on the Bible as it becomes the word of God for me. And Brunner admits reluctantly that the Bible may not be the only means of revelation, leaving us to wonder why it is a means at all.

The difficulty with this category of evasion is its inability to give reason why this encounter experience should point beyond itself to a revelation *ab extra* (from beyond) and not be explained more simply as another mystical experience common to mankind. Existential religious claims are peculiarly liable to sinful distortion and deceit, and stand in great need of objective verification. And if the text which is supposed to mediate the experience is riddled with errors on the subjects where it may be tested, the Thou-truth it allegedly promotes will not be very impressive. The Bible connects theological truths and historical facts, and ties the fate of both together. We must reject this brand of revelation as docetism. Personal encounter and verifiable truth content should not be wrenched apart. To downgrade the conceptual side of revelation is to reduce faith to empty mysticism. There

69. On Barth's view of Scripture, see Klaas Runia, *Karl Barth's Doctrine of Holy Scripture.*
70. Brunner, *The Word and the World,* p. 38. See Paul K. Jewett, *Emil Brunner's Concept of Revelation,* pp. 117-36.

is no reason, on such a basis, to speak only of a "Christ-event"; why not a Mary-event? R. P. Hanson remarks,

> Indeed, Mr. Douglas Hyde, who some years ago joined the Roman Catholic Church after serving on the editorial staff of the *Daily Worker* as an ardent Marxist, *was* apparently converted in what might be called a Mary-event, as existential and as demanding and as full of self-understanding as any "Christ-event" described by the followers of Bultmann.[71]

We *must* not separate the personal meeting from the conceptual knowing aspect in revelation experience. The encounter with God occurs in the context of truth revelation. Revelation is a meeting and a knowing! A meeting without a knowing would not make any sense at all. Revelation is at least informational. We come to know Christ within the conceptual framework of the inspired Scripture.[72] God speaks to our hearts (*Deus loquens*) because and by means of His having spoken to all men in the personal and written Word (*Deus locutus*). The two do not stand in opposition; they are complementary principles.

Category two. Revelation, we are advised, consists of a series of historical events with revelational significance, not an inspired record of divine truths. The divine activity is contrasted to and elevated over the divine speaking. As in the first category, a biblical truth is selected, and then improperly opposed to another biblical truth. Certainly the Bible contains a recital of the acts of God in history, but in no way does it discourage interest in what the prophets and apostles wrote, as though the divine activity alone enjoyed revelational status. On the conservative wing of the *Heilsgeschichte* school, Cullmann and Althaus wish to affirm the close connection of revelation with verifiable historical hap-

71. R. P. C. Hanson, "The Enterprise of Emancipating Christian Belief from History," in *Vindications: Essays on the Historical Basis of Christianity*, p. 69.

72. See especially B. Ramm, *Special Revelation and the Word of God*, pp. 149-60.

penings, and to insist on the miraculous texture of these events.[73] However, they leave open a highly significant gap, in not granting equal revelation status to the recorded meaning of those events. Not only does Scripture encourage us to treat the divine speaking seriously too, but the failure to do so leaves the interpretation of these saving events up to human guesswork.[74] In the hands of existentially oriented theologians, the emphasis falls upon the receiving minds, rather than the acts of God. There is an intercourse of mind and event, which for the left-wing *Heilsgeschichte* scholars means that revelation is not so much a recital of "acts of God" as an anthology of Hebrew religious interpretations of ordinary events! Revelation is a kind of Hebrew *Blik*, a faith interpretation which certain now unidentifiable happenings managed to stimulate. The exodus, for example, was not so much objective evidence of God's redemptive purposes, as it was generated by faith. In principle any event has the power to call forth such a response as may prove to be revelatory. Clearly the emphasis has subtly shifted from what *God* did, to what some ecstatic Israelites *thought* He did! There is no true act of power (*dunamis*), but only ungrounded faith (*pistis*). It is really astonishing to realize that those who talk most about the acts of God in history are not referring to historical events at all, but to an existential *gnosis* derived from an ecstatic mind in the flow of ordinary history. Evidently we have returned to Schleiermacher's view that the religious feeling contacts God in the course of world history. But is it not highly misleading to speak piously of "acts of God" when all that is meant is religious insight? This category of evasion leaves us with an ineradicable doubt as to whether God has in reality revealed Himself at all, or whether Scripture is but the record of Jewish dreams. And even if we allow this bothersome fideism, the meaning of these redemptive events

73. Paul Althaus, *Fact and Faith in the Kerygma of Today*, pp. 19-37.
74. Kantzer, "The Christ-Revelation as Act and Interpretation," in *Jesus of Nazareth*, pp. 252-53.

remains obscure and the biblical interpretation of them a doubtful human one.[75]

Category three. Scripture is not a deposit of divinely revealed truth, we are told, but a medium of Christian existential experience. It is apparent that each evasion shifts the focus from the objective text of Scripture and makes it reside *within* the interpreter. This evasion is simply a more straightforward and honest version of the first two, which attempt to conceal what they are actually propounding. In this case, the principle of authority is the pious self-consciousness of the theologian himself, subject to no external regulating norm. Liberal subjectivism is a major idol-producing factory dedicated to conforming the gospel to the modern taste. The essence of religion is held to be those historical experiences which the Christian faithful have had, which they enshrined for us in the biblical symbolism and traditional belief. Theology becomes the phenomenology of the primordial experiences of the primitive Christian community which are captured in the text of the Bible.[76] The locale of revelation has been shifted from the text of Scripture to the experience of the writers (and readers). In this way, it is hoped, the corrosive effects of negative criticism can be nullified. But the result inevitably is empty mysticism. If belief in plenary inspiration has on occasion produced mere intellectualism and dead orthodoxy, disbelief in it *must* logically and *does* historically lead to contentless mysticism and religious syncretism. The ultimate authority of religious truth then lies within ourselves, and the test of truth is subjective.[77]

This characteristically liberal, egocentric principle of authority lives on in the existential camp. The influential Bultmannian school is in search of a self-understanding, partly revealed, partly concealed, in the text of the Bible. This ap-

75. See Baillie, pp. 62-82; Raymond Abba, *The Nature and Authority of the Bible,* pp. 74-148.
76. See A. Dulles, "Symbol, Myth, and the Biblical Revelation," in *New Theology,* eds. Martin E. Marty and Dean G. Peerman, pp. 66-68.
77. C. H. Dodd, *The Authority of the Bible,* p. 296.

proach lacks a logical and biblical basis. Scripture roots authentic Christian experience in the objective divine act-word event, and refuses to accept a caricature in the existential terms of Heidegger's ontology. If Scripture is replete with myths, errors and fallacies, the teachings which are supposed to commend an authentic manner of living are suspect too. To admit so low a view of biblical integrity certainly does not enhance the Bible's anthropic insights! It is indeed a curious thing why Bultmann feels a need to use the biblical text at all, since according to his theory it is filled with ridiculous examples of prescientific thinking. Certainly he gives us no grounds for distinguishing a Christian existential experience from any other, and no compelling reason to suppose Scripture promotes it.

Category four. The fourth category of evasion takes many forms, and calls for a *limitation* of inerrancy to certain matters held to be central to the Bible, while allowing for errors in the peripheral material. Views of limited inspiration have always been popular because they seem to relieve us of the need to defend the Bible at certain points. The errors occur in respect of things that do not seem greatly to concern the gospel. Inspiration guarantees the sacred, but not the secular, side of Scripture. Such "dualistic" theories of inspiration seek to disentangle the divine and human aspects of Scripture, and thus deny *plenary* inspiration. The inspired parts of the Bible are distinguished from the uninspired parts, the more inspired parts from the less inspired parts, the inspired content from the uninspired form, or the inspired theological from the uninspired secular subjects in Scripture. In each case, the problem is the same. *How* do we distinguish and *where* do we stop? For we have had opportunity to notice that *limited inerrancy* has a tendency to become *unlimited errancy* once admitted. The dichotomy has a way of eating as does a canker. Such theories, proposed as an insurance against certain charges of negative criticism, are in fact no insurance at all. The same criticism which carries off one unwanted miracle will happily carry off another on the next round unless attacked at the root; and the admission of errors in any part of Scripture inevitably affects the credibility of that which remains (cf. Jn 3:12). The moment we allow that the Bible is trustworthy on a limited range of topics and not others, we must be ready for a progressive reduction of its authority and content to a point without magnitude. To accept only truths concerned with salvation, for example, is to accept a steadily shrinking quantity, which grows smaller under the pressure of each succeeding critical discovery.[78] What to one man is an insight of great depth is to another a vulgar commonplace. What remains of the Bible are a few spiritual proverbs which tend to coincide with the religious values of the interpreter himself. Everything in Scripture contributes to the total impact of Scripture, and there is no justification either biblically or logically for accepting some and rejecting other of its teachings. The doctrine of inspiration inductively derived from the testimony of special revelation insists that we treat *all* the matters which Scripture teaches as reliable and true.

Roman Catholic biblical scholarship of late has been moving toward similar evasions of inspiration.[79] Of necessity, the mode of dissent is more modest, owing to the unequivocal statements of the *magisterium* in the recent past concerning unlimited inerrancy. It has thus been necessary to appeal to "literary forms" in order to cloak what is, in fact, a belief in the existence of biblical errors. The turning point was the Encyclical *Divino Afflante Spiritu* (1943, Pope Pius XII) which took note of advances in critical studies, and suggested that

> a knowledge and careful appreciation of ancient modes of expression and literary forms and styles will provide a solu-

78. See Peter de Rosa, *Christ and Original Sin*, p. 87.

79. See L. R. Keylock, "The Bible Controversy in American Catholicism," in *Christianity Today* (March 1, 1963); Montgomery, "The Approach of New Shape Roman Catholicsm to Scriptural Inerrancy: A Case Study for Evangelicals," in *Ecumenicity, Evangelicals, and Rome*, pp. 73-93.

> tion to many of the objections made against the truth and historical accuracy of Holy Writ.

It was the opportunity liberal Catholics were waiting for. Jean Levie took the encyclical as the starting point for his radical revision of the historic Catholic view of Scripture. In his book *The Bible, Word of God in the Words of Men* (French title: *La Bible, parole humaine et message de dieu,* 1958) he manages to advocate critical theories regarding myths, historical mistakes, midrash, form criticism, and pseudepigraphy, all with the apparent approval of the new Roman Catholic view of Scripture. The Evangelical can no longer appeal to the Roman Catholic Church as an ally in defense of the historic doctrine of inspiration, for very serious shifts have taken place in the Catholic atititude.[80] It has now become possible for Catholic progressives to advocate quite radical hypotheses concerning the truth value of the Bible without fear of churchly discipline.[81] Catholic critics are even free to dismiss the historicity of biblical miracles merely by supposing them to be literary devices for the illustration of theological points. The essence of what the Catholic modernists taught and for which they were excommunicated is now perfectly acceptable so long as it is sanctioned by the shibboleth "literary form." This apparent about-face is consonant with the historic Catholic and neo-Protestant view of truth as an evolving, changing entity. Truth for Rome is what Rome says it is; and truth for the neo-Protestants is what the consensus says it is. In either case, Scripture is not allowed to impose its objective authority on anyone today. But to recognize this does not make it so. It is nonsense to talk about an inerrant Bible with errors in it, and a trustworthy book which lies! A student may not claim to be a top

80. See Keylock, "Biblical Inspiration in Roman Catholic Thought Since 1870" (Master's thesis, Wheaton College, Ill., 1964).

81. See R. A .F. MacKenzie, *Faith and History in the Old Testament,* pp. 80-81; John L. McKenzie, *Myth and Realities: Studies in Biblical Theology,* p. 200. The new-shape Catholic biblical scholarship is particularly obvious in the Dutch *New Catechism,* the *Jerusalem Bible,* and the *Jerome Biblical Commentary.*

student if his transcript records only low grades. Similarly, the Roman Church only contradicts herself when she teaches *both* the inerrancy of Scripture and the existence of errors in it. Montgomery remarks, "That is like saying that the presence of corners can't affect a circle."[82]

It seems plain that Catholic biblical scholarship over the past few decades has been heavily influenced by the existential, contentless understanding of revelation. In Benoit, Levie, J. L. McKenzie and others, the locus of revelation has been shifted from an exclusive preoccupation with the text, and relocated in the realm of personal encounter. In so doing they have weakened their view of Scripture, perhaps fatally.

The dissent and attempted evasion of the historic doctrine of inspiration is the saddest chapter in the history of theology. The dissent has been bitter and derogatory, and the evasions incapable of withstanding critical examination. All are desperate to evade the plain teaching of Scripture, and thus end in a dreamworld of untestable religious feelings. The net effect of the modern approaches to Scripture has been, not a liberation of divine truth from bondage to the letter of Scripture, but a questioning of any normative significance for the Bible at all.

82. Montgomery, *Ecumenicity . . .*, p. 89.

5

THE PHENOMENA OF SCRIPTURE

EVANGELICALS ARE OFTEN DIVIDED on how to evaluate the phenomena they discover in Scripture. Sometimes they are even faced with an intolerable choice—doctrinal orthodoxy or critical honesty. The "maximalists" weigh in from the side of dogmatic theology and jealously seek to guard biblical inerrancy, while the "minimalists," immersed in a close study of the text, are hesitant to generalize on their findings. So there is an unfortunate and unnecessary feud between fellow believers, the one suspecting the other of unorthodoxy or dishonesty, respectively. Yet, paradoxically, the "maximalists" (e.g., Warfield) admit that the extant text is not now inerrant, while the "minimalists" often confess that they believe one day all difficulties will be swept away (e.g., Orr). There is no place for mutual suspicion in evangelical ranks. We ought to be concerned in each other's ministry. A careful and minute study of the phenomena of Scripture is the responsibility of one who holds to the high view of inspiration.

THE HUMANITY OF SCRIPTURE

The Bible is the Word of God in the words of men. As C. S. Lewis remarks,

> The same divine humility which decreed that God should become a baby at a peasant-woman's breast, and later an arrested field-preacher in the hands of the Roman police, decreed also that he should be preached in a vulgar, prosaic,

> and unliterary language. If you can stomach the one, you can stomach the other.[1]

God has given us neither a docetic Christ, nor a docetic Scripture, whose humanity is unreal and intangible. We wish to affirm the true and real humanity of Christ and the Bible. The Spirit used significant human authors, particular men in particular cultures, to communicate the divine Word. Without wishing to wrench the human from the divine side of Scripture, as neo-Protestants do, we wish to do as much justice to the humanness of the divine Word as to the divinity of the human record. At the present time, it is more likely that men will mistake the Bible for a merely human book than that they would overlook its humanity, much as the Jewish people in the day of our Lord mistook Him for a mere man. However, it is imperative that we do justice to the human side.[2]

Naturally we reject the puerile maxim: "To err is human—Scripture is human—therefore, Scripture errs."[3] For error is no more required of the Bible's humanity than sin is of Christ's. Inerrancy no more deifies Scripture or makes criticism impossible, than sinlessness renders Christ docetic and makes historical study of His life impossible. A better maxim is this: "To err is human—*ergo,* God gave Scripture by inspiration—so that, it does not err." The fact that all men, including the biblical writers, are sinners, does not obviate the existence of infallible Scripture; it underlines the *need* for it. Without it, sinful men twist revelation to their liking and bend God's Word to coincide with their own. Evangelicals fully recognize the humanity of the Bible, but not in the way negative criticism does. Scripture is simultaneously the product of divine and human authorship, the two factors interpenetrating the text at every point, so that Scripture is never less than human and divine anywhere.

1. Introduction to J. B. Phillips' *Letters to Young Churches.*
2. G .E. Ladd has a very helpful book relating inspiration and criticism, *The New Testament and Criticism.*
3. See Karl Barth, *Church Dogmatics,* vol. 1, pt. 2, pp. 529-30.

Christian Criticism

The shape of Scripture as a historically mediated document requires careful critical study. Evangelicals are against certain conclusions at which negative criticism has arrived, not against criticism itself. Inspiration in no way obstructs valid historical-critical scholarship applied to the Bible. For criticism is the effort, by means of an honest and careful collection and evaluation of the evidence, which seeks to lay bare the structure and meaning of Scripture. Criticism begins, however, with a decision concerning the *kind* of book the Bible is. Evangelicals feel constrained to examine Scripture in the light of the biblical doctrine of inspiration, whereas negative critics do not. If all the evidence were in and if we were flawless exegetes, this initial standpoint would matter a good deal less. But as it is, we continually meet difficulties which we do not know how to treat. Should we take this as mythical, or this as contradiction? The liberal critic is not inhibited in proposing theories which announce errors in the Bible. But Evangelicals, who see the phenomena of Scripture in the light of the whole Christian faith and the authority of our Lord, are loath to do this. They prefer to believe that when all the evidence is in, the "errors" will vanish away. Both liberal and Evangelical, however, *believe* this is the case, and cannot yet demonstrate whether the "errors" are apparent or real. This is not, let us note, fideistic presuppositionalism. Evangelicals have excellent reasons for approaching Scripture as they do (see chaps. 1-2). Christ and the whole of special revelation fix the methods and presuppositions by which the Bible is studied. The *nature* of the Bible helps determine our approach to it, and gives a clue to what the difficulties we meet really are. The difficulty which the Liberal too readily calls an error may in reality be only a temporary problem which a little further thought or a little more evidence would easily solve. Inspiration is our guideline, our hermeneutical *Gestalt,* which we employ in our criticism. We proceed from what we *know* (Scripture is

God's Word) to what we *wish* to know (what does this phenomenon mean?), and consider the latter in terms of the former. We interpret a telephone book in terms of what the book is; and likewise we study Scripture in the light of what God says it is.

Admittedly, evangelical criticism is conservative in a way negative criticism is not. Complete critical freedom is purchased at the price of Christian faith. This is a freedom we do not covet. We are reluctant to consider our inability to solve a given problem as proof that the problem is ultimately real (i.e., an error). Negative critics who do charge errors in Scripture usurp, we believe, the very infallibility for themselves which they deny to Scripture! It is a matter of record that the majority of critical hypotheses charging the Bible with error over the past hundred years have been refuted by facts and withdrawn. How is it then that today's critics can so boldly claim the Bible is error-ridden? Evangelicals are more conservative than that. Our belief in biblical inerrancy rests upon the demonstration that God in Christ teaches it; it does not depend upon our ability to establish it from the extant text. We live in hope that all the difficulties will be solved in our lifetime; but if they are not, we shall not die in despair, for we do not believe the evidence exists to prove God in Christ lied. Often it seems as though the "creativity" of negative criticism depends on how great an amount of the Bible one dares to consider inauthentic and untrue. The evangelical critic feels no compulsion to overturn traditional opinion and interpretation for the sake of mere novelty, or to concoct new hypotheses more radical than before. We are content to let the wisdom of the past, especially the teachings of our Lord and His apostles, teach us.

This patient attitude has been abundantly rewarded of late. Time and again the critical proposals aimed at discrediting the integrity of Scripture have been unmasked for what they were: namely, speculative and a priori theories, concocted apart from the controls of objective research in Near Eastern cultures. C. H. Gordon has shown decisively that the criteria employed in the documentary analysis of the Pentateuch are completely inadequate when evaluated in the context of their cultural-linguistic setting. Thanks to scholars like Gordon and Albright, to name only two, the negative attitude which was almost universal a generation ago is gradually being replaced by a positive respect for the biblical text. The actual cause of the new approach is the availability of fresh archeological material which serves as a welcome check upon the excesses of critical speculations. There has been a virtual revolution in the study of Old Testament history and religion which is due entirely to the willingness of some scholars (far from all as yet) to repudiate outdated theories and to replace them with sound conclusions.[4]

Our method of approach to the dark places of Scripture is synthetic and integrating; that is, in the case of apparent contradictions, we assume as a working hypothesis that both poles are correct and seek to trace connecting wires between them. In most cases where this is carefully done, the data is found to harmonize rather easily. The negative critic, on the other hand, employs an analytic and disjunctive method; that is, he assumes ultimate contradiction and sharpens the difficulties to make his point.[5] The difference in attitude and approach stems from a difference in the basic doctrine of inspiration. The evangelical scholar and the negative critic are both honest investigators of the phenomena of Scripture, and both operate from a precommitment to what Scripture is. The most fundamental hermeneutical rule is always the doctrine of inspiration because it is decisive throughout the work of interpretation. Montgomery comments,

> Harmonization of Scriptural difficulties should be pursued within reasonable limits, and where harmonization

4. The most competent and complete work to appear in decades, if ever, which firmly lays to rest negative critical theories by the score is R. K. Harrison, *Introduction to the Old Testament.*
5. Olav Valen-Sendstad, *The Word that Can Never Die,* pp. 50-51.

> would pass beyond such bounds, the exegete must leave the problem open rather than, by assuming surd error, impugn the absolute truthfulness of the God who inspires all Holy Scripture for our learning.[6]

Undoubtedly there are dark places where the harmony between infallibility and the phenomena of Scripture is difficult to see. But we do not require that every difficulty be cleared up before we will believe God. What doctrine is there which does not confront us with some unanswered question? The tension between inspiration and the difficulties calls not for unbelief, but for a closer scrutiny of the facts. Critical honesty does not commit us to a naïve acceptance of all the results of negative criticism; nor does doctrinal orthodoxy commit us to a suppression of the grand diversity of Scripture. J. C. Ryle writes,

> Let us not give up the great principle of plenary inspiration because of difficulties. The day may come when they will all be solved. In the meantime we may rest assured that the difficulties which beset any other theory of inspiration are tenfold greater than any which beset our own.[7]

Negative Biblical Criticism

Contemporary biblical criticism, called "scientific" by its friends, is the cause of deep division among Christians, who are divided in their opinion how best to cope with the literary phenomena in the Bible. By its friends it is championed as the only truly honest way to analyze the Bible, and by its enemies it is attacked as little more than a novel brand of skepticism. Its friends contend that the results of critical study necessitate a revision of our doctrine of Scripture and our interpretation of its contents, while its enemies insist that criticism is a legacy of liberalism and ought to be destroyed root and branch. Each side distorts the standpoint of the other. It is well to keep in mind: (1) that the historically

6. John W. Montgomery, ed., *Crisis in Lutheran Theology,* 1:103.
7. J. C. Ryle, *Warnings to the Churches,* p. 32.

mediated Scripture makes criticism completely inevitable and desirable; (2) that liberal and conservative critics, with exceptions, are characterized by integrity and scholarship; and (3) that none of us are as free of prejudice as we suppose nor as objective as we would like. Not *all* negative critics are dishonest and not *all* their work as useless as Fundamentalism has implied. As a direct result of critical study, we know a great deal more about the Bible and the conditions of its origin now than we did a century ago. Because Scripture is *historical* revelation, we study it critically; because it is historical *revelation*, we study it reverently. To Evangelicals, the fact that the Bible claims divine authorship in the whole and in the parts is a supremely relevant fact for their critical endeavors. Our complaint with contemporary criticism is not that it is too scientific—it is often not scientific enough—but that its theories seem so frequently to be spun out of alien cloth.[8] So often negative criticism disregards the context of the Christian truth claim in which the phenomena stand, and espouse conclusions which it is impossible for a Christian to entertain if he is to be consistent. James Smart has commented,

> It may be worth noting that missionaries are often in a dilemma because new Christians seem to take most readily to a naive literalistic view of Scripture, so that the missionaries are afraid to introduce them to the modern historical-critical approach lest it undermine their confidence in the Scriptures themselves.[9]

Would that more critics and seminary professors had the sensitivity of a missionary! An antisupernaturalistic bias lurks behind many a critical hypothesis, creating a real problem for those who would read the Bible with believing hearts. Negative critics ought to reflect more on the theology of criticism.

8. K. A. Kitchen has shown this unscientific aspect in the field of Old Testament (*Ancient Orient and Old Testament*) and D. Guthrie in the field of New Testament studies (*New Testament Introduction*, 3 vols.).

9. James Smart, *The Interpretation of Scripture*, p. 167.

For there is nothing particularly new about criticism per se. The older theologians were perceptive, keen exegetes of Scripture who wrestled honestly with the difficulties they encountered and proposed some highly satisfactory solutions to many of them. Calvin, for example, in his commentaries, hardly fails to face any problem in the text of the Bible, and more often than not supplies a convincing (or at least ingenious) solution to them. What is *new* about modern criticism is the neutral, secular stances it pretends to adopt: its autonomy and freedom to act apart from all inhibition, even obedience to Christ, and to propose critical theories incompatible with a Christian view of Scripture. Negative criticism, properly speaking, belongs *outside* the church because it repudiates the truly Christian attitude to the Bible—total trust. Evangelical criticism regards the Bible as a divinely inspired human record; negative criticism regards it as simply a human one. This is the watershed between them. Barth is a less adventurous critic than Brunner, and Brunner than Bultmann, but all of them agree that Scripture is *not* a divinely veracious document. So whatever the complexities are which arise in the discussion of inspiration and criticism, the root issue is rather simple to grasp: do we acknowledge in our criticism the divine authorship of the Bible or not? It is a decision we all must make, and one which, in the course of our work, we must recognize we *have* made.

At this point it is necessary to puncture a piece of critical mythology repeated ad nauseam by countless devotees, to the effect that the "assured results of criticism" have rendered belief in biblical infallibility impossible for any honest, intelligent person.[10] It might as easily be claimed in opposition that criticism has not disproved the authenticity of a single biblical book nor demonstrated the existence of a single biblical error. But both statements arise from the critical attitude

10. So widely is this myth believed that the phrase "to read the Bible precritically" means to believe its literal teachings, while to read it "critically" is to doubt it! In fact, however, criticism has to do with careful discrimination, not with disbelief.

adopted from the outset. Every knowledgeable person knows of the flux of critical opinion, of the reversals of critical theories, and of the serious disagreements on every topic among biblical critics themselves. Obviously the basis of the mythology that infallibility is untenable is not empirical at all, but philosophical. We need not bow at the altar of critical scholarship. Lewis once remarked that he distrusted men who claimed to be able to read between the lines of the Bible when it was apparent they were unable to read the lines themselves! Certainly the real gains in a century of biblical criticism have not been in the slippery field of literary reconstructions, but in the fields of archeology and linguistics. The liberal insistence that criticism has proved the Bible errant is pure propaganda and should be regarded as such. Of course all biblical scholars face difficulties in the text, but the Evangelical is not in a worse position than anyone else. Indeed, considering the promising results of genuinely historical research into Scripture (viz., objective archeological digs, and comparative literary studies), his position is happier than some. At any rate, whatever the varying fortunes of the critical consensus may be, the Evangelical is able to stand beside his Lord in a high view of Scripture, and that will always prove safe. What the negative critic is pleased to call "errors" we prefer to call "difficulties." If only our freedom to do this were not assailed with such invective from the liberal camp, a more congenial atmosphere might develop. We may never achieve perfect clarity in the marginal areas of Scripture, but such dark patches do not upset for us the deep royalty of Scripture.

Negative criticism, because of its refusal to acknowledge the question of preunderstanding, has had disastrous results. Theologically, the basis for constructing a sound theology has vanished. W. N. Clarke stated his dilemma poignantly:

> I tell no secret—though perhaps many a man has wished he could keep it a secret—when I say that to the average

> minister today the Bible that lies on his pulpit is more or less an unsolved problem. He is loyal to it, and not for his right hand would he degrade it or do it wrong. He longs to speak with authority on the basis of its teaching, and feels that he ought to be able to do so. He knows that the people need its message in full power and clearness, and cannot bear to think that it is losing influence with them. Yet he is not entirely free to use it. Criticism has altered the book for his use, but just how far he does not know.[11]

For a time, Liberalism breathed the exhilarating air of freedom from the shackles of biblical infallibility, only to awaken to the sober realization that Scripture had lost its power and the clarity of its message. And apologetically, the only basis for defending the Christian faith as a historically grounded religion was undermined and discredited. As a result, the faith of thousands found itself unable to understand its own truth content, and incapable of defending itself against strong secular criticism. We have not yet felt the full impact of this theological disaster and, sadder still, not even recognized as we should, what a disaster it was and is.

Theology of Criticism

The scientific inquiry into the nature and teaching of the Bible is a notable endeavor, an extension of the reverence which leads every believer to search the Scriptures. Yet, criticism, like everything else that we do, is subject to divine judgment. To be committed to supernatural Christianity and practice naturalistic criticism is intellecual schizophrenia. Criticism should be rooted in the total Christian faith. Many critical theories are little more than popular hypotheses based on the superficial assumption that Scripture frequently errs. Our critical "freedom" is relative and not absolute. It is relative to the total body of facts available. The decision to adopt a critical hypothesis charging the Bible with surd error presupposes the decision to deny the evidence of special revela-

11. Cited in Harry Emerson Fosdick, *Modern Use of the Bible*, p. 2.

tion regarding inerrancy. A person is free to do this; but he is not free to do it and then to proceed under the illusion that what he has decided cannot affect the quality of his Christian faith.

Oscar Cullmann attempts to make a virtue out of what he considers a necessity in arguing that the imperfection of the Bible is part and parcel of the true scandal of the gospel.[12] However, it is no part of the gospel that makes Jesus a sinner or the Bible errant. Nowhere are we asked to exalt the Bible in our preaching and demean it in our scholarship. Jesus Christ assures us that at all times and in all places Scripture is trustworthy. This fact is the reason why, in a certain sense, critical verdicts play a small part in exegesis for us. For whatever the literary history of a given portion may be, it is the finished product, the *graphe* itself, which we heed and obey. We do not really need even to know the precise history of how each text came to be. Our faith in the ultimate divine authorship of the Bible leads us to study the text in its unity and totality. The specific claims of the text command our attention, not the speculative reconstructions which appeal more or less to curiosity.

For Evangelicals, the nature of biblical inspiration is crucial both for criticism and for hermeneutics. The divine authorship and consequent inerrancy of Scripture, is the ruling principle by which we function, the truth of each particular viewed in the light of the whole. Our criticism lacks the luster and glamour of innovation and speculation, but it has one surpassing virtue, namely, its sturdy grasp of the pattern of divine revelation of which the infallible Word is a component part.

Some Critical Issues

There is a set of biblical characteristics which marks the Bible off to be an ancient book, but which in no way impairs

12. Oscar Cullmann, *The Early Church,* pp. 9-10.

its claim to infallibility. The following six theses illustrate this point and create little tension with plenary inspiration.

1. Biblical history, like all history, is written under a careful and purposeful selection and elimination of detail. Drawing is the art of omission, and the lens of a camera must be focused to the correct viewing distance. The integrity of a historical passage is relative to the standpoint of and the degree of magnification required by the writer. There are many ways of writing history, none of which distort truth. Matthew seems to order his material according to a catechetical plan, and Moses wrote about the exodus with a religious purpose in view, though in both cases the facts are not distorted or invented.[13] The chronicler deliberately omitted reference to past events which he felt did not contribute to the kind of work he was writing, and it is entirely artificial for us to impose on him the kind of thoroughness and detachment required of modern historians. Biblical history is truthful in the matters it wishes to convey, not in all the details we might like to know. There is nothing that requires every biblical sentence to be meticulously precise. Pedantic precision is an artificial standard of infallibility. Critics impose it in order to (unsuccessfully) discredit the high doctrine of inspiration. However, it is not necessary that to be truthful an assertion must record *exactly* what is said or done to the letter, if such precision is unnecessary to the purpose in view. Incompleteness and selectivity in historical writing do not negate truthfulness. To the human eye, railroad tracks appear to converge; to a geometer, they are parallel to infinity; under a microscope, the track is jagged and uneven. It depends on the standpoint taken. The perspective and genre of biblical history need to be taken into account when measuring its accuracy.

2. Biblical language employs, as does our own language, popular expressions (the four corners of the earth), and

13. A. Bea has excellent remarks in this vein: *De Inspiratione et Inerrantia Sacrae Scripturae.*

phenomenal descriptions of the natural order (the sun rises). These involve no error. Such terms are entirely serviceable to convey meaning and no one dreams of pressing them literally. The lack of scientific precision in no way hampers their usefulness. The moon *does* appear bigger than the stars to the earth-bound observer (Gen 1:16). There is no effort in the use of such expressions to convey scientific information on cosmology. Inerrancy is unaffected by them.

3. Figurative, symbolic, and even mythological language is employed by Scripture in its expression of doctrine. Literary forms, which are not *deceitful,* are freely used: allegory, fable, proverb, parable. These adorn the text and contribute to its color and its teaching. A striking case of this is the use of certain mythological allusions to clothe the biblical doctrines. For example, Leviathan (Job 3:8, Berkeley; Is 27:1), centaurs and satyrs (Is 34:14), "Rahab's" helpers (Job 9:13, Berkeley). In no case is it apparent that the biblical writer wishes to indicate his personal endorsement of the existence of these creatures or, even if he did believe in them, that he desires all of his readers to be bound to believe them. The mythical element is an incidental allusion, a piece of the clothing of the doctrine, a mere figure of speech, and part of the cultural texture of the Scripture. Poetic description, needless to say, is as respectable a literary form as prose, and both are capable in their different ways of yielding the freight of divine revelation.

4. Often Scripture contains duplicate, parallel accounts of the same event or sermon in which different details occur, a different standpoint is adopted, or a different mode of description is employed. Genesis 1 approaches creation differently than Genesis 2–Job 38 describes creation differently yet–and the small divergencies in the synoptic gospels are legion. But inerrancy does not require standardization of all such accounts, and there is no reason why we should jump to the conclusion that the truth has been violated simply be-

cause differences exist. For it may well be, if everything were known, that all the apparent discrepancies would disappear.

5. There is nothing which says that quotations from the Old Testament or elsewhere must in all cases conform to the original with verbal exactness. The substance of a text, or part of its wording, or even a paraphrase of its thought, may be chosen for the purpose at hand. The variations in the gospels of the wording of the title on the cross, for example, illustrate an attempt to convey the sense and not the exact words. The free and creative use of the Old Testament by the New is not a problem for plenary inspiration; for in addition to presenting the general sense of the texts cited, not necessarily their precise wording, the New Testament teachers sought to indicate the true, Messianic import of the Old Testament. In a sense they not only cite an old text but create a new one through their inspired, Christocentric approach. We should read the Old Testament through their eyes. The very liberty of their use of Scripture indicates their confidence in the *new* revelation they were bearing to the world. The writer is at liberty to use the Old Testament text freely or strictly according to his requirement.

6. The literary quality and polish of the biblical material is not of uniform degree. It varies with the literary style of the author and his stylistic purposes. It is likely that the writer of the Revelation deliberately conforms his Greek to the style of Old Testament translation Greek. The purpose of language is to communicate, and this the biblical language does. There is no reason for the Greek of Matthew to conform to classical Attic grammar. The popular speech of the day served the apostolic missionaries well as they traveled across the world to make Christ known. We should not blame Paul for an anacoluthon (lapse of grammar) if under the rush of strong emotions he presses on to tell us of a thrilling spiritual truth. Grammar is made for man, not man for grammar! A writer enjoys the freedom, where his thought requires it, to

leave normal syntax for a space in order to heighten an emphasis or alter the tone.

These are a few of the characteristics which mark Scripture as a truly human product, but which in no way hamper the will of God to communicate truly to His people. There are, however, critical hypotheses which in various ways charge the Bible with error or deception, and these constitute the *real difficulties* of infallibility. We will discuss literary deceptions, historical blunders, moral blemishes, and scientific mistakes.

Difficulties in Scripture

The careful Bible reader is faced unavoidably with problems of form and content which formerly skeptics, and now skeptics and negative critics, raised to overthrow the reliability of the Bible. Some seem to derive maximum delight from dwelling upon such difficulties, and seek wide publicity for problems on the fringes of Scripture. There is even at times, it seems, a furious search for such contradictions, as if to satisfy some deep hatred of God's Word. It did not however, take skeptics to locate the difficulties—theologians have always recognized them and attempted to resolve them. It took skeptics to use them against the gospel. The Christian approach in such cases has been to offer a plausible explanation of the phenomena, or leave the matter in temporary abeyance, based on the conviction that whatever apparent falsehoods and contradictions are found in the Bible, they did not come from the God of truth and are not ultimately real. Perfectly reasonable solutions have been suggested for most of them and, in view of the great antiquity of Scripture, it is surprising that the difficulties are not more and the solutions less. Scripture was written by many writers over a long period of time, and transmitted even longer, yet there has been no conspiracy to eliminate the tensions. They provide a stimulus to our intelligence to discover a reasonable explanation of the data. If we can, the discrepancy is unreal; if we cannot, it does not mean no one can. Something that perplexes one person does not perplex another. God permitted discrepancies to appear in Scripture. He did not, however, permit them to dull the force or obscure the clarity of its message. It is our *duty* to look such difficulties squarely in the eye and not pretend they do not exist. Scripture should be cleared of reproach, and the charges against her refuted. If we do not face the difficult cruxes of the Bible, the opponents of inspiration will conclude either that our faith in it is irrational or that the doctrine itself is foolish, or both. We must ever seek to close the gap between the doctrine of inspiration deductively formulated from the teaching of Christ and the apostles, and the phenomena of Scripture inductively examined by reverent study.[14] It is our conviction that eventually all tension will be eliminated and all problems solved. To this end we must work if our belief is not to be discredited.[15]

LITERARY DECEPTIONS

Not all critical hypotheses are compatible with biblical inspiration because they accuse Scripture of deliberate deception. Where a myth is dressed up to look like plain history, or an epistle makes claim to an author falsely, the truthfulness and even the morality of Scripture are in doubt. The myth is tainted with historical deception, and the pseudonymity with literary deceit. In each case the truthfulness of Scripture is denied. Preus remarks,

14. I use the words *deductive-inductive* in the manner commonly adopted in this connection. Strictly speaking, both poles involve induction: the doctrine of inspiration is formed by a process of induction from the doctrinal passages.

15. Every one of Beegle's "errors" by which he sought to show that biblical inerrancy was an impossible belief has been shown not to be such by David P. Livingston, "The Inerrancy of Scripture" (Master's thesis at Trinity Evangelical Divinity School, Deerfield, Ill., 1969). For other work on Bible difficulties, see John W. Haley, *An Examination of the Alleged Discrepancies of the Bible;* W. Arndt, *Does the Bible Contradict Itself?* and *Bible Difficulties;* G. W. DeHoff, *Alleged Bible Contradictions Explained;* H. E. Guillebaud, *Some Moral Difficulties of the Bible.*

> Certain alleged forms are not compatible either with the purpose of Scripture or with its inerrancy. For instance, in principle, purely scientific, purely historical, purely salacious literary forms cannot be reconciled with the serious, practical, theological purpose of Scripture. Specifically, any literary genre that would in itself be immoral or involve deceit or error is not compatible with Biblical inerrancy and is not to be found in Scripture, for example, myth, etiological tale, midrash, legend or saga according to the usual designation of these forms. None of these genres fits the serious theological purpose of Scripture.

Later he adds,

> Pseudonymity in the sense of one writer pretending to be another in order to secure acceptance of his own work is illicit and not compatible with inerrancy. That the motives for such action may be construed as good does not alter the fact that fraud or forgery has been perpetrated. The fact that such a practice was carried on in ancient times does not justify it nor indicate that the practice was considered moral.[16]

Parable and proverb are literary forms which occasion no difficulty. The problem arises when the reader is deceived by reading the Bible in its natural sense. Hebrews is no problem because it is anonymous, not pseudonymous. But 2 Peter contains so deliberate a claim to Petrine authorship that falsification would prove deception. No motive, however noble, could make the act less fraudulent. The ethical question is unavoidable. The view that a disciple of Peter's may have reworked his master's notes is less objectionable, but wholly speculative. But if we believe pseudonymity is involved, we have no right to consider the book inspired and canonical. "Pseudonymity and canonicity are mutually exclusive."[17] Two

16. Robert Preus, "Biblical Hermeneutics and the Lutheran Church Today," *Crisis in Lutheran Theology,* 2:42, 45. See also "Epistolary Pseudepigraphy" by Guthrie in *New Testament . . .,* 2:282-94.

17. J. I. Packer, *'Fundamentalism' and the Word of God,* p. 184 . For a defense of Petrine authorship, see E. M. B. Green, *Second Peter Reconsidered.*

alleged epistles of Paul, cited in the Muratorian fragment, were excluded from the canon for precisely this reason—they were considered inauthentic and nonapostolic. Daniel is an example in the Old Testament in which, according to most critics, a second century B.C. author recounts events in prophetic form as if he were speaking from the sixth century. It is difficult to believe the Spirit led this writer to deceive us. The book of Jonah presents the same issues less sharply. Taken by itself it could pass for a piece of didactic fiction. The collateral evidence from the historical books, however, creates a strong impression in favor of a historical interpretation (2 Ki 14:25; Lk 11:29).[18] The central question is always what the Bible means us to understand it to say. It was not written to deceive us.

Ramm, following Orr, contends that we should not balk at accepting whatever literary form Scripture presents. If pseudonymity, or legend and saga, for example, were a recognized form in the culture of the writer, and would not offend the people of his time, we must accept it too.[19] Scripture is expressed in the literary forms current at the time of its composition. Ramm measures veracity by a relative cultural standard, rather than by an absolute truth standard. How far this can go is illustrated in Levie's case, who reduces the fall of man to a myth and the vicarious atonement to primitive thought by invoking such a relative standard. (These were the presuppositions of Paul's thought, and characteristic of the culture of that day and time).[20] However, simple honesty cannot be excluded from any truth criterion. Scripture honors the law of noncontradiction, and operates on the basis of a correspondence idea of truth. Where statements of fact are intentional, we must suppose they do correspond to what is indeed the case. To break the link between biblical affirmations and reality would be disastrous. Of course we will

18. See G. C. Aalders, *The Problem of the Book of Jonah.*
19. B. Ramm, *Special Revelation and the Word of God,* pp. 63-69; J. Orr, *Revelation and Inspiration,* pp. 169-74.
20. J. Levie, *The Bible, Word of God in Words of Men,* pp. 274-76.

accept any literary form Scripture *uses*, but the question whether Scripture uses myth or not can only be answered at an earlier point. Inspiration requires us to accept as historical fact all that Scripture presents as fact (e.g., the fall of man), and forbids us to treat it otherwise. Evangelicals reject the neoorthodox tendency to mythologize scriptural narratives because (1) it is a denial of what Scripture teaches, and (2) it represents a docetic dehistoricizing of redemption. The next step after making Adam everyman is to make Christ everyman. Nowhere does the Bible give us the impression of speaking by myth or saga. Everywhere it is jealous of historical reality. We believe that Scripture has been said to employ certain deceitful literary forms that it does *not*, in fact, use. For instance, the theory that Matthew and Luke employ nativity saga and midrash in their accounts of the birth of Jesus, is *not* an observation of what the literary form is, so much as a *judgment* that the material is legendary. Similarly, the view that Adam is everyman was concocted apart from and contrary to Scripture, and represents a construction which modern science is supposed to permit.

In the field of Old Testament criticism, many theories are currently held which are incompatible with belief in biblical inspiration and cannot be harmonized with it. Miracles are rationalized away, contradictions are uncovered, historical fallacies are exposed, deceptions are charged.[21] Although many of the most radical theories in Old Testament criticism have been reversed by recent scholarship (e.g., the evolutionary scheme of Julius Wellhausen), the attitude of most Old Testament scholars continues to be hostile to the high view of inspiration. Despite the brilliant illumination on the Old Testament narrative from discoveries at Nuzi, Ugarit and Mari, and the confirmation of countless specific details, many

21. For a representative modern treatment of the whole field from the negative critical viewpoint, see Otto Eissfeldt, *The Old Testament, An Introduction;* and Ernst Sellin, *Introduction to the Old Testament,* rewritten by Georg Fohrer. Competent conservative introductions are G. L. Archer, *A Survey of Old Testament Introduction;* and E. J. Young, *An Introduction to the Old Testament.*

critics remain doubtful about the historical reliability of the early accounts. The application of form-critical techniques to the Old Testament (by Noth, von Rad, etc.) has in some measure put the whole matter in even greater doubt. And, although W. F. Albright and others have challenged the unwarranted historical pessimism of this school, even they are far from admitting the complete trustworthiness of the accounts. The Evangelical in this field is still a lonely voice. But there are signs of better things to come. The source criticism of the Pentateuch has been subjected to heavy criticism and rejected by C. H. Gordon and U. Cassuto. Gordon considers the JEDP scheme untenable for a critical scholar, and the failure to question it due to intellectual sloth.[22] K. A. Kitchen, in one of the finest examples of evangelical criticism to appear in years, subjects the whole hypothesis to rigorous examination, and points to the extreme artificiality and unwarranted stylistic criteria adopted in support of the theory.[23] The late date of Deuteronomy, a keystone of the Pentateuchal theory, has likewise been subjected to convincing refutation by Meredith G. Kline and G. T. Manley.[24] There are many other questions to be faced by evangelical scholars, but it is gratifying to note the competence of the men now at work and the success of their alternative proposals.

In New Testament criticism, the situation is far less grave. The radical theories of the nineteenth century have for the most part been completely abandoned. The genuineness of most of the Pauline corpus, the authenticity of the Johannine material, and the trustworthiness of Acts, are all now widely recognized. And there is no New Testament introduction more thorough in scholarship and complete in scope than is

22. C. H. Gordon, "Higher Critics and Forbidden Fruit," *Christianity Today* (Nov. 23, 1959). See U. Cassuto, *The Documentary Hypothesis*.

23. Kitchen, pp. 112-29. See also Archer, pp. 73-165; Young, pp. 107-54; Aalders, *A Short Introduction to the Pentateuch;* O. T. Allis, *The Five Books of Moses*.

24. Meredith G. Kline, *Treaty of the Great King;* and G. T. Manley, *The Book of the Law*.

evangelical Donald Guthrie's three-volume work.[25] There remain, of course, critical hypotheses incompatible with biblical infallibility, notably the form-critical approach to the gospel records, but materials exist for handling these challenges.[26] In both Old and New Testament criticism it seems that attacks on biblical reliability come chiefly from speculative theories most affected by naturalistic presuppositions, whereas the really solid gains in Near Eastern archeology and languages tend to support its integrity. There is reason to believe that as long as our *factual* knowledge broadens, the trend toward Bible-believing criticism will continue.

HISTORICAL DISCREPANCIES

Many critics, even after allowing for the importance of redemptive history to the Bible and taking into account the particular genre of historical writing in the Bible, still insist on the presence of irreducible error in its text. In a great debate of the last century, H. P. Smith drew attention to the highly visible contradictions in the parallel accounts of Samuel-Kings and Chronicles.[27] As a matter of fact, each case but one which Smith cites has distinct textual problems connected with it, and can be resolved.[28] It must be stressed, however, that unless Evangelicals seek to clear the Scripture from such reproach, their position is meaningless, for it would imply that belief in infallibility would not be affected by errors in Scripture. It will not do to greet every discrepancy with a retreat to the autographs, safely out of range of all criticism. No doubt a good number of them may well be due to transcriptional slips and mistakes. Numbers are especially

25. See Guthrie, 3 vols.; see also Paul Feine and Johannes Behm, *Introduction to the New Testament,* edited by Werner G. Kummel, 14th ed.; A. Wikenhauser, *New Testament Introduction.*

26. On form criticism, see A. H. McNeile and C. S. C. Williams, *Introduction to the New Testament,* pp. 46-58; Robert H. Gundry. *The Use of the Old Testament in Matthew's Gospel,* pp. 189-93; D. Guthrie, vol. 1: *The Gospels and Acts,* pp. 178-211; and B. Gerhardsson, *Memory and Manuscript.*

27. H. P. Smith, *Inspiration and Inerrancy,* pp. 124-25.

28. See J. O. Buswell, Jr., *A Systematic Theology of the Christian Religion,* pp. 210-11.

vulnerable to corruption in the course of transmission.[29] But we owe it to friend and foe alike to attempt some theory as to how and why these slips occurred so that their confidence in Scripture will not be shaken. The difficulties, if we are to contend they are apparent and not real, must be grappled with seriously.[30] Admittedly, these minor imperfections in the text do not obscure the message of Scripture. But unless we wish to blame God for man's mistakes, we have an obligation to try to show that these discrepancies are not original errors. For his part, Warfield was right to fall back upon the doctrine of inspiration in refusing to admit Smith's difficulties were surd errors.[31] But we must contest the notion that we have no responsibility to vindicate Scripture in a study of the phenomena themselves. A hypothesis which is compatible with anything and everything means nothing. The difficulties in Scripture *matter* to Evangelicals, and it is our duty to cope with them.[32]

Curiously, while demanding the right to treat the Bible like any other book, negative critics frequently treat it like no other book, bathing it in the acid solution of their historical skepticism. Neither Conzelmann (in the Lietzmann *Handbuch* series) or Haenchen (in the Meyer *Kommentar*) give much credit to Luke's historical acumen in Acts, despite the impressive conversion of both William Ramsay and Adolf Harnack to its substantial integrity. If one's predisposition is skeptical enough, no quantity of facts will sway his opinion![33] In Acts 5:36-37, Conzelmann and Haenchen discover a historical error committed by Luke in the chronological order of Theudas and Judas. Josephus dates a Theudas in A.D. 45, a

29. John W. Haley, *An Examination of the Alleged Discrepancies of the Bible*, pp. 380-92.

30. Young has sought to do this in *Thy Word Is Truth.*

31. B. B. Warfield, *The Inspiration and Authority of the Bible*, p. 220; *Limited Inspiration.*

32. In this connection, see Arndt's two books and Haley, pp. 312-436.

33. A. N. Sherwin-White is astounded at such pessimism, and contends that excellent results are realized in Roman history on data far less impressive historically than the New Testament which he regards highly. See his *Roman Society and Law in the New Testament.*

a full decade after Gamaliel's speech in Acts. Luke's mistake was double: incorrect order and a gross anachronism. There is certainly no reason to treat Luke so cavalierly. His record is a good deal better than Josephus', and it is entirely possible he is referring to another Theudas otherwise unknown to us.

Evangelicals have no ground for complacency in historical studies. John Bright has remarked that no full-length, serious history of Old Testament times has come from an evangelical pen in recent times.[34] Assurance regarding infallibility should not breed complacency, and does not absolve us from the responsibility of digging deeply and evaluating critically genuine historical materials. Indeed, the prospects for writing one are excellent. The older evolutionary approach to Hebrew history has been discredited by the new archeological evidence. The time is past when the work in this field can go on in oblivion to truly objective data.

> In a *New York Times* review of *The Bible as History* by Werner Keller, Glueck stated that he had spent many years in biblical archeology, and in association with his colleagues had made discoveries confirming in outline or in detail historical statements in the Bible. He was consequently prepared to go on record as stating that no archeological discovery has ever been made that contradicts or controverts historical statements in Scripture.[35]

Harrison goes on to cite Orlinsky:

> More and more the older view that the Biblical data were suspect and even likely to be false, unless corroborated by extra-biblical facts, is giving way to one which holds that, by and large, the Biblical accounts are more likely to be true than false, unless clear-cut evidence from sources outside the Bible demonstrates the reverse.[36]

Most accusations to the effect that the Bible is in error are due to a vast oversimplification. More often than not the

34. John Bright, *Early Israel in Recent Historical Writing*, p. 27.
35. R. K. Harrison, *Introduction to the Old Testament*, p. 94.
36. Ibid., p. 532.

charges result from a Western ignorance of ancient Near-Eastern life rather than from an error in reality. In his work on Hebrew chronology, Thiele has clearly shown that the Old Testament historians were very concerned to be accurate in their work and that, in fact, the precision they achieved is amazing as compared with comparable ancient sources.[37]

MORAL BLEMISHES

To the sensitive reader there are actions and attitudes recorded in Scripture which at first glance shock and even outrage his moral conscience. The recounting of wicked deeds is not the problem, for it testifies to the sinful condition of mankind. The difficulty concerns cases of cruelty apparently sanctioned, and even commanded, by God, and postures of hatred and vengeance toward one's enemies by some biblical writers. Many adopt some principle of "accommodation" or "progressive revelation" in order to clear God's character, as though Israel wrongly attributed to Him certain of her own sinful emotions.[38] Such a notion is but a hermeneutical sleight of hand which, though piously clearing God of any blame, asserts that Scripture, His Word, errs in its teaching, as if it were but the record of man's groping after God. An Evangelical can have no part of a theory to clear God's name which does it by smearing the integrity of Scripture! "All those writings of long ago were written for our instruction" (Ro 15:4, Berkeley). If negative critics are outraged by these teachings of the Bible, we are outraged by the audacity which moves them to sit in judgment upon God's Word. Christ set aside nothing in Scripture, and neither should we. There is no place for the expurgating eye. Scripture will not permit modern sentimentality to become its yardstick and inquisitor.[39]

37. Ibid., p. 474.
38. C. H. Dodd, *The Authority of the Bible,* p. 13; R. Abba, *The Nature and Authority of the Bible,* p. 248.
39. See Engelder, *The Scripture Cannot Be Broken,* pp. 226-33; H. E. Guillebaud, *Some Moral Difficulties of the Bible.*

The practice of *herem* in the Old Testament is usually singled out as an example of cruelty ordered by God. This was the holy war conducted by the Israelites at God's command for the extermination of the ancient Canaanites (Deu 20:16-18; Jos 6:17). Certain factors mitigate the harshness of the act—the cruelty of ancient peoples, the actual limitation on the extent of the massacre, the close identification of God and people in Semitic religion—but the fact remains the same, that *herem* was definitely and repeatedly ascribed to the will of the Lord. H. O. J. Brown remarks,

> In the century of extermination camps, atomic and nuclear weapons, and intercontinental rockets, we are hardly in a position to reprove the ancient Israelites for wiping out some of their enemies.[40]

Christian people have approved of the killing in this century of many times the number of their foes in Germany, Japan and Vietnam than were killed by the Israelites, in the absence of any command from the Lord! We cannot allow either that the Old Testament errs in this matter or that the New Testament contradicts it. The two relevant facts for a solution are the fact of judgment in the New Testament and of Canaanite depravity in the Old. The New Testament simply will not be pitted against the Old. If the character of God is compatible with His excluding sinners eternally from Himself (Mt 25:46), it would be petty to suggest that the temporal punishment of sinners in the Old Testament was intolerable. We do not consider the consciences of modern liberals a better guide to absolute morality than the words of Scripture. The religious culture of Canaan during the second millennium B.C. was, by any reckoning, polluted, corrupt and perverted. The Lord punished that culture for its iniquity (Lev 18:24-30; Gen 15:16). It was a display of His holiness and indignation against sin and sinners. It will happen again (2 Th 1:6-10). Only grace prevents it from happening now (Lk 13:1-5). Judgment is indeed God's "strange work" (Is

40. H. O. J. Brown, *The Protest of a Troubled Protestant*, p. 233.

28:21), but its certainty is the teaching of the whole Scripture (Ro 2:5). Grace and wrath are teachings of both Testaments.[41] Gracious sayings and hard words are to be found on every strata and by every author of Scripture. "Any serious critic must recognize that a theory of biblical authority is purely arbitrary that affirms gracious sayings as Word of God and rejects hard sayings as human weakness."[42]

For many, the psalms of imprecation have caused a similar difficulty (Ps 55, 59, 69, 79, 109, 137). And there are expressions of similar force in the New Testament (2 Ti 4:14), especially in Revelation (6:10; 18:20).[43] In them is detected a sub-Christian spirit of revenge and vindictiveness contrary to Jesus' teachings (Mt 5:43-48). This judgment is far too superficial. Jesus Himself promised that God will vindicate His elect who cry unto Him day and night (Lk 18:7). These prayers represent an outcry against those who are truly reprobate, the seed of unrighteousness "ripe for destruction" (Ro 9:22, Williams). They are addressed against the public enemies of God, the foes of justice and truth. Such righteous indignation against sin and evil may well indicate the moral *superiority* of the psalmists to our own relativistic, languid generation. At least they were not guilty of reducing wickedness to a neurosis. Lacking a clear teaching on retribution after death, the Old Testament writers viewed this life to be the principal stage on which ethical imbalances are to be corrected. And Paul himself employed the language of imprecatory psalms to indict the enemies of God whose sin rendered them liable to the eschatological wrath of God (Ro 3:10-18). These utterances are proleptic of the fate of all the godless when the final reckoning comes (Ps 2:4-9; Rev 19:11-21; 20:11-15). The central point is clear: whatever allowance we make for Semitic hyperbole and the agonized cries of

41. See Edwyn Bevan, *Symbolism and Belief*, pp. 188-89.
42. E. E. Ellis, "The Authority of Scripture: Critical Judgments in Biblical Perspective," *Evangelical Quarterly* 39 (1967): 197.
43. See R. L. Thomas, "The Imprecatory Prayers of the Apocalypse," *Bibliotheca Sacra* 126 (1969): 123-31.

those in sore distress, God's holy anger rightly rests on those who obey not the truth (Jn 3:36; Ro 1:18-19). Biblical imprecations are to be understood in terms of God's ultimate vindication of His people. As Job said, "I know that my Vindicator [*go'el*] lives" (19:25). The prayers reflect a proper abhorrence of sin, the leaving of judgment in God's hands, a concern for the glory of God, and an anticipation of divine judgment.[44] It will not help at all to invoke progressive revelation, for if these expressions are due to human vindictiveness, all we have in Scripture is the account of a moral crudity. Inspiration requires that we take the Bible much more seriously than that.

But is there not, it might be asked, a reversal and contradiction of the Old Testament ethic respecting marriage in the teaching of Jesus? Christ Himself declared a point of Mosaic legislation outdated and then rescinded it (Deu 24:1-4; Mt 19:8). However, the situation is not quite one of reversal and contradiction, for Jesus appealed to the prior creation ordinance, and viewed the Mosaic command as divine permission for a time of a lower standard.[45] After all, even Deuteronomy 24:1-4 itself does not explicitly sanction divorce, but seeks to proscribe even greater moral outrages stemming from it.[46] God allowed polygamy for a time, but "from the beginning it was not so." But, what God once tolerated, He no longer permits. Furthermore, polygamy in the Old Testament was nothing like promiscuity today. Each wife a man took was his *wife,* and his was the obligation to care for and to maintain her and her children. The notion that further revelation *contradicts* and *corrects* earlier revelation is a confusing and mistaken assumption. Revelation is a

44. See J. Barton Payne, *The Theology of the Older Testament,* pp. 197-204. For articles on the imprecatory psalms, see *Westminster Journal of Theology* 4 (1942) and *Princeton Theological Review* 1 (1903). Guillebaud, pp. 156-68.

45. Christ was no biblical critic. He did not oppose biblical teachings, but perverted interpretations and misapplications of them. See N. B. Stonehouse, *The Witness of Matthew and Mark to Christ,* pp. 188-225.

46. J. Murray, *Divorce,* pp. 3-16.

cumulative, organic disclosure of God to men in history; it is progressive and unfolding, but it is *not* self- contradictory.

SCIENTIFIC MISTAKES

Even after one allows for the peculiar *Weltbild* of Scripture wherein the world is described from the standpoint of an ancient Hebrew observer on the earth, there are assertions in Scripture which conflict unavoidably with much current opinion. The presence of miracle in Scripture, for example, offends the naturalistic and existential mood of our day. To the not-quite modern men of Newtonian physics, miracles appear to violate immutable natural laws, and cannot be considered factual. In reality, however, what are called "natural laws" are empirical constructs based upon experiment and testimony. These constructs describe what has been observed to have taken place; they do not legislate what may or may not happen! Whether a miracle happened is a question of history, not philosophy. No one can dogmatically say "Miracles do not occur"; for how could he know, except by revelation? On Hume's basis, the Lilliputians should have refused to acknowledge Gulliver's existence because *their* universal experience was against it! Biblical miracles occur in the context of the great miracle, the incarnation and the resurrection of Jesus Christ. They function in this context as part of God's total discourse. The credibility of that miracle, based upon the historical testimony of eyewitnesses, is very high. Science which denies the possibility of miracle is bad science because it is closed to the implications of truly relevant data. Belief in "the uniformity of natural causes in a closed system" is blind faith, and Christians are justified in rejecting it.[47]

Belief in the existence of demons, an almost universal conviction shared by our Lord (Mk 1:25; Lk 11:20), is now held by naturalistic psychology to be erroneous and superstitious. The dogmatic insistence that man has no unseen neighbors, certainly no *superior* ones, is an illustration of humanistic

47. Cf. a major work by H. van der Loos, *The Miracles of Jesus.*

pride. Denial of demons and angels is prejudice, not science. For a considerable body of evidence exists which points to their reality.[48] The phenomena of the occult cannot be so easily dismissed. They have metaphysical implications. Observations have been made which refuse to be explained by science as we know it (according to H. H. Price, J. B. Rhine, S. G. Soal), which means such a criticism of Scripture cannot be made.[49] Current prejudice against our unseen neighbors is not based upon any scientific discoverey but rather upon a vague climate of opinion which persists despite the lack of any substantial reason to think that man is the highest intelligent life there is. Even apart from biblical revelation, and on a naturalistic standpoint, there is no reason to scoff at the idea that there are creatures which transcend man in the hierarchy of being.

The doctrine of creation is the point of biblical teaching around which most of the warfare between religion and science has raged. No doubt both scientists and theologians have often spoken rashly or prematurely. The theologian has been guilty of faulty exegesis or overexegesis, and the scientist of leaping to conclusions far ahead of the evidence. However, the danger today is that theologians will abandon the facticity of creation altogether, in order to placate the dogmas of the "church-scientific," to which the realm of nature is thought exclusively to belong. Most modern theologians have eagerly dropped belief in a historical creation out of nothing and a historical fall of man into sin, and clambered aboard the neo-Darwinian bandwagon. We must warn against this foolhardy tactic. Enormous issues are involved in the doctrine of creation and fall. New Testament soteriology is poised upon the truth of the Genesis narratives (Ro 5:12-

48. John L. Nevius, *Demon Possession and Allied Themes;* Kurt Koch, *Christian Counselling and Occultism* and *Between Christ and Satan;* J. S. Wright, *Man in the Process of Time,* pp. 123-37; Merrill F. Unger, *Biblical Demonology.*

49. See C. W. K. Mundle, "ESP Phenomena, Philosophical Implications of," *Encyclopedia of Philosophy* 3:49-58.

21).[50] Hermeneutics collapses if Genesis 1-3 does not describe what had happened historically. The mythology of modern scientism contends that the biblical teaching is beset with insoluble problems. However, it must be said strongly that naturalistic evolution itself is full of unanswered questions and has come under heavy criticism of late.[51] When distinguished biologist W. R. Thompson was invited to supply the introduction to the Everyman edition of Darwin's *Origin of Species* in 1956, he was extremely hesitant to accept the invitation because he doubted the value of its effects on scientific and public thinking. He took the opportunity of that introduction to subject the theory of evolution to a withering, critical appraisal. He refers to its "elusive" character, its implausible arguments, its serious omissions, and its deleterious effects. The success of Darwin's theory was accompanied by a decline of scientific integrity, he said, its motives primarily theophobic and antireligious, and its popularity chiefly due to its importance to the humanistic liturgy![52] C. S. Lewis and R. J. Rushdoony hold that the theory of evolution as it is popularly believed today is a cultural myth, not a scientific statement at all.[53] Resistance to evolution, contrary to popular opinion, has not been the preserve to fundamentalism, though it has performed a valuable service in this regard. G. A. Kerkut, in the International Series of Monographs in Pure and Applied Biology, has set forth seven assumptions which lie at the basis of evolutionary theory and are incapable of experimental verification.[54] He wrote his book out of the frustration he felt from students who were *unable* to free their minds

50. Belief in evolution has led a Catholic theologian to reject the doctrine of the fall and original sin. See Herbert Haag, *Is Original Sin in Scripture?* Granted, he is opposed by Rahner and Scheffczyk who maintain the historicity of Adam, but Haag represents a growing number of Catholic progressives.

51. John C. Greene, *Darwin and the Modern World View;* A. E. Wilder Smith, *Man's Origin, Man's Destiny.*

52. W. R. Thompson, *Introduction to The Origin of Species,* by Charles Darwin, Everyman Library No. 811. See R. E. D. Clark, *Darwin: Before and After.*

53. C. S. Lewis, "The Funeral of a Great Myth," *Christian Reflections,* pp. 82-93; R. J. Rushdoony, *The Mythology of Science.*

54. G. A. Kerkut, *Implications of Evolution.*

from the dogma of scientism and look at the question objectively. When he would assign an essay to assess the evidence for and against evolution, his students could never find any problems with it. Kerkut did not write (nor did Thompson) because he was a biblical creationist. Honesty simply required that he distinguish science from science-fiction, and speculation from legitimate theory. There is *no* evidence for biogenesis. It is a matter of faith on the part of the evolutionary biologist that it occurred. The relative appearance chronologically of the animal stocks and their relation to one another have not been factually established. Kerkut objects to the arrogance of scientists who speak as if they got their theories by revelation! Evolution is a working hypothesis, not a proven theory. Its security will be decided by future experimentation, not by propaganda.

Christians must not be intellectually intimidated by the church scientific, that humanist-scientist complex which pretends to know everything there is. We should be bold to say that Scripture accounts for the existence of the world by a special creation of God, and that to believe as modern men do, that the spacio-temporal order can account for its own existence on the basis of chance, is *absurd,* contrary to all man has ever experienced. Liberalism has committed a gross tactical error in surrendering the doctrine of creation and aligning itself with irrational, man-centered thought. The notion that the universe can be accounted for by materialistic determinism and blind chance requires a faith far greater than any the Bible requires. To reject the Genesis account on scientific grounds is prejudice. Evolution is the theory which results from extrapolating backward in time, assuming a "uniformity of natural causes in a closed system." But, if there was, for example, a creation 50,000 years ago, it would still be possible to extrapolate back millions of years, because we stand *within* creation. For wherever we start, that which is created will seem to have existed before! This is simply to say that the date and manner of creation are, in principle, hidden from us. Denial of the Genesis picture of origins is philosophical, not scientific.[55]

Most of the difficulty would vanish if (1) the scientists would admit to the difficulties inherent to the evolutionary cosmogeny and recognize the danger of confusing evolution as religious philosophy with evolution as a possible biological hypothesis to explain certain phenomena; and (2) the theologians would acknowledge the importance of science as a fact-gathering and generalizing activity which can serve Scripture well, much like archeology as a meaningful commentary upon the text. Scripture and science are not on the same plane; the former is a divinely given language revelation, and the latter an empirical investigation of the natural world. Yet, there is a meaningful interplay between them. Science can function ministerially for the Christian and illuminate for him the requirements of the biblical text.

Particular questions aside, a principle of considerable importance is at stake. We cannot allow that any subject is biblically irrelevant just because it happens to fall within the field of the profane sciences. The authority and competence of Scripture is self-determined and not artificially restricted. The matters taught by Scripture refuse to be banished to an "existential" beyond from which they can pose no threat to science or be disturbed by it. The fear of making faith in any way vulnerable to criticism is a characteristic of dialectical theology. But, for historic Christianity, all that Scripture teaches is significant; and where the teaching penetrates into a realm treated by some branch of science, it is proper to expect validation from that quarter.

Conclusion

No one wishes to deny that certain difficulties face the believer in plenary inspiration. However, these are not as numerous, as novel, or as recalcitrant, as our theological critics

55. *Man's Origin, Man's Destiny* by Wilder Smith is to the author's mind a most helpful book written on this subject.

seek for some reason to make out. The supposedly "incontrovertible" evidence for biblical errors is, upon careful scrutiny, not that at all. Without wishing to minimize any of them, we regard none as insuperable, and the whole collection of difficulties as unable to shake the strong basis for the verbal inspiration of Scripture. We are open to all facts and threatened by none; but, as Evangelicals, we are still unconvinced that the evidence has yet been fairly set forth which undermines belief in the total trustworthiness of the Bible.

6

SACRED HERMENEUTICS

Every verbal utterance and every written document invites, even demands, interpretation. Hermeneutics is the art of understanding or interpretation. The need for principles of interpretation increases in proportion to the distance which the text is in time and culture from our own. A gap is to be bridged, and obstacles to understanding removed. Reading the daily paper requires little conscious reflection on hermeneutics because the literary genre and material are familiar. But if the content is strange and the literary genre unfamiliar, spontaneous understanding is hindered, and attention must be given to hermeneutics. A document should be interpreted according to the kind of text it is. A dictionary is determined by the alphabet and may be read in any order; a novel is structured around a plot development and should be read from the beginning. Because Scripture is capable of being twisted and mishandled (2 Pe 3:15-16; 2 Co 2:17), it is imperative to observe rules of a sound hermeneutic. A loose hermeneutic can destroy the meaning of inspiration altogether, and may be a cloak for a denial of biblical teachings. An orthodox stand on Scripture profits not at all if the truth of Scripture is short-circuited by perverse interpretation (e.g., Jehovah's Witnesses).

Part One: Traditional Hermeneutics

The interpretation of Scripture is a stewardship which we have from God. It is a part of the "ministry of the word" (Ac 6:4). After His resurrection, Christ "interpreted" the Scriptures to the apostles in reference to Himself as Messiah (Lk 24:27). We are to "cut a straight line" down the word of truth (2 Ti 2:15). Hermeneutics is the science of correctly interpreting God's Word, of observing principles whereby the Scriptures are devoutly and profoundly read. It is a process of meaning-extraction, of bringing out the sense of the Bible by means of principles Scripture itself supplies. The task is never done, for God always has yet more light and truth to give from His Holy Word. Our hermeneutic is never exhaustive and never infallible. It can always be enlarged with new insight and improved by sharper insight. Just because we listen to Scripture from a different setting in time and space from our fathers, our perspective is unique and we notice things not seen before. As Berkouwer has taught us, "listening, unlike remembering, is always a thing of the present moment."[1] Thus we would be "hearers" of God's Word, charged with the interpretation and proclamation of this message among all nations. This involves determining exactly what the biblical text means to say (exegesis), assessing the results of exegetical study in the light of the whole Bible (theology), and directing the message to men's lives for correction and instruction (application). We wish to discuss five of the most important hermeneutical principles.[2]

INSPIRATION IS BASIC TO HERMENEUTICS

The most important thing about the New Testament writers' attitude to the Old was simply that they trusted and believed it *all* as God's written Word. Consequently, they took the historical material seriously, accepted its doctrine as proof for their own, perceived a divine unity pervading the whole, and in every way subjected themselves to its authority. The preunderstanding proper to our hermeneutics is belief in the divine authorship of Scripture. Our interpretive method will

1. G. C. Berkouwer, *Faith and Justification*, p. 9.
2. See Bernard Ramm, *Protestant Biblical Interpretation;* A. Berkeley Mickelsen, *Interpreting the Bible;* M. S. Terry, *Biblical Hermeneutics;* L. Berkhof, *Principles of Biblical Interpretation;* M. C. Blackman, *Biblical Interpretation;* James D. Smart, *The Interpretation of Scripture.*

reflect what we consider the Bible to be. Where it is regarded as merely a human document, the interpretations will be shaped accordingly. But when we approach Scripture as Christ did, in an attitude of total trust in all that it teaches, a sound hermeneutic results. We strive to discern the truth of each particular scripture in the light of the whole Scripture, regardless of what extrabiblical fact or idea may be bearing upon the text. Divine authorship implies complete reliability and assures us the Bible will not ultimately contradict itself.

> Extra-biblical linguistic and cultural considerations must be employed ministerially, never magisterially, in the interpretation of a text; and any use of extra-biblical material to arrive at an interpretation inconsistent with the veracity of the scriptural passage is to be regarded as magisterial and therefore illegitimate. Extra-biblical data can and should put questions to the text, but only Scripture itself can in the last analysis legitimately answer questions about itself.[3]

The decision about the nature of Scripture ought to be made before interpretation even begins. The conviction that the Bible is God's written Word, having its origin in the divine acting and speaking, and cast into writing by inspiration, cannot but revolutionize our entire approach.

THE LITERAL SENSE

The *sensus literalis* is the backbone of Reformation hermeneutics. Scripture is to be read in its natural sense and proper context. We are to ascertain what the writer wished to say by interpreting his words according to the customary, socially accepted meaning of those words.[4] To abandon this principle of literal interpretation is to forsake all serious exegesis. Christian theology rests on what the biblical writers meant to teach, not on what some interpreter might wish to imagine they meant. What we have left when we leave the literal sense is generally non-sense. Luther confessed,

3. John W. Montgomery, *Ecumenicity, Evangelicals, and Rome,* p. 92.
4. Ramm, p. 90.

> When I was a monk, I was an expert in allegories. I allegorised everything.[5]
>
> Since that time when I began to embrace the historical meaning I have always abhorred allegories and have not used them unless either the text itself exhibited them or [allegorical] interpretations could be cited from the New Testament.[6]

The literal sense is the starting point for all further reflection, and the only check against willful tampering with truth. All nonliteral methods of interpretation, whether the Alexandrian allegorical or the Bultmannian demythologizing approach, suppress or deny the actual teachings of Scripture. They transform events and doctrines into myths and symbols, and thus escape and evade the meaning of Scripture. What is needed is careful historical-grammatical exegesis for extracting the meaning out of the text. Nonliteral methods of interpretation have been responsible for countless perversions of biblical truth. Luther rejected the theory of a *multiplex intelligentia* because he saw that the idea of Scripture having many senses implied it had no certain sense, and the door was open for the suppression of truth. For God's Word lies not behind or above or apart from the text, but in the text itself.

Needless to say, the literal sense does not commit anyone to a literalistic interpretation. The two are frequently confused, sometimes deliberately. The idea is that the orthodox view of Scripture leads to proof-texting and an atomistic, piecemeal approach whereby passages are wrested from their contexts and quoted at random.[7] This charge is a deliberate distortion. The high view of Scripture makes us *more,* not less, careful to ascertain the actual meaning of a text in context. In fact, there is evidence to suggest that it is the low view of the Bible which leads to a sidestepping of biblical teaching. How often we hear an appeal to what the "whole

5. Martin Luther, *The Table Talk of Martin Luther,* 1:136.
6. Luther, *D. Martin Luthers Werke,* 42:173.
7. See Harry Emerson Fosdick, *Modern Use of the Bible,* pp. 10, 27.

Bible says" or what "the Hebrew view of man" is, which is, in fact, a subterfuge for bypassing the doctrine of an actual text! The "biblical concept of love" is supposed to cancel the specific texts on judgment and hell, and "the deepest strains of biblical teaching" to expunge the actual evidence of vicarious atonement. The liberal appeal to the mysterious *Schriftganze* (totality of Scripture) is very convenient, for it permits one to silence actual biblical teaching on the strength of a standpoint not explicitly sanctioned by Scripture. The idea of "the whole Scripture" is a subterfuge to substitute what the text actually says with what the interpreter wants it to say. Scripure proof is the proper method of theology, and proof texts are perfectly acceptable if they do in fact prove the point in question. Engelder remarks,

> We can understand what "the whole of Scripture" or "Scripture as a whole" means, but we cannot understand what "the whole of Scripture" as put into opposition to the component parts of Scripture means.[8]

It would be like claiming, "Nature teaches the earth is flat, only the facts deny it!" Denial of the literal sense of the text itself is an attack on Scripture as a whole. In this we simply remind ourselves that it is the text of Scripture we are expounding, not our own thoughts. We must not surrender the Bible to interpreters who would make it say whatever they will. The Bible is our critic and master; and we are its servants and hearers.

THE UNITY OF SCRIPTURE

The unity of Scripture follows from the fact that God is the principal Author of it, and implies that the meaning of the parts agrees with the meaning of the whole, so that one passage sheds light upon another (*analogia Scripturae*). The Bible is not simply a collection of assorted religious writings from many periods; it is a single book with a single Author,

8. T. Engelder, *The Scripture Cannot Be Broken*, p. 351.

a perfect unity growing out of its integrating theme, Jesus Christ. "The testimony of Jesus is the spirit of prophecy" (Rev 19:10).

Because it comes from one divine Author, Scripture is its own interpreter.[9] This means that one passage illumines the sense of another. Such is the Reformation's hermeneutical circle.

> The infallible rule of interpretation of Scripture, is the Scripture itself; and therefore, when there is a question about the true and full sense of any Scripture (which is not manifold, but one), it may be searched and known by other places that speak more clearly.[10]

Scripture is in agreement with itself. God who is eternal truth does not contradict Himself.[11] Only Scripture has the right to tell us the true meaning of a difficult passage. Neither the inspired magisterium of Rome nor the existential insight of a modern interpreter has any right to determine for us what the Bible says.

In Marcion and Bultmann we have an unchristian reduction of the Old Testament and a breaking up of the unity of Scripture. Both were radical Paulinists, and insisted on seeing only law and not gospel in the Old Testament. There is a radical discontinuity between the Testaments. The use made of the Old Testament in the New, however, makes it impossible to cut the bond between them. In Origen and Barth (and especially Vischer) we see a slurring over of the differences, and a Christian inflation of the Old Testament. This overaffirmation of unity has led to exegesis and a revival of fanciful typology. What is needed is the recognition of the progressive-revelation process in Scripture, and its completion in the Christ event. In this way the original sense of the text is respected and the unity of the whole recognized.

9. *Scriptura sacra sui ipsius interpres* (Holy Scripture is its own interpreter).
10. Westminster Confession 1. 9.
11. Formula of Concord SD 11. 35.

Theological unity is not theological uniformity. But all the diverse strands of teaching weave together in testimony to Christ.

CUMULATIVE REVELATION

The phrase *progressive revelation* is tainted by its frequent use to describe the evolution of biblical religion from primitive stages to advanced forms. It is based upon a naturalistic theory of the origins of biblical faith, that Procrustean bed onto which liberals have made redemption history to rest. The term leaves the distinct impression that the later ideas in Scripture contradict the earlier, which is a flat denial of divine inspiration. Even James Orr comes close to this:

> Revelation has to take man as it finds him, with his crude conceptions, his childlike modes of thought and expression, his defective moral ideas and social institutions and has to make the best of him it can.[12]

However, Orr stops short of accusing the Old Testament of fallibility in its teachings, and holds to progressive revelation without false teaching.

The term *cumulative revelation* is better. It signifies the *teleological* direction of revelation with the emphasis on the building up of the total truth picture. That which is patent in the New Testament lies latent in the Old. The revelation increases from dimness to pure light. It was not complete all at once, but moved toward ever clearer expression. Because revelation was given gradually in chronological progression, Scripture needs to be read with regard for the place each passage occupies in the revelation process.

The climax of cumulative revelation was the appearance of Jesus Christ. He is the divine amen to all that went before (2 Co 1:20). He stands at the summit of a series of divine disclosures through word and deed (Heb 1:1-2), the antitype

12. James Orr, *Revelation and Inspiration*, p. 103. See pp. 101-8; 175-79.

of every type and the reality of every shadow (Heb 10:1). All the promises are fulfilled in Him. Cumulative revelation does not mean a repudiation of the word of promise, but its fulfillment. Christ is the focus and true unity of all divine revelation. Holy Scripture is Christocentric (Jn 5:39; Lk 24:27; 2 Ti 3:15). Unhappily, even this grand principle is capable of being abused. It is often employed wrongly to warrant the rejection of a portion of Scripture. Kantzer provides a corrective:

> Jesus Christ becomes *not a critical principle* to divide between the acceptable and the unacceptable, but a *hermeneutical principle* to enable us to understand fully and adequately what is the true meaning of Scripture.[13]

The mode of revelation which is *Christ* does not contradict the mode of revelation that is *Scripture!*

THE ILLUMINATION OF THE SPIRIT

As the Author of Scripture, the Spirit is its best Interpreter, and He assists our interpretation in a special sense. Philological and exegetical research is not rendered useless by His operation, for it is in the heart of the interpreter himself that He works, creating that inner receptivity by which the Word of God is really "heard." All of us are prone to disbelieve and misconstrue divine matters until a new heart is placed within us (1 Co 2:14). An unbeliever can comprehend the letter of Scripture, but is not inclined to commit himself to the appropriation of its truth for his life until the Spirit creates a new disposition within, rendering the Word of God effective in men's lives (2 Co 3:14-18). Before conversion, the natural man "sees many things, but does not observe them; his ears are open, but he does not hear" (Is 42:20, RSV; cf. Jer 5:21) As Luther said, "Whosoever does not understand the subject matter of Scripture [Christ], cannot elicit the mean-

13. Kenneth S. Kantzer, "The Communication of Revelation," in *The Bible; Living Word of Revelation*, p. 77.

ing of the words."[14] To which the Westminster Confession 1.6 adds,

> Nevertheless we acknowledge the inward illumination of the Spirit of God to be necessary for the saving understanding of such things as are revealed in the Word.

Our subjective disposition does affect the results of our exegesis. Unless we are in fellowship with the living Christ, the "penny does not drop," and the Scriptures are confusing. The objective, divine revelation is accompanied by a subjective divine Revealer; the Word *and* the Spirit, a duality not to be disregarded. The Spirit *speaks* in Scripture. He is responsible for *two* miracles in regard to it: the miracle of inspiration by which revelation was infallibly recorded, and the miracle of illumination by which the book is understood and believed. The Protestant principle of authority is that a divine objective revelation (the external principle) is accompanied by an interior divine witness (the internal principle.)[15]

> There are, therefore, left before the conversion of man two efficient causes only, that is to say, the Holy Spirit and the Word of God, which is the instrument of the Holy Spirit whereby he effects the conversion of man.[16]

We have the written testimony (1 Jn 5:13) and the inner witness (v. 7), and they are not to be divorced. To appeal to the Spirit apart from Scripture is sub-Christian fanaticism; to appeal to Scripture apart from a humble dependence on the Spirit is presumption. The Spirit gives us a mind to see and hear His Word (cf. Deu 29:4). Liberalism is a form of sub-Christian mysticism which likes to conflate inspiration and illumination in order to make revelation an immanent,

14. Qui non intelligit res, non potest ex verbis sensum elicere." (He who does not understand the subject matter is unable to discover the meaning of the words.) Gadamer uses this citation to justify his existential hermeneutical circle. Luther may not be used in this way, however.
15. Ramm, *Pattern of Authority*, p. 29.
16. *Formula of Concord*, 2:9.

evolving entity, so that liberal ideas themselves may be effectively canonized.[17]

Despite the abuse of this term, there is a real sense in which the Bible does "become" the Word of God for us when the Spirit makes its message personally effective. Truth available (revelation past: Scripture) becomes truth personal (revelation present: experience) through His ministry. But, Scripture *becomes* the Word of God *for us* because it *is* the Word of God *in itself*. The Spirit takes the text, infallible and true, and prepares our hearts to receive its message. It is the recipients, and not the Word, which need to be criticized and corrected! Hearts must be prepared for the reception of divine truth. The vision is sealed because men *will* not see (Is 29:11). Our prayer must always be: "Open my eyes, that I may contemplate the wonders of Thy law" (Ps 119:18, Berkeley).

Part Two: The New Hermeneutic

Traditional hermeneutics sought to extract the meaning from Scripture by careful exegesis in accord with the original writer's intention. The New Hermeneutic is quite a different ball game with another set of rules.[18] It is an *existential* hermeneutic, an effort at this level to carry forward the anti-metaphysical program of liberal theology. Like pietism, which it resembles more than superficially, it seeks to lead us to the real questions of personal faith. (Christians have always been concerned to make the Bible relevant, so the "New" Hermeneutic is not new in that sense.) The novelty

17. In the case of the biblical writers, we may assume that inspiration and illumination usually coincided, but not always (see 1 Pe 1:10-12).

18. J. M. Robinson and J. B. Cobb, eds., *The New Hermeneutic;* C. Braaten, *History and Hermeneutics;* R. W. Funk, *Language, Hermeneutics, and Word of God;* G. Ebelıng, "Hermeneutik," *Religion in Geschichte und Gegenwart,* 3d ed., 3:242-62; E. Fuchs, *Hermeneutik,* 2d ed.; C. E. Braaten, "How New Is the New Hermeneutic?" *Theology Today* 22 (1965): 218-35; Paul J. Achtermeier, "How Adequate Is the New Hermeneutic?" *Theology Today* 23 (1966): 101-19; R. T. Osborn, "A New Hermeneutic?" *Interpretation* 20 (1966): 400-11; R. G. Alexander, "On the Language of the New Hermeneuticians." *Lutheran Quarterly* 20 (1968): 52-60; Achtemeier, *An Introduction to the New Hermeneutic.*

of this approach, and our objection to it, resides in the *manner* in which the text is handled, often in direct contradiction to its plain and intended sense. The approach is obsessed with the anthropological question: How does this text help me to relate myself to my own being? How is man's existence understood in this passage?

There are elements in the Bible which people today find strange and unfamiliar. It is important that we ask how Scripture is relevant to us. Hermeneutics is the attempt to grapple with this problem. Karl Barth insisted that the exegesis of Scripture was influenced by the theological presuppositions of the interpreter. An unbreakable hermeneutical circle joins text and reader. R. Bultmann hailed this discovery. The text and our self-understanding interact with one another.[19] Objective exegesis is impossible. What was formerly regarded as a *danger* in interpretation—the fusing of our mental concepts with the text of Scripture—is now hailed as a virtue and a discovery! The subject-object distinction is almost dissolved. This idea of involvement with the text goes back to Schleiermacher, for whom exegesis requires an intuitive grasp of the text, which is, after all, an expression of the writer's experience. By means of a sort of psychological hermeneutic, the attempt is made to reproduce the original experience today.[20]

Bultmann's program is rather well known. The Bible presupposes a mythical world view which contradicts our understanding of things and must be rejected.[21] Modern science will not permit us to think of miracles, the fall, judgment and resurrection. We must set aside this mythical world view if

19. Bultmann, "Ist voraussetzungslose Exegese möglich?" (Is exegesis possible without presuppositions?) *Theologische Zeitschrift* 13 (1957): 409-17.

20. In theology as in science it is perilous to disregargd the subject-object distinction. When the sinful interpreter and his milieu are at liberty to determine what the teaching of Scripture is, revelation data is bent in that direction, and the Bible can no longer function as rule and standard.

21. Bultmann, "The New Testament and Mythology," in *Kerygma and Myth*, ed. H. W. Bartsch, 1:1-44. On Bultmann's hermeneutic, see especially Walter Schmithals, *An Introduction to the Theology of Rudolf Bultmann*, chap. 10.

the *kerygma* is to be credible today. This is not to say the text is to be discarded, however. It stands in need of *existential reinterpretation.* Myth alone, he contends, could express for men of that day, the vision of reality they experienced. Myth is rejected as literal fact, but embraced as the *poetic* vehicle of the "transcendence" inherent in the gospel. Biblical myths are to be interpreted anthropologically, not cosmically.[22] Bultmann seeks, by use of Heidegger's categories, to translate the meaning of the Bible into the idiom of modern man.

The preunderstanding (*Vorverständis*) Bultmann adopts is a curious mixture of deistic, existential and gnostic elements: deistic in its antipathy to the miraculous, existential in its fundamental view of truth as personal, and gnostic in its portrayal of redemptive history as only accessible to the eye of enlightened faith. It is a preunderstanding which leads directly to serious exegetical crimes against Scripture. His attitude toward miracles belongs to nineteenth century positivism, and his view of truth and objectivity to existential philosophy. If he would subject his own preunderstanding to Scripture, he would discover how foreign to the gospel it is. Marriage to the spirit of any age will leave one a widow in the next! Barth has vigorously and wisely protested this existentialist conquest of the gospel, which Bultmann is in danger of dekerygmatizing.[23] We may not reduce the resurrection, for example, to a subjective event. Barth cannot, however, carry through his criticism effectively because he, too, shares the existential assumptions of Bultmann regarding objective history and cognitive faith. Thus when Bultmann asks for evidence to justify belief in the facticity of the resurrection,[24] Barth cannot provide it because, for him, revelatory acts in history are not historically verifiable.[25] Cullmann, however,

22. Ibid., p. 10.
23. Karl Barth, *Church Dogmatics,* vol. 3, pt. 2, pp. 536-37.
24. Bultmann, *Glauben und Verstehen,* 2:234-35.
25. Barth, *The Doctrine of the Word of God,* p. 188; and "Rudolf Bultmann—An Attempt to Understand Him," in *Kerygma and Myth,* 1:83-132.

is less squeamish and seeks to support Barth's position exegetically. For him, revelation takes place in real, historical events. Bultmann (and, to that extent, Barth also) errs in making the gospel a subjective affair. Salvation depends upon historical facts.[26] The setting of the gospel in space and time is essential to it.

For Bultmann, however, the prescientific mythology, including the temporal framework of redemption in history, must be stripped away by a process called "demythologizing," so that the "religious intent" of the text may remain. It is a search for the Word behind the words, a kind of "psychoanalysis" of Scripture. In place of the antiquated ballast of the mythical world view, the gospel must be remythologized in contemporary categories.[27] What was once widely regarded as a heresy of the deepest dye (the denial of biblical teachings) is now presented as a spiritual responsibility no minister dare disregard. Three strong criticisms are in order:

1. The program of Bultmann and the New Hermeneutic is essentially *pietistic*. It is concerned exclusively with personal involvement in the text, with *my* existence and *my* self-understanding. The actual message of Scripture is sacrificed to what modern man can experience today. It attempts to zero in on the "real" subject matter of the New Testament, and determine what the basic *experience* was which the writers sought to express in such an antiquated apparatus. Scripture becomes an existential springboard, and hermeneutics the search for a text that "inspires" me. Factual and doctrinal statements are reduced to existential ones. The verb "to understand" is repeatedly used without a direct object in gnostic manner. This is a pietistic, anthropological conquest of the gospel.[28]

26. Oscar Cullmann, *Christ and Time*, 3d ed., pp. 32, 38, etc.

27. See Bultmann, *Jesus Christ and Mythology*. Roman Catholic theology faces the same challenge in regard to Scripture *and* dogma. The same repugnance of propositional truth appears in the form of the dehellenization of dogma. Bernard Lonergan subjects Dewart to searching criticism in "The Dehellenization of Dogma," in *New Theology No. 5*, pp. 156-77.

28. H. M. Kuitert brings this out most clearly in *The Reality of Faith*, pp. 39-83.

2. The dependence of Bultmann's program on an alien (to the New Testament) philosophy is a serious liability. The deliberate similarity of his theology to the philosophy of the early Heidegger is well known.[29] It seems highly arbitrary to us for Bultmann to select a philosophy which few understand and fewer follow as the critical principle for editing the New Testament. No doubt it is possible to force some biblical teaching into this mold; but in view of the extensive demolition carried out throughout the whole extent of biblical and doctrinal teaching, we wonder whether it is the best mold after all. It is certainly surprising how both Bultmann and McLuhan can speak for "modern man," and disagree violently in their view of what man is! We really have no right to kidnap the terminology and ideology of the Bible and turn it into a fanciful version of existential philosophy.[30] This is a crime against language. To take "resurrection," which has reference to the glorification of Jesus' body, and psychologically reinterpret it in terms of the "new freedom" the disciples felt, and then not to admit that one has made an important change, is intellectually dishonest. The dishonesty is compounded with absurdity when men are asked to believe in a "resurrection" which never happened and to study a text full of prescientific crudities. It is no accident that the theological program which was launched for the purpose of making Christianity intelligible to modern man has failed to do so, and those who talk most about clarity and understanding complain most about being misunderstood![31]

3. The existential approach to the New Testament is diametrically opposed to its explicit message. No Evangelical

29. See John Macquarrie, *An Existentialist Theology*.

30. To employ the thought of a secular philosopher who stands in the flux of the human situation to interpret the Word of God which comes from beyond it is deeply ironical. McLuhan and Heidegger need the guidance of Scripture more than it needs them!

31. See Cleon L. Rogers, "Modern Theology and Modern Man," *Bibliotheca Sacra* 126 (1969): 53-69. Braaten remarks: "And my own opinion is that the development cannot proceed further along the Fuchs-Ebeling line, if for no other reasons than that Fuchs lacks clarity (no one understands him) and Ebeling lacks substance (the objective *content* of faith is reduced to a bare minimum)" *Theology Today* 22 (1965): 220.

would deny that preaching the gospel in the modern world is a challenging, exacting task, nor that it is our duty to make the gospel as relevant as we can. But this program is less a preaching of the gospel than a *denial* of it. The New Testament writers sought to record sober history (Lk 1:1-4) and revealed truth (Gal 1:12; 1 Jn 1:1-3) concerning the Christ event, the birth, death, resurrection and ascension of God's only Son in time and space. They opposed the category of *myth* as pagan. Stahlin writes, "The firm rejection of myth is one of decisions characteristic of the New Testament."[32] It simply will not do to reject the historicity of these events and the truthfulness of these teachings and still go on calling one's theology Christian. Bultmann refuses to believe the matters the New Testament emphasizes and puts all the weight on aspects of its thought which are secondary. His pietistic concerns cause him to push God's saving activity into the background. The biblical spokesmen reflected on *Christ*, not on their own experiences. They resisted all attempts to reduce His reality to a faith apparition. We must respect the true intentionality of the biblical accounts. We may believe it is wrong, but we may *not* distort what the New Testament is trying to say. The Christ event took place outside of us (*extra nos*) for our sakes (*pro nobis*). The existential dimension is the *result* of the factual, and depends on it. To evaluate the resurrection as an objectification of the experience of the disciples is not to interpret the New Testament seriously, but deny its claim. The astonishing thing is why, if the modern world view requires Bultmann to demythologize the incarnation, it does not compel him to demythologize the Godhead too. After all, God Himself is the largest element of the supernatural in the Bible! It would be more "authentic" for Bultmann to proclaim the death of God than to occupy this halfway house.[33]

32. *TDNT*, 4:793. See Mickelsen, pp. 71-73.
33. Milton D. Hunnex, *Existentialism and Christian Belief*, pp. 35-51.

The New Hermeneutic operates on the basis of Bultmann's program and is an insidious *enemy* of genuine biblical interpretation. Creation, fall, incarnation, atonement, resurrection and *parousia* are *all* discarded after being reinterpreted because they are judged prescientific. Everything offensive to modern man is stripped away. This is the *antithesis* of traditional hermeneutics! For what the biblical writers intended to say (the goal of traditional hermeneutics) is dismissed from the outset by this neoallegorical, neopietistic approach! Honest, painstaking exegesis is discarded. The text can mean whatever one wishes. Preus has noted,

> When one has abandoned the high doctrine of the infallibility of Scripture and no longer believes Scripture to be reliable in its claims and assertions, then the quest for the genuine, literal sense of Scripture, is no longer so important. For if there are errors in Scripture, then the interpreter will wish somehow to avoid the implications of the literal sense of Scripture and find a "new" meaning which will be more congenial to his world view or more "relevant" to his day.[34]

Bultmann is guilty of two hermeneutical sins: he denies the meaning Scripture gives, and imposes meanings on Scripture which are external to itself. The *intent* of the text is secondary to the *needs* of the interpreter. The Bible no longer rules us; we rule it!

The story of the Bultmannian movement is a sad chapter in the chaotic history of modern theology. At the very time when the gospel should be presented forcefully in opposition to secular mythology, it is emasculated and mutilated by its friends.[35] In the past, Christians have always managed to

34. Robert Preus, "Biblical Hermeneutics and the Lutheran Church Today," in *Crisis in Lutheran Theology*, p. 110. There is one view of the New Testament worse than Bultmann's in which the writers were well meaning, though mistaken: it is that of *Tendenzkritik*, the view that holds that the writers consciously manipulated the facts to "help" the readers. They deceived the people for their own good! They were deceived and deceivers.

35. Tillich also holds that the New Testament is relative to its historical situation, and its message is constructed mythologically. Tillich wants to make it explicit that myth is the dramatic, symbolic expression of transcendent reality. His position is no less radical with regard to literal biblical truth. *Systematic Theology*, 1:6-7.

excuse their failure to preach the gospel in one way or another, but not until now have they had a full-blown theology which would condone their sinful omission. Here is a theology calculated to keep a conscience easy which ought to be troubled. The popular thing to do is to conform the gospel to the world's philosophy, rather than the difficult task of converting the world to Christ. Evangelical Christians believe there is a war on between God's truth and man's apostate ideas. We refuse to admit modern man has successfully banished God from his world, and intend to continue to preach the unaltered biblical gospel as the only antidote to modern pessimism and hopelessness.

We have devoted considerable space to a discussion of the demythologizing program because it is the foundation and starting point of the New Hermeneutic. Bultmann's intent was hermeneutical, to assist men in understanding the gospel aright.[36] The aim of the New Hermeneutic is to comprehend the movement of the "word" from the text to the contemporary hearer. The unique emphasis lies in the theory of language adopted. Language itself is an interpretation! It represents man's attempt to put into words his encounter with reality. The text is a performative word which illumines man's real situation and serves to evoke faith. Language is an acoustical event. Dilthey comments,

> In language alone does what is inside man find its complete, exhaustive and objectively intelligible expression. Hence the art of understanding has its center in the interpretation of the remains of human existence contained in writing.[37]

As for the later Heidegger, man is the loudspeaker for the silent tolling of being, the hermeneut of the gods, so the biblical text serves as the word-event spoken by faith, and

36. E. M. Good, "The Meaning of Demythologization," in *The Theology of Rudolf Bultmann*, pp. 21-40.
37. Cited in *The New Hermeneutic*, p. 21.

capable of affecting our lives. The text is the precipitate of a vision of reality religiously conceived!

Fuchs and Ebeling have taken a step beyond Bultmann in the direction of an even more radically existential interpretation. For Bultmann, the text still remained the object to be reinterpreted; but for Fuchs the text is in motion! The text addresses and interprets us.[38] It stands in dynamic, existential relation with its interpreter, and may be interpreted in the opposite way from that which the writer intended (*contra versionem explicatam*). The "word" is a flash of lightning that strikes, according to Gadamer. The text serves to create the same opening in us as was once created in the author of it. The text represents a self-interpretation by early Christians in response to ecstatic revelation which, it is hoped, may be reproduced in us today. What the practitioners of the New Hermeneutic seek from the New Testament is not the *work* Christ *did* for our redemption, but the *faith* He *had* in "being as gracious."[39] Christ becomes a pious appellation of a quality of human experience, says Braun. The New Hermeneutic is a *linguistic mysticism*. Faith arises in an encounter with words.

It is by no means clear why, considering all its liabilities, the existential theologians do not cut loose from the text altogether and philosophize freely. Their pietistic hermeneutics has to do with a psychological event the *text* sets in motion. But need it? The new hermeneuts possess the reality they seek before they approach the text itself. All the text does is to name an existential event long ago. There is no need to be bound to it. Pietism generally ends up discarding Scripture as the necessary creative source of faith.[40] The New Hermeneutic admits that the New Testament text contains

38. E. Fuchs, *Hermeneutik*, p. 13.
39. Ebeling, *Theologie und Verkündigung*, p. 90.
40. Kuitert, pp. 81-82. Certainly Schleiermacher objected strenuously to the idea that the Bible alone mediated God's Word. The intuition of the infinite is the ultimate theological norm, and the Bible authoritative only as it conforms to this. It is not uniquely inspired, nor the only source of divine revelation. For Tillich the "word of God" is *any* reality by means of which the eternal breaks with unconditioned power into our lives.

largely misleading teachings. Surely there must be another language deposit that could bring us to understanding more efficiently than this. The same may be said about Jesus. No doubt His certainty even in the face of death was admirable, even inspiring. Yet, if His resurrection can be confessed as an expression of our faith without its having to be historical, surely Christ can be named as "witness" to faith without His needing to have existed. Christ and Scripture bear a somewhat accidental relation to the Christian faith, and can be dispensed with easily. H. Braun freely admits that the *only* historical fact of which we have certainty is that there once existed a community that confessed Jesus as the Christ. Everything else is a mythological construction scooped out of the hellenistic world. Indeed, what the New Hermeneutic needs more than text or Christ is the Roman Catholic Church! For, as Raymond S. Brown observes, when the interpreter is flying high in existential encounters, he needs a hermeneutical *place* to land. If the meaning of the Bible is always modified by the historical context of the present-day reader, that reader had better be in the right place; and only an infallible church can guarantee for him what the contemporary meaning of Scripture ought to be![41] Otherwise, there is no way to distinguish a Christian interpretation from a nonchristian one. The Evangelical is caught in no such dilemma because he has a perspicuous, inerrant and noncontradictory Bible.

The Christian faith is solidly grounded in supernatural reality, in divine revelation in word and event. The existential theology contends that God does not act in ordinary history, but in the "history" (*Geschichte*) of our own "personhood." Thus it reroutes the entire Christian message in an anthropological, mystical direction. However, it is biblically and logically inadmissible to attempt to retain the joyful self-understanding the early Christians experienced while at the

41. Raymond S. Brown, "Hermeneutics," *Jerome Bible Commentary*, vols. 1-2. For the new-shape Roman Catholic theologian, doctrine can be mutable and truth-in-motion because the church is infallible. See G. Baum, *Faith and Doctrine: A Contemporary View*.

same time repudiating the substance of the good news they believed. The only reason they had this inspiring faith was because they believed what they did. We can fly across the oceans because airplanes exist. If they no longer existed, our confidence in being able to fly would melt. These theological supermen think themselves able to fly to the heights of Christian experience when the historical wings of the gospel have been crushed (mostly by their own historical skepticism). Instead, they will but tumble into the bottomless abyss of subjectivity and solipsism.

CONCLUSION

"It is better," writes Athanasius, "to incur the blame of redundancy than to omit anything which ought to have been written."[1] In our study of aspects of the doctrine of inspiration, we have seen that the issue here runs very deep. The battle for the plenary inspiration of the Bible is part of the larger struggle for authentic biblical religion. To cast doubt on the complete veracity and authority of Scripture is a criminal act creating a crisis of immense proportions for theology and faith. The cost of losing the battle for the Bible is the loss of all theology and truth. Everything stands in question. Packer remarks,

> The fact is that here we are faced in principle with a choice between two versions of Christianity. It is a choice between historic Evangelicalism and modern Subjectivism; between a Christianity that is consistent with itself, and one that is not; in effect, between one that is wholly God-given and one that is partly man-made.[2]

We will not admit that the debate over plenary inspiration is an insignificant and out-of-date squabble. It is a matter of life and death. In the last analysis, there are only two alternatives: either we put the Bible above all else, or we put something above the Bible. To scrap the authority of Scripture is to corrupt the gospel and pervert it with human doctrine. If the church allows her truth base to slip away, she will embark upon a quest for certainty which will never succeed, and will become, not "the pillar and ground of the truth," but a debating society for the discussion of ideas. Modern preaching has lost its ring of authority because the key to the divine mysteries has been lost. The solution lies in a return to the

1. *Athanasius, De Incarn.* 20.3.
2. J. I. Packer, *'Fundamentalism' and the Word of God,* p. 170.

pattern of divine revelation and its primary product, infallible Scripture.

Sadly, many of the evangelical streams from the Reformation are at this moment forsaking their mighty biblical commitments. Instead of loyalty to the Word of God, theologians dally with unbiblical speculations and reveal a reverence to expressions of modern unbelief that approaches idolatry. Robert Preus observes,

> There is today in our Church as much as anywhere a fawning, almost servile attitude toward what is called scholarship and a reluctance, even fear, of questioning the "assured results" of what is called modern scholarship and going against the stream. . . . We seem incapable of distinguishing facts from hypotheses and interpretations; and we are timid (if not altogether silent) in exposing the clay feet, the sub-Christian presuppositions, of much modern Biblical scholarship. . . . Twenty years ago when I was a seminarian the kindest compliment you could pay a theologian was to call him either pious or orthodox; now we praise him by calling him scholarly. Now we know that scholarship is a gift of God. But we also know that scholars have been wrong again and again. Scripture is a gift of God, too, and Scripture has never been wrong.[3]

A revival of life in the church must be accompanied by a reformation of truth. The loss of biblical authority is the cause of the doubt and uncertainty which plague the modern church. Faith as walking in the light of God's promises has been replaced by the empty existential leap. No longer is the Bible the touchstone of truth, but itself stands in need of one. The move toward mystical subjectivism will result in the demise of authentic Christianity. Jesus Christ has located for us the Word of God in the Holy Scripture. God's truth does not need to be improved or corrected. A revival of true religion will not take place until God's people acknowledge His holy Word.

3. Robert Preus, "Biblical Hermeneutics and the Lutheran Church Today," in *Crisis in Lutheran Theology,* 2:118.

The infallible Word is the golden grail of all philosophical thought because it affords a perspective upon life and history which originates beyond the flux of human situation. It is, therefore, the clue to the meaning of life and reality, the only sure antidote to the rootlessness of modern man cut off from his transcendent ground. The relevance of Scripture extends far beyond the narrow concerns of the church, and speaks effectively to a sick culture which has lost its way. It testifies to the Lord of heaven and earth, and directs our feet on the path to the eternal city. We ought to close on a less abstract, more practical, note. No doubt the credentials of biblical inspiration are so high that it will be forever impossible for unbelief to destroy faith in it. Yet Scripture speaks to us with a demand that we heed and obey God's Word. Scriptural truth is to shape our minds, correct our judgments, and direct our paths. John emphasizes the *doing* of the truth. Lip service to the ideas of the Bible is not enough if its truth does not grip us and change our lives.

The Bible is an authority which rightfully and worthily commands our obedience and loyalty. It alone has final, normative power over us because it is the inspired record of the revelation of God in Christ. The proper response to legitimate authority imposed upon us by God is humble and joyful obedience. We stand in defense of something which is infinitely precious. If ever an age needed a sure Word from God, it is our own. There is a critical lack of perspective on man's life and upon human history. People are searching for a place to stand. The Christian faith knows of a God who has invaded our world in the person of Jesus Christ and has left us a Word of truth and transforming power. The Bible possesses the most extraordinary relevance for the twentieth century. But every low view of its inspiration ends up robbing us of that Word and leaving behind a mere approximation of it. Out of the great silence of eternity the Lord has spoken:

> The grass withers, the flower fades; but the word of God shall stand for ever! (Is 40:8, Berkeley).

BIBLIOGRAPHY

Aalders, G. C. *The Problem of the Book of Jonah.* London: Tyndale, 1948.

———. *A Short Introduction to the Pentateuch.* London: Tyndale, 1949.

Abba, Raymond. *The Nature and Authority of the Bible.* London: Clarke, 1958.

Achtemeier, Paul J. *An Introduction to the New Hermeneutic.* Philadelphia: Westminster, 1969.

———. "How Adequate Is the New Hermeneutic?" *Theology Today* 23 (1966): 101-19.

Ahlstrom, Sydney E. "Theology in America." In *The Shaping of American Religion,* ed. James Ward Smith and A. Leland Jamison. Vol 1. Princeton, N.J.: Princeton U., 1961.

Alexander, R. G. "On the Language of the New Hermeneuticians." *Lutheran Quarterly* 20 (1968): 52-60.

Allis, O. T. *The Five Books of Moses.* Philadelphia: Presbyterian & Reformed, 1943.

Althaus, Paul. *Fact and Faith in the Kerygma of Today.* Philadelphia: Muhlenberg, 1960.

Altizer, Thomas J. J. and Montgomery, John W. *The Altizer-Montgomery Dialogue.* Chicago: Inter-Varsity, 1968.

Archer, G. L. *A Survey of Old Testament Introduction.* Chicago: Moody, 1964.

Arndt, W. *Does the Bible Contradict Itself?* St. Louis: Concordia: 1926.

———. *Bible Difficulties.* St. Louis: Concordia, 1932.

Babbage, Stuart Barton. *The Mark of Cain.* Grand Rapids: Eerdmans, 1962.

Baillie, John. *The Idea of Revelation in Recent Thought.* New York: Columbia U., 1956.

Baillie, John and Martin, H., eds. *Revelation.* New York: Macmillan, 1927.
Barr, J. "Revelation Through History in the OT and in Modern Theology." *Princeton Seminary Bulletin* 56 (May 1963): 4-14.
Barth, Karl. *Against the Stream.* London: SCM, 1954.
———. *Church Dogmatics.* 12 vols. Edinburgh: T. & T. Clark, 1956-62.
———. *The Doctrine of the Word of God.* Edinburgh: T. & T. Clark, 1936.
———. "Rudolf Bultmann—An Attempt to Understand Him." In *Kerygma and Myth,* ed. H. W. Bartsch. London: SPCK, 1960.
———. *The Word of God and the Word of Man.* Boston: Pilgrim, 1928.
Baum, G. *Faith and Doctrine: A Contemporary View.* Baltimore: Newman, 1969.
Bavinck, Herman. *Gereformeerde Dogmatiek.* Kampen: Bos, 1895-1901.
Bea, A. *De Inspiratione et Inerrantia Sacrae Scripturae.* Rome: Pontifical Biblical Institute, 1954.
Beegle, D. M. *The Inspiration of Scripture.* Philadelphia: Westminster, 1963.
Benz, Ernst. *The Eastern Orthodox Church.* New York: Doubleday, 1963.
Berger, Peter. *Rumor of Angels.* New York: Doubleday, 1969.
Berkhof, L. *Principles of Biblical Interpretation.* Grand Rapids: Baker, 1950.
Berkouwer, G. C. *Faith and Justification.* Grand Rapids: Eerdmans, 1954.
———. *De Heilige Schrift.* 2 vols. Kampen: Kok, 1967.
Bevan, Edwyn. *Symbolism and Belief.* London: Allen & Unwin, 1938.
Blackman, M. C. *Biblical Interpretation.* Philadelphia: Westminster, 1957.
Bochenski, I. M. *Contemporary European Philosophy.* Los Angeles: U. California, 1957.
Bohlmann, Ralph A. *Principles of Biblical Interpretation in the Lutheran Confessions.* St. Louis: Concordia: 1968.
Bornkamm, Günther. "The Theology of Rudolf Bultmann." In *The Theology of Rudolf Bultmann,* ed. C. W. Kegley. New York: Harper, 1966.

Bornkamm, H. *Luther and the Old Testament.* Philadelphia: Fortress, 1969.

Braaten, Carl E. *History and Hermeneutics.* Philadelphia: Westminster, 1966.

———. "How New Is the New Hermeneutic?" *Theology Today* 22 (1965): 218-35.

Bratsiotis, P. "An Orthodox Contribution." In *Biblical Authority for Today,* ed. A. Richardson and W. Schweitzer. Philadelphia: Westminster, 1951.

Bright, John. *Early Israel in Recent Historical Writing.* London: SCM, 1956.

Bromiley, G. W. "The '1967 Confession' and Karl Barth." *Christianity Today* (Mar. 4, 1966).

———. "The Church Doctrine of Inspiration." In *Revelation and the Bible,* ed. Carl F. H. Henry. Grand Rapids: Baker, 1958.

Brown, H. O. J. *The Protest of a Troubled Protestant.* New Rochelle, N.Y.: Arlington, 1969.

Brown, Raymond S. "Hermeneutics." *Jerome Bible Commentary.* Vols. 1-2. Englewood Cliffs, N.J.: Prentice-Hall, 1968.

Brown, Robert McAfee. "Secular Ecumenism: The Direction of the Future." In *The Religious Situation 1969,* ed. Donald R. Cutler. Boston: Beacon, 1969.

Bruce, F. F. *Are the New Testament Documents Reliable?* Grand Rapids: Eerdmans, 1965.

Brunner, H. *The Christian Doctrine of God.* Philadelphia: Westminster, 1950.

———. *Divine-Human Encounter.* Philadelphia: Westminster, 1943.

———. *The Mediator.* Philadelphia: Westminster, 1957.

———. *Revelation and Reason.* Philadelphia: Westminster, 1946.

———. *The Word and the World.* London: SCM, 1931.

Bryant, Robert H. *The Bible's Authority Today.* Minneapolis: Augsburg, 1968.

Bultmann, Rudolf. *Existence and Faith.* Ed. S. M. Ogden. London: Hodder, 1961.

———. *Glauben und Verstehen.* Tübingen: Mohr, 1933-52.

———. "Ist voraussetzungslose Exegese moglich?" *Theologische Zeitschrift* 13 (1957): 409-17.

———. *Jesus Christ and Mythology.* New York: Scribner, 1958.

———. "The New Testament and Mythology." *Kerygma and Myth,* ed. H. W. Bartsch. London, SPCK, 1960.

Burnaby, John. *In What Sense Is the Bible Inspired?* London: SPCK, 1960.

Burrows, Millar. *An Outline of Biblical Theology.* Philadelphia: Westminster, 1946.

Burtchaell, James T. *Catholic Theories of Biblical Interpretation Since 1810.* Cambridge: U. Press, 1969.

Buswell, J. O., Jr. *A Systematic Theology of the Christian Religion.* Grand Rapids: Zondervan, 1962.

Buttrick, George A. *The Christian Faith and Modern Doubt.* New York: Scribner, 1935.

Cadoux, C. J. *The Case for Evangelical Modernism.* New York: Willett, Clark, 1939.

Calvin, John. *Commentaries on the Catholic Epistles.* Grand Rapids: Eerdmans, 1948.

———. *Commentaries on the Epistles to Timothy, Titus, and Philemon.* Grand Rapids: Eerdmans, 1948.

———. *Institutes.* Philadelphia: Presbyterian Board of Christian Education, 1852.

Campbell, C. A. *On Selfhood and Godhead.* New York: Macmillan, 1957.

Carnell, E. J. *The Case for Orthodox Theology.* Philadelphia: Westminster, 1959.

———. *Philosophy of the Christian Religion.* Grand Rapids: Eerdmans, 1954.

Cassuto, U. *The Documentary Hypothesis.* Jerusalem: Magnes, 1961.

Chang, Lit-sen. *Zen-Existentialism, The Spiritual Decline of the West.* Philadelphia: Presbyterian & Reformed, 1969.

Clark, Gordon, H. *Religion, Reason, and Revelation.* Philadelphia: Presbyterian & Reformed, 1961.

———. et al. *Can I Trust My Bible?* Chicago: Moody, 1963.

Clark, R. E. D. *Darwin: Before and After.* London: Paternoster, 1948.

Cleobury. F. H. *Christian Rationalism and Philosophical Analysis.* London: Clarke, 1959.

Cobb, John B. Book review of E. J. Carnell's *Case for Orthodox Theology. Interpretation* 14 (1960): 96.

Congar, Y. M.-J. *Tradition and Traditions.* London: Burns & Oastes, 1966.

Costello, C. J. *St. Augustine's Doctrine on the Inspiration and Canonicity of Scripture.* Washington, D. C.: Catholic U., 1930.

Cranmer, Thomas. *Works.* Vol. 1. Cambridge: U. Press, 1842.

Creed, J. M. *The Divinity of Jesus Christ.* London: CUP, 1938.

Cullmann, Oscar. *Christ and Time.* 3d ed. Philadelphia: Westminster, 1964.

———. *The Early Church.* London: SCM, 1956.

———. *Salvation in History.* New York: Harper, 1967.

Cunningham, William. *The Reformers and the Theology of the Reformation.* 1862. London: Banner of Truth, 1967.

Custer, Stewart. *Does Inspiration Demand Inerrancy?* Nutley, N.J.: Craig, 1968.

Cutler, Donald R., ed. *The Religious Situation 1969.* Boston: Beacon, 1969.

Davies, R. E. *The Problem of Authority in the Continental Reformers.* London: Epworth, 1946.

Davies, W. D. *Christian Origins and Judaism.* London: Darton, Longman & Todd, 1962.

Decision of the Synod of 1961 of the Christian Reformed Church on Infallibility and Inspiration in the Light of Scripture and Our Creeds. Grand Rapids: Christian Reformed, 1961.

DeHoff, G. W. *Alleged Bible Contradictions Explained.* Grand Rapids: Baker, 1950.

Denzinger, Heinrich. *Sources of Catholic Dogma.* 30th ed. St. Louis: Herder, 1957.

deRosa, Peter. *Christ and Original Sin.* Milwaukee: Bruce, 1967.

Dewart, Leslie. *Future of Belief.* New York: Herder, 1966.

Dialog. 2 (1963): 307-13.

Dodd, C. H. *The Authority of the Bible.* New York: Harper, 1929.

Douglas, J. D., ed. *The New Bible Dictionary.* London: Inter-Varsity, 1962.

Downing, F. G. *Has Christianity a Revelation?* Philadelphia: Westminster, 1964.

Duchrow, U. "Die Klarheit der Schrift und die Vernunft." *Kerygma und Dogma* 15 (1969): 1-17.

Dulles, A. "Symbol, Myth, and the Biblical Revelation." In *New Theology No. 4,* ed. Martin E. Marty and Dean G. Peerman. New York: Macmillan, 1964.

Ebeling, G. "Hermeneutik." In *Religion in Geschichte und Gegenwart,* ed. Kurt Galling. 3d ed. Tübingen: 1957.

———. *Theologie und Verkündigung.* Tübingen: Mohr, 1962.

Edwards, Paul, ed. *Encyclopedia of Philosophy.* New York: Macmillan, 1967.

Edwards, Paul. "Professor Tillich's Confusions." *Mind* 74 (1965): 192-214.

Eissfeldt, Otto. *The Old Testament, An Introduction.* Oxford: Blackwell, 1965.

Ellis, E. E. "The Authority of Scripture: Critical Judgments in Biblical Perspective." *Evangelical Quarterly* 39 (1967): 196-204.

———. *Paul and His Recent Interpreters.* Grand Rapids: Eerdmans, 1961.

———. *Paul's Use of the Old Testament.* London: Oliver & Boyd, 1957.

Engelder, T. *The Scripture Cannot Be Broken.* St. Louis: Concordia, 1944.

Erickson, Millard. *The New Evangelical Theology.* Westwood, N.J.: Revell, 1968.

Feine, Paul and Behm, Johannes. *Introduction to the New Testament.* Edited by Werner G. Kummel. 14th ed. Nashville: Abingdon, 1966.

Ferre, Frederick. *Basic Modern Philosophy of Religion.* New York: Scribner, 1967.

Ferre, Nels F. S. *The Christian Understanding of God.* New York: Harper, 1951.

———. *The Universal Word.* Philadelphia: Westminster, 1969.

Flew, A. and MacIntyre, A., eds. *New Essays in Philosophical Theology.* London: SCM, 1955.

Forsyth, P. T. *The Principle of Authority.* London: Independent, 1952.

Fosdick, Harry Emerson. *The Modern Use of the Bible.* New York: Macmillan, 1924.

———. *A Guide to Understanding the Bible.* New York: Harper, 1938.

Fuchs, E. "Hermeneutik." In *Religion in Geschichte und Gegenwart,* ed. Kurt Galling. 3d ed. Tübingen: Mohr, 1957.

———. *Hermeneutik.* 2d ed. Bad Cannstatt: Muellershoen, 1958.

Fuller, Daniel P. *Easter Faith and History.* Grand Rapids: Eerdmans, 1965.

———. "Warfield's View of Faith and History." *Journal of the Evangelical Theological Society* 11 (1968): 80-81.

Funk, R. W. *Language, Hermeneutics, and Word of God.* New York: Harper, 1966.

Gaussen, L. *Theopneustia.* 1840. Chicago: Moody, n.d.

Geisler, Norman L. and Nix, William E. *A General Introduction to the Bible.* Chicago: Moody, 1968.

Geldenhys, J. N. *Supreme Authority.* London: Marshall, Morgan & Scott, 1953.

Gerhardsson, B. *Memory and Manuscript.* Copenhagen: Christensen, 1964.

Gerstner, John H. *A Bible Inerrancy Primer.* Grand Rapids: Baker, 1965.

Gilkey, Langdon. *Naming the Whirlwind: The Renewal of God-Language.* Indianapolis: Bobbs-Merrill, 1969.

———. "Cosmology, Ontology, and the Travail of Biblical Language." *The Journal of Religion* 40 (1961): 197.

Gill, Jerry H. "Talk About Religious Talk." In *New Theology No. 4,* ed. Martin E. Marty and Dean G. Peerman. New York: Macmillan, 1964.

Gill, John. *Body of Divinity.* 1769. Atlanta: Lasseter, 1965.

Glicksberg, Charles I. *Modern Literature and the Death of God.* The Hague: Martinus Nijhoff, 1966.

Glock, C. Y. and Stark, R. *American Piety: The Nature of Religious Commitment.* Vol. 1. Berkeley: U. California, 1968.

Good, E. M. "The Meaning of Demythologization." In *The Theology of Rudolf Bultmann,* ed. C. W. Kegley. New York: Harper, 1966.

Gordon, C. H. "Higher Critics and Forbidden Fruit." *Christianity Today* (Nov. 23, 1959).

Graef, Hilda. *Modern Gloom and Christian Hope.* Chicago: Regnery, 1959.

Grant, F. C. *Introduction to New Testament Thought.* Nashville: Abingdon, 1950.

Grant, R. M. *The Bible in the Church.* New York: Macmillan, 1948.

Green, E. M. B. *Second Peter Reconsidered.* London: Tyndale, 1961.

Greene, John C. *Darwin and the Modern World View.* Baton Rouge: LSU, 1961.

Guillebaud, H. E. *Some Moral Difficulties of the Bible.* Chicago: Inter-Varisty, 1941.

Gundry, Robert H. *The Use of the Old Testament in Matthew's Gospel.* Leiden: Brill, 1967.

Guthrie, Donald. *New Testament Introduction.* Rev. ed. London: Tyndale, 1970. Vol. 1: The Gospels and Acts; Vol. 2: The Pauline Epistles; Vol. 3: Hebrews to Revelation.

Haag, Herbert. *Is Original Sin in Scripture?* New York: Sheed, 1969.

Haley, John W. *An Examination of the Alleged Discrepancies of the Bible.* 1874. Grand Rapids: Baker, 1958.

Hamilton, Kenneth. *The System and the Gospel.* London: SCM, 1963.

———. *Revolt Against Heaven.* Grand Rapids: Eerdmans, 1965.

Hanson, R. P. C. "The Enterprise of Emancipating Christian Belief from History." In *Vindications: Essays on the Historical Basis of Christianity,* ed. Anthony Hanson. New York: Morehouse-Barlow, 1966.

Harnack, A. *History of Dogma.* Vol. 7. London: Williams & Norgate, 1899.

———. "Fifteen Questions to Those Among the Theologians who are Contemptuous of the Scientific Theology." In *The Beginnings of Dialectical Theology,* ed. James M. Robinson. Richmond: Knox, 1968.

Harris, R. Laird. "How Reliable Is the Old Testament Text?" In *Can I Trust My Bible?,* ed. Howard F. Vos. Chicago: Moody, 1963.

———. *Inspiration and Canonicity of the Bible.* Grand Rapids: Zondervan, 1957.

Harrison, Everett F. "Criteria of Biblical Inerrancy." *Christianity Today* (Jan. 20, 1958).

———. "The Phenomena of Scripture." In *Revelation and the Bible,* ed. Carl F. H. Henry. Grand Rapids: Baker, 1958.

Harrison, R. K. *Introduction to the Old Testament.* Grand Rapids: Eerdmans, 1969.

Hebert, A. G. *The Authority of the Old Testament.* London: Faber, 1947.

Hedegard, David. *Ecumenism and the Bible.* London: Banner of Truth, 1964.

Henry, Carl F. H. *Frontiers in Modern Theology.* Chicago: Moody, 1964.

———. ed. *Jesus of Nazareth: Saviour and Lord.* Grand Rapids: Eerdmans, 1966.

———. *Revelation and the Bible.* Grand Rapids: Baker, 1958.

———. "Divine Revelation and the Bible." In *Inspiration and Interpretation,* ed. J. F. Walvoord. Grand Rapids: Eerdmans, 1957.

Hick, John, ed. *Faith and the Philosophers.* London: Macmillan, 1964.

———. *Philosophy of Religion.* Englewood Cliffs, N.J.: Prentice-Hall, 1963.

———. "Revelation." In *Encyclopedia of Philosophy,* Vol. 7. ed. Paul Edwards. New York: Macmillan, 1967.

Hodge, Charles. *Systematic Theology.* Vol. 1. London: Clarke, 1960.

Holmes, A. F. "Ordinary Language Analysis and Theological Method." *Journal of the Evangelical Theological Society* 11 (1968): 137-38.

Hordern, William. *A Layman's Guide to Protestant Theology.* New York: Macmillan, 1955.

Hughes, Philip E. *Theology of the English Reformers.* Grand Rapids: Eerdmans, 1965.

Hunnex, Milton D. *Existentialism and Christian Belief.* Chicago: Moody, 1969.

Jay, E. G. "The Church as the Locus and Medium of Revelation." *Canadian Journal of Theology* 11 (1965): 94-105.

Jenkins, D. *Tradition and Spirit.* London: Faber, 1951.

Jewett, P. K. *Brunner's Concept of Revelation.* London: Clarke, 1954.

Kantzer, Kenneth S. "The Authority of the Bible." In *The Word for This Century*, ed. Merrill C. Tenney. New York: Oxford U., 1960.

———. "Calvin and the Holy Scriptures." In *Inspiration and Interpretation*, ed. J. F. Walvoord. Grand Rapids: Eerdmans, 1957.

———. *Christ and Scripture. His* magazine offprint, n.d.

———. "The Christ-Revelation as Act and Interpretation." In *Jesus of Nazareth: Saviour and Lord*, ed. Carl F. H. Henry. Grand Rapids: Eerdmans, 1966.

———. "The Communication of Revelation." In *The Bible; Living Word of Revelation*, ed. Merrill C. Tenney. Grand Rapids: Zondervan, 1968.

Kaufman, G. D. *Relativism, Knowledge and Faith*. Chicago: U. Chicago, 1960.

———. *Systematic Theology: A Historicist Perspective*. New York: Scribner, 1968.

Kelly, J. N. D. *Early Christian Doctrines*. New York: Harper, 1958.

Kerkut, G. A. *Implications of Evolution*. London: Pergamon, 1960.

Kerr, David W. "Augustine of Hippo." In *Interpretation and Inspiration*, ed. J. F. Walvoord. Grand Rapids: Eerdmans, 1957.

Keylock, L. R. "The Bible Controversy in American Catholicism." *Christianity Today* (Mar. 1, 1963).

———. "Biblical Inspiration in Roman Catholic Thought Since 1870." Master's thesis, Wheaton College, Ill., 1964.

Killan, R. Allen. *The Ontological Theology of Paul Tillich*. Kampen: Kok, 1956.

Killinger, John. *The Failure of Theology in Modern Literature*. Nashville: Abingdon, 1963.

Kitchen, K. A. *Ancient Orient and Old Testament*. Chicago: Inter-Varsity, 1966.

Kittel, Gerhard, ed. *Theological Dictionary of the New Testament*. Trans. and ed. G. W. Bromiley. 7 vols. Grand Rapids: Eerdmans, 1964-71.

Klassen, William. "Anabaptist Hermeneutics: The Letter and the Spirit." *Mennonite Quarterly Review* 40 (1966): 83-96.

Kline, Meredith G. *Treaty of the Great King*. Grand Rapids: Eerdmans, 1963.

Knox, J. *Criticism and Faith.* New York: Abingdon, 1952.

Koch, Kurt. *Between Christ and Satan.* Grand Rapids: Kregel, n.d.

———. *Christian Counselling and Occultism.* Grand Rapids: Kregel, 1965.

Kraft, R. "Contributions of Jesus to a Modern Discussion of Inspiration." Master's thesis, Wheaton College, Ill., 1957.

Kuitert, H. M. *The Reality of Faith.* Grand Rapids: Eerdmans, 1968.

Kuyper, A. *Encyclopedia of Sacred Theology.* Vol. 3. New York: Scribner, 1898.

———. *Principles of Sacred Theology.* Grand Rapids: Eerdmans, 1963.

Kysar, Robert. "Toward a Christian Humanism." *Christian Century* (May 21, 1969).

Ladd, G. E. *The New Testament and Criticism.* Grand Rapids: Eerdmans, 1967.

Lake, Kirsop. *The Religion of Yesterday and Tomorrow.* Boston: Houghton, 1926.

Latimer, Hugh. *Works.* Vol. 1. Cambridge: U. Press, 1842.

Levie, J. *The Bible, Word of God in Words of Men.* London: Chapman, 1961.

Lewis, C. S. *Christian Reflections.* Grand Rapids: Eerdmans, 1967.

———. *A Grief Observed.* New York: Seabury, 1961.

———. *Mere Christianity.* London: Fontana, 1955.

———. *Surprised by Joy.* New York: Harcourt, Brace, 1956.

Lightner, Robert P. *Neo-Evangelicalism.* Des Plaines, Ill.: Regular Baptist, 1965.

———. *The Saviour and the Scriptures.* Philadelphia: Presbyterian & Reformed, 1966.

Litton, E. A. *Introduction to Dogmatic Theology.* London: Clarke, 1960.

Livingston, David P. "The Inerrancy of Scripture: A Critique of Dewey Beegle's Book, *The Inspiration of Scripture.*" Master's thesis, Trinity Evangelical Divinity School, Deerfield, Ill., 1969.

Lonergan, Bernard. "The Dehellenization of Dogma." In *New Theology No. 5*, ed. Martin E. Marty and Dean G. Peerman. New York: Macmillan, 1968.

Loos, H. van der. *The Miracles of Jesus.* Leiden: Brill, 1965.

Lumpkin, W. L. *Baptist Confessions of Faith.* Chicago: Judson, 1959.

Luther, Martin. *Bondage of the Will.* London: Clarke, 1957.

———. *D. Martin Luthers Werke.* Weimar: Böhlaus, 1914.

———. *The Table Talk of Martin Luther.* London: H. G. Bohn, 1857.

MacKenzie, R. A. F. *Faith and History in the Old Testament.* New York: Macmillan, 1963.

Macquarrie, John. *An Existentialist Theology.* London: SCM, 1955.

———. "How Is Theology Possible?" In *Studies in Christian Existentialism.* London: SCM, 1965.

———. *Principles of Christian Theology.* New York: Scribner, 1966.

———. *Scope of Demythologizing.* Gloucester, Mass.: Peter Smith, 1969.

Malcolm, Norman. *Ludwig Wittgenstein, A Memoir.* London: Oxford U., 1958.

Manley, G. T. *The Book of the Law.* Grand Rapids: Eerdmans, 1957.

Martin, C. B. "A Religious Way of Knowing." In *New Essays in Philosophical Theology,* ed. A. Flew and A. MacIntyre. London: SCM, 1955.

Marty, Martin E. "The American Situation in 1969." In *The Religious Situation 1969,* ed. Donald R. Cutler. Boston: Beacon, 1969.

Mascall, E. L. *Christian Theology and Natural Science.* London: Longmans, Green, 1956.

———. *Existence and Analogy.* Hamden, Conn.: Archon Books, 1967.

Masters, D. *The Rise of Evangelicalism.* Toronto: Evangelical Press, 1961.

Mavrodes, G. "The Inspiration of the Autographs." *Evangelical Quarterly* 41 (1969): 19-29.

McDonald, H. D. *Ideas of Revelation.* London: Macmillan, 1959.

———. *Theories of Revelation.* London: Allen & Unwin, 1963.

McKenzie, John L. *Myth and Realities: Studies in Biblical Theology.* Milwaukee: Bruce, 1963.

McNeile, A. H. and Williams, C. S. C. *Introduction to the New Testament.* Oxford: Clarendon, 1953.

Metzger, B. M. *The Text of the New Testament.* New York: Oxford, 1964.

Meyendorff, John. "The Meaning of Tradition." In *Scripture and Ecumenism,* ed. L. J. Swindler. Pittsburgh: Duquesne U., 1965.

Meyerhoff, H. *The Philosophy of History in Our Time.* New York: Doubleday, 1959.

Mickelsen, A. Berkeley. *Interpreting the Bible.* Grand Rapids: Eerdmans, 1963.

———. "Is the Text of the New Testament Reliable?" In *Can I Trust My Bible?,* ed. Howard F. Vos. Chicago: Moody, 1963.

Mill, J. A. "The Bible and Non-Inspired Sources." *Journal of the Evangelical Theological Society* 3 (1960): 78-81.

Montgomery, John W. *Chytraeus on Sacrifice.* St. Louis: Concordia, 1962.

———. "Clark's Philosophy of History." In *The Philosophy of Gordon H. Clark,* ed. Ronald H. Nash. Philadelphia: Presbyterian & Reformed, 1968.

———., ed. *Crisis in Lutheran Theology.* Vols. 1-2. Grand Rapids: Baker, 1967.

———. *Ecumenicity, Evangelicals, and Rome.* Grand Rapids: Zondervan, 1969.

———. *History and Christianity. His* magazine offprint, n.d.

———. "Inductive Inerrancy." *Christianity Today* (Mar. 3, 1967).

———. *The 'Is God Dead?' Controversy.* Grand Rapids: Zondervan, 1966.

———. "The Relevance of Scripture Today." In *The Living Word of Revelation,* ed. Merrill C. Tenney. Grand Rapids: Zondervan, 1968.

———. *The Shape of the Past.* Ann Arbor: Edwards, 1962.

———. "The Theologian's Craft: A Discussion of Theory Formation and Theory Testing in Theology." *Concordia Theological Monthly* 37 (1966): 67-98.

———. "Tillich's Philosophy of History." *Gordon Review* 10 (1967): 130-49.

———. *Where Is History Going?* Grand Rapids: Zondervan, 1969.

Morris, Leon. *The Apostolic Preaching of the Cross.* 3d ed. Grand Rapids: Eerdmans, 1965.

———. *The Cross in the New Testament.* Grand Rapids: Eerdmans, 1965.
Morrison, Frank. *Who Moved the Stone?* London: Faber & Faber, 1958.
Mueller, T. J. "Luther's Canon Within the Canon." *Christianity Today* (Oct. 27, 1961), pp. 179-80.
Mundle, C. W. K. "ESP Phenomena, Philosophical Implications of." In *Encyclopedia of Philosophy*, ed. Paul Edwards. New York: Macmillan, 1967.
Murray, John. *Calvin on Scripture and Divine Sovereignty.* Philadelphia: Presbyterian & Reformed, 1960.
———. *Divorce.* Philadelphia: Orthodox Presbyterian Church, 1961.
———. "The Attestation of Scripture." In *The Infallible Word*, ed. N. B. Stonehouse and P. Woolley. Grand Rapids: Eerdmans, 1946.
———. *Principles of Conduct.* Grand Rapids: Eerdmans, 1957.
Nash, R. H. *The New Evangelicalism.* Grand Rapids: Zondervan, 1963.
Navone, J. J. *History and Faith in the Thought of Alan Richardson.* London: SCM, 1966.
Nevius, John L. *Demon Possession and Allied Themes.* 1894. Grand Rapids: Kregel, 1968.
Niebuhr, H. R. *The Meaning of Revelation.* New York: Macmillan, 1946.
Nielsen, Kai. "Can Faith Validate God-Talk?" In *New Theology No. 1*, ed. Martin E. Marty and Dean G. Peerman. New York: Macmillan, 1964.
New Catholic Encyclopedia. New York: McGraw-Hill, 1967.
Oepke, Albrecht. "apokalupsis." In *Theological Dictionary of the New Testament*, ed. Gerhard Kittel. Trans. and ed. G. W. Bromiley. Grand Rapids: Eerdmans, 1964.
Ogden, Schubert. *Christ Without Myth.* New York: Harper, 1961.
Orr, J. *Progress of Dogma.* London: Clarke, 1901.
———. *Revelation and Inspiration.* Grand Rapids: Eerdmans, 1951.
Osborn, R. T. "A New Hermeneutic?" *Interpretation* 20 (1966): 400-11.

Otten, Herman. *Baal or God.* New Haven, Mo.: Leader, 1965.

Outler, Albert C. "Scripture, Tradition and Ecumenism." In *Scripture and Ecumenism,* ed. L. J. Swindler. Pittsburgh: Duquesne U., 1965.

Packer, J. I. *Evangelism and the Sovereignty of God.* London: Inter-Varsity, 1961.

———. *'Fundamentalism' and the Word of God.* London: Inter-Varsity, 1958.

———. *God Speaks to Man.* Philadelphia: Westminster, 1965.

———. "The Necessity of the Revealed Word." In *The Bible: The Living Word of Revelation,* ed. Merrill C. Tenney. Grand Rapids: Zondervan, 1968.

———. "Revelation." In *The New Bible Dictionary,* ed. J. D. Douglas. London: Inter-Varsity, 1962.

Pannenberg, W. *Jesus—God and Man.* Philadelphia: Westminster, 1968.

Paton, H. J. *The Modern Predicament.* New York: Macmillan, 1955.

Payne, J. Barton. "The Biblical Interpretation of Irenaeus." In *Inspiration and Interpretation,* ed. J. F. Walvoord. Grand Rapids: Eerdmans, 1957.

———. "Faith and History in the Old Testament." *Journal of the Evangelical Theological Society* 11 (1968): 111-20.

———. "Hermeneutics as a Cloak for the Denial of Scripture." *Journal of the Evangelical Society* 3 (1960): 93-100.

———. *The Theology of the Older Testament.* Grand Rapids: Zondervan, 1962.

Phillips, J. B. *Letters to Young Churches.* London: Bles, 1947.

Pieper, Francis. *Christian Dogmatics.* Vol. 1. St. Louis: Concordia, 1950.

Piepkorn, A. C. "What Does Inerrancy Mean?" *Concordia Theological Monthly* 36 (1963): 577-93.

Pilkington, James. *Works.* Cambridge: U. Press, 1842.

Pinnock, Clark H. "Cultural Apologetics: An Evangelical Standpoint." *Bibliotheca Sacra* 127 (Jan.-Mar. 1970): 58-63.

———. *A Defense of Biblical Infallibility.* Philadelphia. Presbyterian & Reformed, 1967.

———. "A Long Night's Journey into Day." *His* (June 1970).

———. *A New Reformation.* Tigerville, S. C.: Jewel Books, 1968.

———. "The Secular Wasteland." *His* (May 1970).
———. *Set Forth Your Case.* Chicago: Moody, 1971.
———. "Toward a Rational Apologetic Based upon History," *Journal of the Evangelical Theological Society* 11 (1968): 147-51.
Polman, A. D. R. *The Word of God According to St. Augustine.* Grand Rapids: Eerdmans, 1955.
Preus, Robert. "Biblical Hermeneutics and the Lutheran Church Today," "The Doctrine of Revelation in Contemporary Theology," and "Notes on the Inerrancy of Scripture." In *Crisis in Lutheran Theology,* ed. John W. Montgomery. Grand Rapids: Baker, 1967.
———. *The Inspiration of Scripture: A Study of the Theology of the Seventeenth Century Lutheran Dogmaticians.* London: Oliver & Boyd, 1955.
———. "The Word of God in the Theology of Lutheran Orthodoxy." *Concordia Theological Monthly* 33 (1962): 469-83.
Prust, Richard C. "Was Calvin a Biblical Literalist?" *Scottish Journal of Theology* 20 (1967): 312-28.
Radhakrishman, Sarvepalli. *The Hindu View of Life.* New York: Macmillan, 1927.
Rahner, Karl. *Theological Investigations.* 5 vols. Baltimore: Helicon, 1961.
Rahner, Karl and Ratzinger, Joseph. *The Episcopate and the Primacy.* New York: Herder, 1962.
Ramm, Bernard. "The Continental Divide in Contempory Theology." *Christianity Today* (Oct. 8, 1965).
———. *Pattern of Authority.* Grand Rapids: Eerdmans, 1957.
———. *Protestant Biblical Interpretation.* Boston: Wilde, 1956.
———. *Special Revelation and the Word of God.* Grand Rapids: Eerdmans, 1961.
———. *The Witness of the Spirit.* Grand Rapids: Eerdmans, 1959.
Ramsey, I. T. *Christian Discourse: Some Logical Explorations.* London: Oxford U., 1965.
Reid, J. K. S. *The Authority of Scripture.* London: Methuen, 1957.
Rengstorf, Karl H. "apostello." In *Theological Dictionary of the New Testament,* ed. G. Kittel. Grand Rapids: Eerdmans, 1964.
Reu, M. *Luther and the Scriptures.* Columbus, O.: Wartburg, 1944.

Richardson, Alan. *The Bible in the Age of Science.* London: SCM, 1961.

———. *A Preface to Bible Study.* Philadelphia: Westminster, 1954.

———. *History Sacred and Profane.* London: SCM, 1964.

Richardson, Alan and Schweitzer, W., eds. *Biblical Authority for Today.* Philadelphia: Westminster, 1951.

Ridderbos, H. N. "An Attempt at the Theological Definition of Inerrancy, Infallibility, and Authority." *International Reformed Bulletin* 32/33 (1968): 27-41.

———. *The Authority of the New Testament Scriptures.* Philadelphia: Presbyterian & Reformed, 1963.

Ritschl, Dietrich. *Memory and Hope: An Inquiry Concerning the Presence of Christ.* New York: Macmillan, 1967.

Robinson, James M., ed. *The Beginnings of Dialectical Theology.* Richmond: Knox, 1968.

Robinson, James M. and Cobb, J. B. *The New Hermeneutic.* New York: Harper, 1964.

Rogers, Cleon L. "Modern Theology and Modern Man." *Bibliotheca Sacra* 126 (1969): 53-69.

Rogers, Jack. *Scripture in the Westminster Confession.* Grand Rapids: Eerdmans, 1967.

Rowley, H. H. *The Unity of the Bible.* Philadelphia: Westminster, 1953.

Runia, K. "The Authority of Scripture." *Calvin Theological Journal* 4 (1969): 165-94.

———. *Karl Barth's Doctrine of Holy Scripture.* Grand Rapids: Eerdmans, 1962.

Rushdoony, R. J. *Foundations of the Social Order.* Nutley, N. J.: Craig, 1968.

———. *The Mythology of Science.* Nutley, N. J.: Craig, 1967.

Ryle, J. C. *Warnings to the Churches.* London: Banner of Truth, 1967.

Ryrie, C. C. "The Importance of Inerrancy." *Bibliotheca Sacra* 120 (1963): 137-44

Sayers, Dorothy. *Creed or Chaos.* London: Methuen, 1954.

———. *The Mind of the Maker.* New York: Harcourt, Brace, 1941.

Sasse, Herman. "The Inspiration of Holy Scripture." In *Crisis in Lutheran Theology,* ed. John W. Montgomery. Grand Rapids: Baker, 1967.

Sauer, E. *From Eternity to Eternity*. London: Paternoster, 1954.
Schaeffer, Francis A. *Escape from Reason*. Chicago: Inter-Varsity, 1968.
———. *The God Who Is There*. Chicago: Inter-Varsity, 1968.
Scharlemann, Martin H. "The Inerrancy of Scripture." Paper delivered to the faculty of Concordia Seminary, St. Louis (Feb. 25, 1968).
Schleiermacher, F. D. E. *The Christian Faith*. Edinburgh: T. & T. Clark, 1928.
Schlink, Edmund. *Der kommende Christus und die kirchlichen Traditionen*. Gottingen: Vandenbook & Ruprecht, 1961.
———. *Theology of the Lutheran Confessions*. Philadelphia: Fortress, 1961.
Schmid, Heinrich. *The Doctrinal Theology of the Evangelical Lutheran Church*. Minneapolis: Augsburg, 1875.
Schmithals, Walter. *An Introduction to the Theology of Rudolf Bultmann*. Minneapolis: Augsburg, 1968.
Schulte, Hannelis. *Der Begriff der Offenbarung im Neuen Testament*. Munich: C. Kaiser, 1949.
Scott, E. F. *The New Testament Idea of Revelation*. New York: Scribner, 1935.
Sellin, Ernst. *Introduction to the Old Testament*. Rewritten by Georg Fohrer. Nashville: Abingdon, 1965.
Seynaeve, J. *Cardinal Newman's Doctrine on Scripture*. Oxford: Blackwell, 1953.
Sherwin-White, A. N. *Roman Society and Law in the New Testament*. Oxford: U. Press, 1963.
Simons, Francis. *Infallibility and the Evidence*. London: Templegate, 1968.
Skilton, John H. "The Transmission of the Scriptures." In *The Infallible Word*, ed. N. B. Stonehouse and P. Woolley. Grand Rapids: Eerdmans, 1946.
Smart, James D. *The Interpretation of Scripture*. Philadelphia: Westminster, 1961.
Smith, H. P. *Inspiration and Inerrancy*. New York: Clarke, 1893.
Stevick, Donald B. *Beyond Fundamentalism*. Richmond: Knox, 1964.
Stonehouse, N. B. *The Witness of Matthew and Mark to Christ*. London: Tyndale, 1944.

Subilia, V. *The Problem of Catholicism.* London: SCM, 1964.

Swidler, L. J., ed. *Scripture and Ecumenism.* Pittsburgh: Duquesne U., 1965.

Taber, M. E. "Fundamentalist Logic." *Christian Century* 84 (1957): 817-18.

Tavard, G. H. *Holy Writ or Holy Church: The Crisis of the Protestant Reformation.* New York: Harper, 1959.

Temple, William. *Nature, Man and God.* London: Macmillan, 1949.

———. "Revelation." In *Revelation,* ed. John Baillie and Hugh Martin. New York: Macmillan, 1927.

Tenney, Merrill C., ed. *The Bible; The Living Word of Revelation.* Grand Rapids: Zondervan, 1968.

———. *The Word for This Century.* New York: Oxford U., 1960.

Terry, M. S. *Biblical Hermeneutics.* Grand Rapids: Zondervan, n.d.

Thielicke, Helmut. *Between Heaven and Earth.* New York: Harper, 1965.

Thomas, R. L. "The Imprecatory Prayers of the Apocalypse." *Bibliotheca Sacra* 126 (1969): 123-31.

Thomas, W. H. Griffith. *The Holy Spirit of God.* Grand Rapids: Eerdmans, 1964.

Thompson, W. R. *Introduction to The Origin of Species* by Charles Darwin. Everyman Library, no. 811. London: Dent, 1956.

Tillich, Paul. *Systematic Theology.* Chicago: U. Chicago, 1951. Vols. 1-3.

Turner, George A. "John Wesley as an Interpreter of Scripture." In *Inspiration and Interpretation,* ed. J. F. Walvoord. Grand Rapids. Eerdmans, 1957.

Turner, H. E. W. *The Pattern of Christian Truth.* London: Mowbray, 1954.

Unger, Merrill F. *Biblical Demonology.* Wheaton, Ill.: Scripture Press, 1952.

Valen-Sendstad, Olav. *The Word that Can Never Die.* St. Louis: Concordia, 1966.

Van Til, C. *The Doctrine of Scripture.* Philadelphia: Dulk Foundation, 1967.

Vos, Gerdhaus. *Biblical Theology.* Grand Rapids: Eerdmans, 1948.

Walvoord, J. F., ed. *Inspiration and Interpretation.* Grand Rapids: Eerdmans, 1957.

Warfield, B. B. "Apologetics." In *Studies in Theology.* New York: Oxford U., 1932.

———. *Calvin and Augustine.* Philadelphia: Presbyterian & Reformed, 1948.

———. Introduction to *Apologetics,* by F. R. Beattie. Vol. 1. Richmond: Presbyterian Committee of Publication, 1903.

———. *The Inspiration and Authority of the Bible.* Philadelphia: Presbyterian & Reformed, 1948.

———. *Limited Inspiration.* 1894. Philadelphia: Presbyterian & Reformed, 1962.

Werrell, R. S. "Authority of Scripture for the Anglican Reformers." *Evangelical Quarterly* 35 (1963): 79-88.

Wesley, John. *An Earnest Appeal. The Works of the Rev. John Wesley.* Vol. 5. New York: Lane & Scott, 1850.

———. *Journal.* New York: Eaton & Mains, 1909-16.

Wilder Smith, A. E. *Man's Origin, Man's Destiny.* Wheaton, Ill.: Shaw, 1968.

Wilkenhauser, A. *New Testament Introduction.* New York: Herder, 1958.

Wittgenstein, Ludwig. *Tractatus Logico-Philosophicus.* Trans. D. F. Pears and B. F. McGuiness. New York: Humanities, n.d.

Wood, A. S. *The Principles of Biblical Interpretation as Enunciated by Irenaeus, Origen, Augustine, Luther and Calvin.* Grand Rapids: Zondervan, 1967.

Wright, G. E. and Fuller, R. H. *The Book of the Acts of God.* London: Duckworth, 1960.

Wright, J. S. *Man in the Process of Time.* Grand Rapids: Eerdmans, 1956.

Young, E. J. "The Authority of the Old Testament." In *The Infallible Word,* ed. N. B. Stonehouse and P. Woolley. Grand Rapids: Eerdmans, 1946.

———. *An Introduction to the Old Testament.* Grand Rapids: Eerdmans, 1949.

———. *Thy Word Is Truth.* Grand Rapids: Eerdmans, 1957.

INDEX OF SUBJECTS AND PERSONS

SELECTED SCRIPTURE INDEX